Adobe® GoLive® CS2 TIPS and TRICKS

Adobe® GoLive® CS2 TIPS and TRICKS

THE 250 BEST

Adam Pratt
Lynn Grillo

Adobe Press

Adobe GoLive CS2 Tips and Tricks
The 250 Best

Adam Pratt
Lynn Grillo

This Adobe Press book is published by Peachpit

For information on Adobe Press books, contact:
Peachpit
1249 Eighth Street
Berkeley, CA 94710
510/524-2178
800/283-9444
510/524-2221 (fax)

To report errors, please send a note to errata@peachpit.com

Peachpit is a division of Pearson Education

For the latest on Adobe Press books, go to www.adobepress.com

Copyright © 2005 by Adam Pratt and Lynn Grillo

Editors: Corbin Collins, Becky Morgan
Production Editor: Simmy Cover
Copyeditor: Corbin Collins
Compositor: Danielle Foster
Indexer: James Minkin
Cover design: Maureen Forys
Interior design: Maureen Forys

This book was designed and laid out in Adobe InDesign.

ISBN 0-321-33541-4

9 8 7 6 5 4 3 2 1

Printed and bound in the United States of America

Acknowledgements

Writing the acknowledgements for a book is a joy, not only because of the opportunity to thank those whose input helped bring the project to fruition, but also because it means the book is finally done! Given the hectic travel schedules we had during the writing of this book, we are somewhat amazed it made it to press at all. Certainly, that feat would not have been accomplished without the gentle but persistent prodding from our stellar editorial and development team at Peachpit, especially Corbin Collins, Simmy Cover, and Becky Morgan, whose attention to graphic detail and fine crafting of the English language gave polish to these pages.

But there are plenty of people at Adobe we want to thank as well. First and foremost, we'd like to give a standing ovation to the entire GoLive engineering team for consistently developing innovative and amazing new tools in GoLive. But more importantly, thank you for quickly and thoroughly answering our technical questions about those tools during our writing process. You cleared up many foggy moments for us as we worked with early betas and no help files. Special thanks to Jens C. Neffe for being accessible at pretty much all hours of the day and night, and to Mark Erickson for input on the GoLive SDK.

Grazie *mille* to members of the GoLive Product and Marketing teams: Whitney McCleary, George Arriola, and Devin Fernandez, for their support and dedication. Big thanks to Terry White, Technical Resources Manager at Adobe (in other words, our boss) for cutting us some slack when we had too much to do in too little time. Thank you to Jeffery Warnock of Adobe Press who helped initiate the project with the first edition of this book. Thanks also to the third-party GoLive developers who gave us assistance and access to their software during our testing.

Both authors would like to thank their spouses for not pulling the plug during our late-night writing sessions. We're grateful you put up with us and we promise to stay off the computer after midnight for at least two weeks. Finally, Lynn would like to thank Adam, and Adam would like to thank Lynn. It's always great fun working together.

Contents

Foreword

This book is an act of devotion, created by two extraordinary Adobe evangelists and educators, Adam Pratt and Lynn Grillo, out of their mutual love for Adobe GoLive. Huddling over keyboards and phones late at night, snatching time between flights and after customer presentations, these two have managed—with grace and humor—to collaborate once again on a lucid, insightful introduction to designing Web sites with Adobe GoLive CS2 and Adobe Creative Suite 2.

If you're serious about putting GoLive to work, this book is for you. It breaks down complex Web concepts into manageable blocks and then helps you assemble these pieces into a coherent workflow. You'll go from novice to natural faster than you think possible, while uncovering the depth and richness of GoLive CS2's powerful Web-design tools. And if you're a GoLive enthusiast already, you'll pick up a wealth of detail about the latest features.

I speak from experience, having dipped deep into their last volume, *Adobe GoLive CS Tips and Tricks*. I carted it to three continents, jotted all manner of notes in it, sprinkled food and coffee on it, and dog-eared it into a well-loved state. Through it, I got the hands-on view of mastering the GoLive Site window, working with Smart Objects, building CSS pages, incorporating interactivity, and so much more. What appealed most was learning in the company of such stimulating teachers. Their love of GoLive shines on every page and will inspire you to your best Web-design work.

This release of Adobe GoLive is as packed as ever with rich features, from its innovative new drag-and-drop approach to CSS authoring to its deepened integration into the Creative Suite. The GoLive team is indebted to Adam and Lynn for their energy and enthusiasm in educating people about our favorite product. *Adobe GoLive CS2 Tips and Tricks* is a treasure trove of information about getting the most from GoLive. Enjoy!

Whitney McCleary
Adobe GoLive Senior Product Marketing Manager

CHAPTER ONE

Getting Started

Adobe's new Creative Suite 2 Premium (Photoshop CS2, Illustrator CS2, InDesign CS2, GoLive CS2, and Acrobat 7.0 Professional) has significantly changed the industry in terms of graphic-design software. Now designers are able to purchase all the software they might need for print, Web, and PDF publishing in one box. Although there are hundreds of thousands of GoLive users around the world, many new users are being introduced to the GoLive for the very first time through the Creative Suite. GoLive is an incredibly powerful and fun Web authoring application. GoLive on its own is pretty impressive, but combining it with the rest of the Creative Suite is truly sweet!

In this second edition of the book, we've done our very best to write something that will teach beginners the basics and show seasoned users some special tips. We'll even wow the most experienced users with power tips that will save them time and enable them to be more creative as they build sites with GoLive.

This first chapter introduces the interface, shows you how to optimize GoLive for optimum performance and productivity, and even teaches the pros a few cool tips. Let's get started!

TIP 1

Getting Started with the Welcome Screen

Welcome to GoLive CS2! To kick things off, launch GoLive, and you'll see the Welcome screen, which is similar to the Welcome screens in the other Creative Suite applications. The Welcome screen gives you several easy ways to get started with the software, so let's start at the top and work our way down (**Figure 1**).

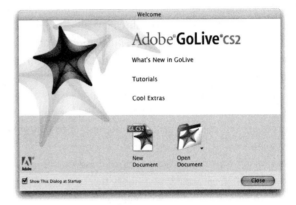

Figure 1 The Welcome screen opens when you launch GoLive and helps get you started with common tasks.

There are three important options in the top portion of the Welcome screen: What's New in GoLive, Tutorials, and Cool Extras. Clicking any of these links loads a Web page about that topic in your default Web browser.

Clicking the New Document button invokes the New... window where you can create individual pages of various file types, begin an entirely new site, base a site on a template, or choose from a list of Favorites. The New... screen is explained in detail in Tip 14.

If you click the Open button in the Welcome screen you'll see a standard Open dialog where you can locate any file GoLive can edit and open the file. If you click and hold the Open icon you'll see a list of the most recently used files in the pull-down menu. This is a really handy shortcut to sites and pages you edit frequently.

Picking Up Where You Left Off

To open all the sites and pages you had open the last time you quit GoLive, press the Shift key and click the Close button in the Welcome screen or choose Last Session from the Open menu in the Welcome screen. Voila!

Turn It Off!

You'll probably like the Welcome screen at first, but after a while it might start to annoy you. To turn it off, just uncheck the Show This Dialog at Startup option in the bottom left corner. You can always turn it on again in the General Preferences in the At Launch pull-down or open it from the Help menu.

TIP 2 Customizing Keyboard Shortcuts

We strongly believe that software should be flexible and allow the user to customize as much as possible. One practical way that GoLive allows you to make the software adapt to how you work is through customizable keyboard shortcuts. If there's an obscure menu command you happen to use frequently, there's no need to send a feature request to Adobe to change it. Open the Keyboard Shortcuts Editor from Edit menu to assign a custom keyboard shortcut (**Figure 2**).

Figure 2 The Keyboard Shortcuts Editor lets you add, remove, and reassign custom keyboard shortcuts for the menu commands you use most often.

Notice at the very top of the dialog there is a default set in place called GoLive Factory Defaults. To create your own set, just click the New Set... button, name the set, and click OK.

Now select the command in the menu listing that you want to customize and type the new shortcut in the Press New Shortcut field at the bottom of the dialog. If you assign a menu command a keyboard shortcut that is already assigned to another command, you'll see a warning at the bottom of the dialog that tells you what the shortcut is currently assigned to. In most cases you'll want to find a unique shortcut that isn't already taken, but if you want to make the change anyway, click the Assign button, and the shortcut will be removed from the old command and assigned to the new command.

Returning to Default Shortcuts

If a friend or coworker ever needs to use GoLive on your computer, and your custom keyboard shortcuts are confusing them, just temporarily switch back to the GoLive Factory Default set. You can always switch back to your custom set.

Sharing Shortcuts

If you create a great set of keyboard shortcuts you'll want to make them the same on every computer you work on and maybe even share them with coworkers. Copy the shortcuts setting file from User/Library/Preferences/Adobe/GoLive/Settings8/Shortcuts on Mac or Documents and Settings/User/Application Data/Adobe/Adobe GoLive/Settings8/Shortcuts on Windows to the same location on the other machine.

Understanding Modules

To understand what a module does, select the module in the list and twirl up the Show Item Information option at the bottom of the window. If you are unsure whether or not you need a module, err on the side of caution and leave it on. Turning off a necessary module can cripple GoLive.

Before you start working in GoLive CS2, we recommend you familiarize yourself with the application preferences. You'll only change a few things now, but when you need to make further adjustments in the future, you'll know where to look. Open the preferences by selecting Adobe GoLive > Preferences... on the Mac or Edit > Preferences... on Windows (**Figure 3**).

Figure 3 The application preferences are a good place to start customizing the software to meet your needs.

In the General section are At Launch options. You could have GoLive create a new blank page every time you launch the application, but you'll probably just want to set it to Do Nothing and open the sites you need to work on. If you turned off the Welcome screen as described in Tip 1, you can turn it back on here.

Another set of preferences to become familiar with is under the Modules heading on the left. You can enable and disable features of GoLive by clicking the On/Off checkbox and restarting the application. Disabling features in the application can speed up launch times and reduce the amount of RAM GoLive requires.

Finally, you'll need to edit the browser preview options. Select Browsers on the left and click the Find All button to let GoLive scour your drives for any Web browsers it can find; or click the Add button to select a browser manually. The browsers listed are added to the File > Preview In menu. If you enable a checkbox next to a browser name, that browser will be launched when you click the Preview in Browser button. If you check more than one, then clicking the button opens multiple browsers at the same time.

TIP 4 Using the Objects Palette

The Objects palette contains both tools and objects that you use when working on a Web page or a Web site. The gray icons at the top of the Objects palette represent tools that help you quickly select and move objects.

Click and hold the color icon below the tools to reveal a list of object categories. Select a category in the list, and all the objects in that category are displayed below. To place an object, drag it from the Objects palette onto a Web page or into a Web site. The default Object categories are seen in **Figure 4**.

Figure 4 The Objects palette stores everything you might add to a page or site.

- **Basic:** Basic page elements such as tables, images, and multi-media files (see Chapter 3).

- **Smart:** Advanced page elements such as native Adobe image file formats (see Chapter 7) and JavaScript Actions (see Chapter 9).

- **CSS:** CSS-based page elements such as multi-column boxes (see Chapter 3).

- **Forms:** All the form elements you'll ever need (see Chapter 9).

(continued on next page)

Configuring for Compliance

If you need to target a specific W3C code specification, such as HTML 3.2, HTML 4 Strict, or XHTML 1.1, use the Configure submenu in the bottom right corner of the Objects palette to limit the available objects and help ensure your source code is compliant.

- **Head:** Web page head items such as keywords and other meta tags (see Tip 36).

- **Frames:** iFrames, frames, and pre-built framesets are stored here (see Chapter 4).

- **Site:** Objects you'd add to the site window such as blank pages, email addresses, and folders (see Chapter 2).

- **Diagram:** Dozens of different objects you might use to create a site map with the Diagram feature (see Tip 200).

- **QuickTime:** 20 different multimedia formats you can use to create interactive QuickTime movies (see Tip 198).

- **SMIL:** Synchronized Multimedia Integration Language. Objects used to create interactive, multimedia presentations.

TIP 5 Introducing the Toolbar

New in this version of GoLive is a small but extremely useful set of tools located in the top portion of the Objects palette. These tools make selecting, moving and drawing objects easier than ever before. Click on a tool to use it, or press its associated keyboard shortcut to activate it. The shortcut is shown in parentheses at the right of the Tool Tip that appears when you hover your mouse pointer over the tool.

Let's explore the six new tools as shown in **Figure 5**. The Standard Selection tool is used for selecting text, while the Object Selection tool makes grabbing and moving CSS layers a breeze. You can now easily draw layers anywhere on your page using the Layer tool and then pick up and apply colors with the Eyedropper tool. Use the Hand tool to pan around the page and the Zoom tool to zoom in on page objects.

Figure 5 The six new tools in GoLive CS are the Standard Selection tool, the Object Selection tool, the Layer tool, the Eyedropper tool, the Hand tool, and the Zoom tool.

For greater detail on how to use any of these fabulous new tools, have a look in Chapter 3.

Toolbar Tricks

Click the Toggle Orientation button in the bottom left corner of the palette to separate the tools and the objects into two individual palettes. Click and drag the bottom right corner of the Objects palette to resize it.

TIP 6 The Inspector Palette

The Inspector palette in GoLive is where you edit and customize selected objects (**Figure 6**). The cool thing about the Inspector palette is that it's context-sensitive and changes depending on what is selected. For example, if you select an HTML table, you'll see options for adjusting rows, columns, and borders, but if you select a page in the Site window, you'll see options for adjusting the filename and page title.

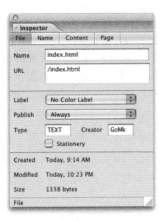

Figure 6 The context-sensitive Inspector palette lets you adjust any selected object.

When there are too many options to fit in the Inspector palette, the settings are distributed across multiple tabs in the palette, as seen in Figure 6. If you're looking for a setting in the Inspector, but can't find it, make sure to look in the other tabs. If you're not sure you're inspecting the right object, just look in the bottom left corner of the palette where it shows the name of the Inspector, such as Image, Text, or Table.

TIP 7 Managing Palettes

GoLive CS2 lets you stash palettes on the left and right edges of your monitor to save precious screen real estate. We really like the Adobe palettes, but let's face it—you want to look at *documents*, not a clutter of palettes. To stash a palette, grab its tab and drag it to the left or right edge of the monitor (**Figure 7a**).

Figure 7a Palettes can be neatly stashed on the right or left edges of your computer screen.

Click the tab of a stashed palette, and it slides into view. Click the tab again, and it slides back to its stashed position. To stash more than one palette together in a group, just drag another palette by its tab into a stashed palette. To adjust the height of a stashed palette, click its bottom edge and slide it up or down (**Figure 7b**).

Figure 7b When your cursor turns into a two-sided arrow, you can drag the edge of a stashed palette to lengthen or shorten it. That's great when you want to stash several palettes together.

(continued on next page)

Stashing and Unstashing All Palettes

No doubt you'll really like the way GoLive CS2 stashes palettes to maximize your usable screen real estate. But opening and closing lots of palettes can still be tedious. A cool power user trick is to Option/Alt-Click on a stashed palette to open or close all stashed palettes simultaneously.

Rearranging Palette Tabs

This might not seem like a big deal, but if you've used Adobe applications as long as we have, you'll appreciate the following attention to detail: GoLive lets you rearrange palettes that are grouped together without having to ungroup them first! That's correct, you can grab a palette tab and move it to the left or right of any other tab in the group until you have it situated just how you like it.

Note

Mac OS X users should note that it's not possible to stash palettes on the same monitor edge as the OS X dock.

GoLive CS2 also has docked palettes that match the behavior of other Adobe applications, including Photoshop, Illustrator, and InDesign. To dock a palette, grab its tab and hold it over the bottom edge of another palette until you see a highlight line appear and then let go (**Figure 7c**). Now when you move the top palette, any palettes docked along with it will move, too.

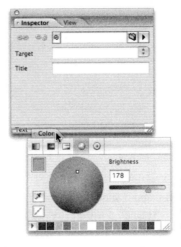

Figure 7c A highlight appears when the palettes overlap. If you let go, the palettes will be docked together.

Docking groups of palettes top to bottom is a great way to manage your palettes, and it makes it easy to move them all around at one time. The problem with docking palettes is that if you dock too many tall ones, the lower ones can get lost off the bottom of the screen. To remedy that problem, click the triangle to the left of the palette names to twirl open or close a palette set (**Figure 7d**).

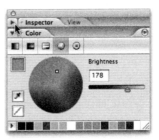

Figure 7d Click the handy-dandy arrow button on the upper left of a palette group to collapse the entire group.

TIP 8 Finding Palettes

We've shown how to take charge of your palettes by stashing, docking, and twirling them, but let's not forget an even more fundamental function: finding them. Where are the rest of the palettes hiding? They're in the Window menu, of course! Simply choose Window and then select the name of the palette you want to open from the list (**Figure 8**).

Figure 8 There's a plethora of palettes in the Window menu.

Notice that plenty of palettes have keyboard shortcuts associated with them, so when you become familiar with which palettes are used for which tasks, you'll be able to invoke your favorite palette by pressing its keyboard shortcut.

Also nested in the Window menu are options for Workspaces (see Tip 9) and for Cascade and Tile. Choose Window > Cascade and Tile > Cascade to place all open Windows in a neat stack; choosing Window > Cascade and Tile > Tile Horizontally (or Vertically) lines all of the open windows up next to one another.

TIP
9 Customizing the Workspace

After you have set up your GoLive palettes exactly as you like, you can save the workspace so that you may revert to it at any time. This is extremely helpful if you find that after a work session you've got palettes strewn all over the place. Choose Window > Workspaces > Save Workspace and then give your workspace a name (**Figure 9a**).

Figure 9a By using workspaces, you can always have your favorite palettes just where you want them. Simply give your workspace a name.

Go ahead and get as messy as you'd like with your palettes. To tidy up the workspace again, simply choose Window > Workspace, select the name of your saved workspace from the list, and then watch as all the palettes jump back into position (**Figure 9b**).

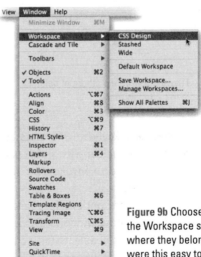

Figure 9b Choose a workspace name from the Workspace submenu to put palettes back where they belong. If only our real desks were this easy to straighten up.

There's more to workspaces than simply creating or using one. To go back to the default palette location, choose Window > Workspace > Default Workspace. To remove a workspace, Choose Window > Workspace > Manage Workspaces and then create, delete, or rename a workspace.

Introducing the Adobe Help Center

Every now and again you may be unsure about how to accomplish a specific task in GoLive CS2. Adobe Help Center to the rescue. GoLive CS2, like all the applications in the Adobe Creative Suite 2.0, includes a fully searchable help system that is installed by default and accessible from the Help menu. Choose Help > GoLive Help, and the GoLive help system is launched in the Adobe Help Center (**Figure 10**).

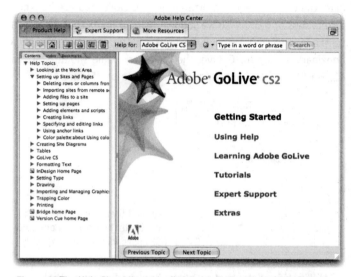

Figure 10 The Help files automatically launch in the Adobe Help Center.

A common misconception is that you need to be online in order to access the Adobe Help Center. It's not true. The pages themselves are local HTML files that are rendered in the Help Center window.

The fastest way to find help on a specific topic is to use the Search field in the upper right corner and choose from the search results, which are ranked according to relevance. You can also browse the help files in the Contents tab or alphabetically through the Index tab. Click on any of the search results or help listings in the left pane to load the corresponding information into the right pane. Use the navigation links at the bottom to go to the next or previous related topic.

PDF User Guides

What if you'd like to print a part or even all of the User Guide? Your best bet would be to print from the included PDF version of the User Guide, which can be found on the installation CDs that came with your purchase of GoLive or the Creative Suite.

Using Bookmarks in the Help Center

The new Adobe Help Center is easy to use and full of helpful resources, and to make it easier to access common pages you can use the bookmark feature to remember information you access frequently. Previous versions of GoLive used a Web browser to display its Help files, but it was difficult to bookmark pages for frequent access. It's now a piece of cake in the Help Center.

Click the Bookmark icon 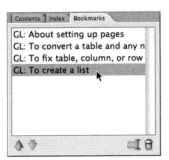 in the Help Center toolbar to bookmark the current page. Unfortunately, you can't organize bookmarks into folders or groups, so we suggest using a prefix that corresponds to the application help you're bookmarking. For example, if you bookmark a page for GoLive, the bookmark name should start with GL. For Photoshop you could use PS, and so on (**Figure 11**).

Figure 11 Create bookmarks in the Help Center for GoLive or any other CS2 application you use regularly.

Also notice at the bottom of the Bookmarks section that you can delete, rename, and even change the order of the bookmarks you create. This makes it easy to organize your bookmarks over time.

TIP 12 Accessing Expert Support from the Help Center

Adobe offers free phone support to registered users for all installation, crashing, and bug problems for the life of the current version of GoLive. However, if you have "How To" questions or cross-application workflow issues, you might consider the new Adobe Expert Support programs. You even get toll-free phone numbers, unlimited calls, and extended support hours.

If you use Adobe Expert Support, you can click on Support Plan Details in the left pane, store your account information in the Help Center, and even submit support requests via the Internet. Expert Support plans last one year, and the Help Center will remind you when your plan is about to expire so you don't miss out on the help you need (**Figure 12**).

Sign Up for Expert Support

To find out more about Expert Support, visit www.adobe.com/expertsupport or call 1-866-MYADOBE (866-692-3623).

Figure 12 You can store your Expert Support plan details in the Help Center for easy access from GoLive or any other CS2 application.

Though the Expert Support program is pretty cool, we realize that some of your favorite technical support experts very well may be your coworkers, friends, family members, or even Web sites. If that's the case, click the More Resources button at the top of the Help Center window and enter your support-related contacts in the Personal Contacts section. Also make sure you check out the Online Resources category, which includes hyperlinks to Support options, Adobe User-to-User Forums, Tips and Tutorials, and various Training options.

TIP

13
Updating Software Automatically

To ensure you have the most recent version of GoLive, use the Updates feature built into the Help menu (**Figure 13a**).

Figure 13a From the Help menu, choose Updates to check for any new patches or updates.

If you already have the latest version, you'll see a dialog box stating that there are no updates available. If you do need an update, you'll get a dialog box showing the name of the update and asking if you'd like to download it. You can then download and install the update (**Figure 13b**).

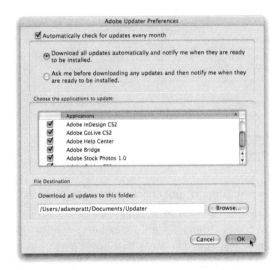

Figure 13b Use the Update Manager to download and install new GoLive updates.

If you're not sure which version of GoLive you're using, select Help > About GoLive... on Windows or GoLive > About GoLive... on Mac, and the exact version of GoLive will appear in the upper left portion of the About screen.

CHAPTER TWO

Working with Sites

GoLive is not merely an application for building Web pages—it's an unstoppable powerhouse of site management. Let's face it: You build Web sites with tons of pages and images and links, not individual Web pages. Without reliable site management you can forget the idea of a hyperlinked "web" of files.

Using GoLive without the Site window makes about as much sense as driving a car without wheels—you could try it, but why make your work so hard? Site management is an area where GoLive really shines, and understanding the Site window will help you get the very most out of the software.

Once you grasp how the Site window works, you'll see why it makes it almost impossible to have missing images or broken links in your Web site. You'll marvel at GoLive's three site-mapping modes. Your heart will race at the thought of multiple undos!

Learn the ways of the Site window. Trust the Site window. Be one with the Site window. Oh yeah, and save yourself tons of time and frustration, too. All right, let's get going.

TIP
14 Creating New Sites

Start the GoLive Site Wizard by selecting File > New... and you'll see a dialog box that lets you create many types of documents, including a new site. On the far left are several categories, the first of which is Site. Select Site to see the available options in the center pane, such as Create Site, Connect to Site, and samples you can use to begin building a site.

When you select Create Site, the Site Creation Wizard on the right side of the New window gives you three options. If you're starting from scratch, choose Blank Site. If you already have some files or an old site on your hard drive that you want to start managing with GoLive, select Site from Existing Content. If you have been given a site locator file, used by hosting companies that partner with Adobe, choose Site from a "Site Locator" file. The site locator file will automatically fill in all the FTP info for you.

If you've inherited an existing site that's on a server somewhere, but you don't have a copy of the files, choose the Connect to Site option in the center pane, and you can download the files via FTP or HTTP.

To create a new, blank site, choose Create Site from the list, check the Blank Site radio button, and click Next (**Figure 14a**).

Figure 14a When beginning a new site from scratch, click the Blank Site radio button.

In the next screen you'll be asked to give your site a name and browse to a spot on your hard drive or network where the site will reside (**Figure 14b**). When finished, click Next.

Figure 14b Give your site an appropriate name and choose a location for it by clicking the Browse button. The site name you enter doesn't have to match the domain name of the site.

If you need to collaborate with other GoLive users on the same site or need a version control system, choose Use Version Control and then select one of the options in the Version Control System pop-up menu. You'll then need to enter the necessary information, such as Username and Password, into the input fields. Otherwise, choose Don't Use Version Control and click the Next button (**Figure 14c**).

Figure 14c Select Don't Use Version Control if you are not collaborating with others and don't need versioning tools.

(continued on next page)

TIP 14: Creating New Sites

Acquiring the FTP Information

If you've never created a Web site before, you may be wondering where in the world you come up with the information needed in the Publish Server settings. The company you have chosen to host your Web site should supply the settings to you.

Finally, you need to enter the publish server information for your site (**Figure 14d**). This is where you specify the Web server that will host your site. Choose a nickname for the server so you can easily recall it later. Select the protocol, such as FTP or HTTP from the protocol pop-up list and then add your username and password.

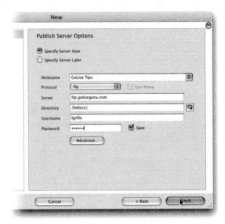

Figure 14d Enter the publish server information including your server name, username, and password so you'll be ready to upload your work from within GoLive CS2.

To select the directory where you'll place your pages, click the small folder button at the right end of the Directory field. You'll be able to browse through the folders on the server until you find the correct one. When you select it, the Directory field will automatically be filled in with the correct path. And here's a little tip: In the Web world, the terms *directory* and *folder* mean the same thing.

TIP 15 Starting with Site Samples

You know that feeling when you're faced with a blank sheet of paper and need to come up with fabulous ideas to fill it up? It's often easier to jump start your creative juices if you have a starting point. To that end, GoLive CS2 offers a number of site samples that allow you to get up and running with a site in minutes and learn the features at the same time.

Choose File > New to bring up the New dialog. Select Site from the category list on the left and then in the center pane, select one of the five types of samples: Web Samples, Mobile Samples, Scripting Samples, Co-Author Samples and Further Samples. In the right pane, choose the first item in the list and then use the down or up arrow on your keyboard to navigate through the list (**Figure 15**). Each sample includes a little preview image that shows the visual design of the site and a bit of text that describes the content of the site.

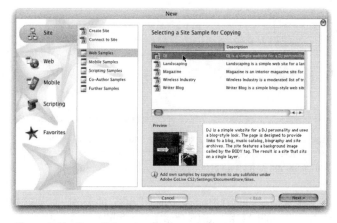

Figure 15 The New dialog gives both a preview image and a description of the site samples included in GoLive CS2.

When you've found a site sample that you like, click the Next button and continue through the setup screens as described in Tip 14.

A Sample of Your Own

If you have a site that you'd like to use as the basis of additional sites, you can save it as a site sample by copying it to a subfolder in this location: Adobe GoLive CS2/Settings/DocumentStore/Sites. When you restart GoLive, your site will appear in the New dialog along with the pre-installed samples.

TIP 15: Starting with Site Samples

Often people have existing sites that were created with other Web-authoring applications or even coded by hand that they want to bring into GoLive. GoLive CS2 imports such sites effortlessly, builds a new GoLive site file to get you going, and begins monitoring all your links from that point forward.

To import an existing site into GoLive, choose File > New, select Site from the category list on the left, select Create Site in the center pane, and then click the Site From Existing Content radio button in the Site Creation Wizard on the right. When you click Next, you'll be shown three options for how the site will be imported (**Figure 16**).

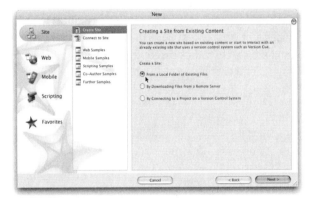

Figure 16 When importing an existing site into GoLive CS2, you'll be asked whether the site is coming from a folder on your drive, from a server, or from a version control system.

If you select Import from a Local Folder of Existing Files and click Next, you'll be asked to locate the folder in question. Click the Browse button and choose the root folder of the site—that is, the one containing the home page. Proceed through the rest of the Wizard as described in Tip 14.

The other two options require a bit more attention. To import a site from a server or version control system, you'll need to know the server name and location as well as the username and password to access the system. If you are not sure where to acquire that information, ask your Web hosting service, IT department, or system administrator. Once you input the required account information, you'll proceed through the Site Wizard as shown in Tip 14.

TIP 17 Understanding the Site File Structure

GoLive has a specific way of organizing directories so that every item can be tracked via the built-in site-management tools. Let's define what each folder is called and what each one does.

In this example, the Web site being built is called *magazine*. All the documents that make up the site, both those that get uploaded to the server and those that stay on the local computer, are housed inside an enclosing folder named magazine.

Inside the magazine folder you will find:

- The Root folder (named web-content). These are the HTML pages, images, multimedia files, and so on that make up your Web site. These items get uploaded to your server.

- The Data folder (named web-data). Inside are items you work with to create your Web site such as Components, Stationeries, Templates, Smart Objects, InDesign Packages, Site Trash, and so forth. These items do not get uploaded to the server. They are for you to work with locally on your computer.

- The Settings folder (named web-settings). GoLive stores settings files in this folder. There is no need for you to access them, though. GoLive will use them when necessary.

- The Site file (magazine.site). This is the workhorse of GoLive. It is the brain that keeps track of all the things in all the folders listed previously. It manages your links, your URLs, your File Transfer Protocol (FTP) settings, your site colors; it also tracks errors and does much more. When you open the Site file, it becomes the Site Window.

Double-click the Site file, and it opens up as the Site window. The contents of the Root folder (web-content) are listed in the left pane under Files. The contents of the Data folder (web-data) are listed in the right pane (**Figure 17**).

(continued on next page)

The Site File Backup

The Site file backup is created when you open a site. It is, very simply, a backup of the Site file. When you close the site, a back-up is automatically created. We suggest that you open the Site file from the original whenever possible. If the original has become corrupt, then try the backup.

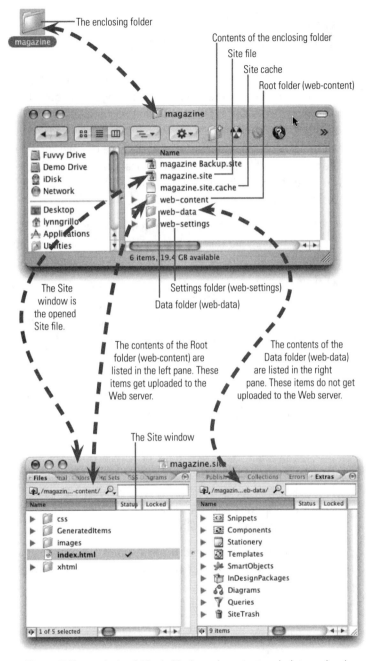

Figure 17 The enclosing folder holds the web-content, web-data, and web-settings folders, as well as the Site file. The Site file, when opened, shows a window separated into two panes and lists the items inside the web-content (left side) and web-data (right side) folders.

TIP 18 Adding Files to a Site

Creating a new site in GoLive is a great place to start, but soon you'll need to add other files, such as images, PDFs, and other documents to your Web site. GoLive offers several easy ways to add existing files to a Web site. Pick the method you like best.

Drag and Drop

Lazy people like us prefer the drag and drop method because it's definitely the easiest. Just select the files in the operating system (Finder on the Mac or My Computer on Windows) and drag them into the Files tab of the Site window (**Figure 18**). If you see a dialog asking you to confirm the copy, just click OK. Note that dragging and dropping copies the files into the site instead of moving them, which means you end up with two copies of the files.

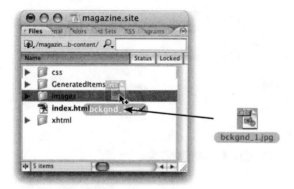

Figure 18 Drag and drop files to add them to your site.

Import Files

If you prefer to work with the menus, make sure the Files tab of the Site window is active by clicking it and select File > Import > Files to Site.... Select the files you want to add (Shift-click to select multiple files at once) and click OK. The selected files are copied to the site, and the originals are still where you found them.

Save and Refresh View

Did you know that in GoLive you can save the files into the root (web-content) folder and they will automatically appear in the Site View? For example, use Photoshop to create a Web Photo Gallery and save the results in the site's root folder. When you switch to GoLive and refresh the Site window, the new files appear in the Files tab.

**Navigating the
Site Window**

If you've opened a subfolder
in your site and want to get
back to the top of your site, click
the up arrow button in the top
left corner.

TIP 19 Moving, Renaming, and Deleting Files

If you move a file to a new place on your hard drive outside of GoLive, you'll end up with broken links, missing images, and heartburn. Instead, manage all the assets in your Web site from the Files tab of the Site window, and GoLive will handle all the dirty work for you. As long as you manage the files from the Site window, GoLive will update all the hyperlinks and references inside HTML, CSS, JavaScript Actions, PDF, QuickTime, and SWF for you. This even works with third-party actions and extensions!

Moving

To move a file, drag it into the folder where you want to put it. To move a file up a level in the file structure, drag the file on top of another file at the same level you want to move to, as seen in **Figure 19a**.

Figure 19a Drag a file over another file to move it to that level.

You can also use the Edit > Copy and the Edit > Paste commands to copy and paste files from one folder to another.

Renaming

To rename a file in the Files tab of the Site window, click on the filename, wait a second, and then click again until the filename (but not the extension) is highlighted. Now type the new filename and press Return or Enter. Notice you can also rename files and folders in the Name field of the Inspector.

When you move or rename a file or folder that is referenced by another file in the site, you'll see a confirmation dialog (**Figure 19b**). When you're ready to confirm the change, click OK and watch GoLive automagically update your entire site for you.

Figure 19b When you move or rename a file or folder, GoLive makes sure all your links are correct.

Deleting

To delete a file or folder in the Files tab, select it and click the trashcan icon in the toolbar (**Figure 19c**). You can also delete selected files with the keyboard by pressing Command-Delete on the Mac or Delete on Windows. When you delete files, you'll see a dialog asking you to confirm the change. Even after you delete the files, you can always retrieve them from the Site Trash over in the Extras tab of the Site window.

Figure 19c Click the trashcan icon in the toolbar to delete selected files.

Make a Mistake?

Have you ever moved a file into the wrong folder? Made a typo? Accidentally deleted a file? If so, then you'll love the fact that GoLive's Site window gives you 20 levels of undo. Just hit Command-Z (Mac) or Control-Z (Windows), and GoLive will undo the most recent file manipulation *and* all the site management to make sure everything's back in order.

TIP 19: Moving, Renaming, and Deleting Files

20 Changing File View Modes

The default view in the Site window shows files in a simple list view (called Details on Windows), but GoLive CS2 includes three other helpful options: icons, thumbnails, and tiles. Access these view options with the Site > View menu or with a Control-click (Mac) or right-click (Windows) in the Files or Extras tabs of the Site window (**Figure 20**).

Helpful Icon View

If you forget what the folders in the Extras tab of the Site window are for, change the view to Icons in the Extras tab. Now the big beautiful icons will make it easier to remember the different features.

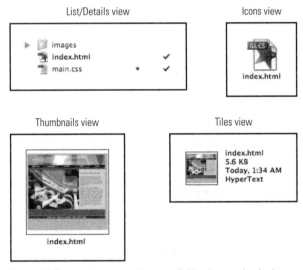

Figure 20 Choose from one of four available view modes in the Site window.

These four view modes make GoLive work like the file browser in the new Adobe Bridge and they even reveal helpful metadata about your files. Just hold your cursor over a file, and you'll see a Tool Tip popup with information including name, file size, date modified, and file status.

Working with Sites

TIP 21 Understanding the Site Window Tabs

Before we get much further into our exploration of GoLive, let's do a quick rundown of all the different tabs in the Site window. We'll begin on the left side and work our way across (**Figure 21a**).

Figure 21a The left side of the Site window is where you'll perform most of your day-to-day site-management tasks.

- **Files:** Think of this tab as the root folder of your Web site. Everything that you upload to your Web server needs to be stored here (see Tips 17 through 20).

- **External:** Store all the email addresses and Web site addresses you'll link to in here (see Tip 26).

- **Colors:** To keep the colors throughout a site consistent, you can store frequently used color swatches here (see Tip 71).

- **Font Sets:** Whether you use font tags or CSS (Cascading Style Sheets), this is where you store your favorite font groupings for Web-friendly type.

- **CSS:** This tab is new in GoLive CS2 and helps you track all your CSS files, classes, and IDs from one central location (see Tip 117).

- **Diagrams:** GoLive includes integrated site-mapping tools, and this is where you store those diagrams (see Tip 200).

(continued on next page)

Simplifying the Site Window

You can hide and reveal the right side of the Site window by clicking the Toggle Split View icon  in the bottom left corner of the window. You can also Toggle Split View from the flyout menu in the upper right corner of the window.

Now, the right side of the Site window is also really important, but it's responsible for behind-the-scenes tasks such as storing templates, tracking errors, and saving settings files (**Figure 21b**). You'll definitely use these tabs, but less frequently than the ones on the left.

Figure 21b The right side of the Site window is where you upload files to a server, fix errors, and store library items.

- **Publish Server:** Use this tab to upload and download files to your Web server right within the Site window (see Tips 212–224).

- **Collections:** Store aliases (or shortcuts) to frequently used files here (see Tip 210).

- **Errors:** The real-time error checking in GoLive instantly flags any broken links, missing images, or orphaned files and displays the errors here (see Tip 202).

- **Extras:** The assets available in the Library palette (templates, components, snippets, and so on) are stored here in the Site window (see Tip 129).

TIP 22 Managing the Site Window Tabs

Considering how many tabs there are in the Site window, it should relieve you to know they're completely customizable. For starters, you can rearrange the order of the tabs and even move them from the left to the right and vice versa. If you want to move the Extras tab next to Files, just drag the tab to the left side of the window and then drag it between the Files and External tabs (**Figure 22a**).

Figure 22a Customize the Site window for maximum productivity.

If you have multiple displays or a huge LCD attached to your computer, then you might have enough screen real estate to pull some tabs out of the Site window so you can see them all at the same time. Just drag one of the tabs out of the Site window until it separates into its own window. If the tab is a feature you don't use often, you can even tear it out and close it to get it out of your way.

In case you tear off or close a tab and then need it back again, select the name of the tab from the flyout menu in the top right corner of the Site window (**Figure 22b**). You can also use this flyout menu to open the Navigation and Links views for site mapping and link tracking.

Figure 22b Reopen closed tabs with the flyout menu.

> **Resetting the Site Window**
>
> To reset the tabs in the Site window to their default locations and restore that factory fresh scent, select the Default Configuration option at the bottom of the Site window flyout menu.

TIP 22: Managing the Site Window Tabs

TIP 23 Selecting Multiple Files

To make it as easy as possible to learn and use GoLive, the brilliant GoLive engineering team has made the Site window look and behave just like your operating system. That means that although the features are identical between the Mac and Windows versions, GoLive behaves like a Mac on a Mac and like Windows on a Windows PC.

For example, to select multiple contiguous files in the Site window, select the first file, press and hold the Shift key, and then click on the last file in the sequence. This is new behavior for many Mac users, but it works exactly like the new Finder in Mac OS X (**Figure 23**).

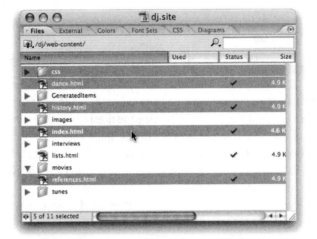

Figure 23 Command-click (Mac) or Control-click (Windows) to select multiple discontiguous files. Shift-clicking will select all the files in the range.

To select multiple discontiguous files in the Site window, Mac users Command-click and Windows users Control-click on the files.

TIP 24: Viewing Content in the Inspector

You can see your files in the Site window, but to see a really nice preview without opening the files, look in the Content tab of the File Inspector. You can view just about any file format, including GIF, JPEG, HTML, QuickTime, Photoshop, Illustrator, and PDF.

If you have a large image like the one in **Figure 24a**, you'll only be able to see a small portion of the file. Notice the numbers in the bottom left corner of the Inspector—those numbers tell you the dimensions of the selected file.

Figure 24a You can preview Web pages and graphics in the Content tab of the Inspector.

The scale-to-fit icon 🔍 in the bottom left corner of the Inspector makes it easy to see all of a large image at once. Just click the scale-to-fit icon, and GoLive changes the preview dimensions (but not the actual image size) so that it fits perfectly in the Inspector (**Figure 24b**).

Figure 24b The scale-to-fit option lets you see the entire image at once.

When you're sure you've located the right file, just drag and drop it from the Inspector into your Web page to place the image.

TIP

25 Counting File Usage

Have you ever wondered how many times a page, graphic, or PDF file is referenced throughout a site? If you look in the Used column in the Files tab of the Site window, you can see a little tick mark if the file is referenced. For more detailed reporting, just widen the Used column by dragging the column header dividers with your mouse pointer, and you'll see that GoLive actually keeps a running tally of how many times a file is referenced throughout the site (**Figure 25**). This is just one more reason GoLive users rave about the awesome site-management capabilities.

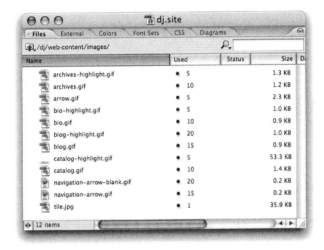

Figure 25 Widen the Used column in the Site window to get more detailed information.

While we're tinkering around in the Site window, try widening the Status column in the Files tab. You'll see nicely written explanations of what the various status icons mean.

TIP 26 Managing URLs and Email Addresses

GoLive does an amazing job of managing files in a Web site, and it's also very adept at managing external references such as email and Web site addresses. To add an external reference to your site, make sure the External tab is active. Then click the Create New Address ⬛ or Create New URL ➡ icons in the toolbar or drag the Address or URL objects from the Site section of the Objects palette. Customize the external reference in the Inspector so that it looks something like **Figure 26**.

Figure 26 Edit external references in the Inspector palette.

To apply an external reference as a hyperlink in a page, just drag it from the Site window onto a selected image or text in a Web page in GoLive's Layout Editor. (See Tip 42 for more information on linking.)

If you have an existing site in GoLive and you want to see what email addresses and external URLs are hyperlinked throughout the site, choose Site > Update > Add Used > External Links. All the detected references are added to the External tab of the Site window where you can organize and update them.

To update every instance of an email address throughout a site, just select it in the External tab and make the change in the Inspector. For example, if somebody in your organization gets a promotion, you can change his email address from peewee@company.com to bigshot@company.com in one central location instead of in each instance.

Checking External Links

Instead of verifying every external link individually by hand, select the External tab and choose Site > Check External Links. Checkmarks in the Status column are good. If you see a red bug, you should doublecheck the address.

Importing Favorites as Externals

If you have favorites from Internet Explorer you want to use as links in a Web site, try the File > Import > Favorites as Site Externals… and select your favorites.html file. If you use a different browser such as Safari, Firefox, or Opera, you can drag and drop URLs from the address bar or the bookmarks list directly into the External tab in GoLive.

TIP 27 Adding File Metadata with XMP

Learn More About XMP

To learn more about Adobe's open-source metadata technology visit the Web site at http://www.adobe.com/xmp.

Metadata is a labeling technology that frequently includes fields such as keywords and a description. Metadata may not sound very exciting, but it makes your images more valuable because they become easier to find and use, especially in large projects with lots and lots of files.

Some of the things that make Adobe's Extensible Metadata Platform (XMP) so great are that it's based on XML, it's an open and documented standard, and anybody can implement it in their software. A wide variety of file formats support XMP metadata, including JPEG, GIF, Photoshop, Illustrator, PDF, EPS, and TIFF.

To add or edit metadata to a file, select the file or files in the Site window and choose File > File Info. Edit the desired fields and click OK (**Figure 27**). It's really that easy, and now those fields can be accessed by the Adobe Bridge (see Tip 225), Adobe Version Cue (see Chapter 12), and several third-party digital asset management systems.

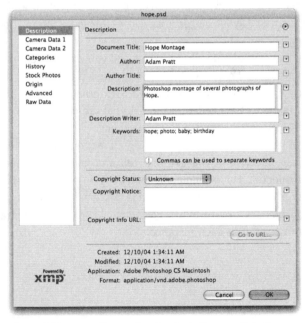

Figure 27 You can edit metadata for single file or multiple files all in one dialog box.

TIP 28 Using Quicksearch to Find Files

When you're working on a large Web site with lots of files, it's hard to quickly locate a specific file, even if you know the filename. The new Quicksearch field in the Files tab of the Site window makes it easy to instantly locate the files you're looking for.

Just type into the Quicksearch field, in the upper-right corner of the Files tab, and you'll see the list of files filtered to match your search criteria as seen in **Figure 28**.

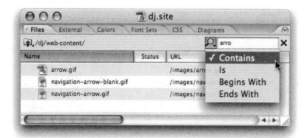

Figure 28 Use Quicksearch to quickly locate files in the Files and Extras tabs of the Site window.

The options are pretty self-explanatory, but notice that if you click the magnifying glass icon, there are four different search types: Contains, Is, Begins With, and Ends With. These options make it easy to narrow your search and find the files you need.

To edit a file you find with Quicksearch, just double-click its icon in the filtered list of search results. To revert back to the normal file view, click the X icon next to the Quicksearch field.

Where Did All My Files Go?

If you look at the Files tab in your Site window, and your heart skips a beat because of all the missing files, it's probably because of Quicksearch. If you're not seeing all the files you expect, make sure the Quicksearch field is empty by clicking the X icon. This will revert your list of files to the normal view.

CHAPTER THREE

Working with Pages

We remember the early days of the Web when we had to walk to work in four feet of snow in our bare feet, uphill both ways, and type all of our source code by hand. Back then, the two biggest competitors in the Web-design software market were SimpleText and Notepad. Fortunately, Web-design software such as GoLive has come a long way and makes the process of building interactive, visually compelling Web sites easier than ever.

You can still write code in GoLive, but it's usually much more efficient to work in GoLive's Layout Editor and let the software write all the HTML for you. GoLive offers six different ways to edit and preview your Web pages, but many users will spend most of their time in the Layout Editor. The accurate layout of this visual authoring environment makes it simple for anybody to build Web sites with the ease of drag and drop.

Because you, too, will spend most of your time in the Layout Editor, we decided to make this the longest chapter in the book. We start by covering some basic layout tools such as zooming, panning, guides, and rulers. We also cover different layout techniques including layout grids, tables, and CSS layers. Toward the end, we cover the use of color in GoLive and sharing color swatches and settings between all the Creative Suite applications.

TIP 29 Touring the Six Document Modes

When you open a Web page in GoLive you see six tabs across the top of the document window. Each tab offers a different way to edit or view your page. To change modes, click on the document tabs. Let's start on the left side and work our way across.

Figure 29 There are six powerful ways to edit and preview your Web pages in GoLive.

- **Layout Editor:** Visual designers spend most of their time using GoLive's Layout Editor. When you add and edit objects in this mode, GoLive writes all the source code for you (see Tips 36–60).

- **Frame Editor:** HTML frames are not nearly as popular as they used to be, but if you need to create frames pages this is the mode you work in (see Tip 75).

- **Source Code Editor:** GoLive includes a very full-featured source code editor that is chock-full of timesaving features (see Tips 77–82).

- **Outline Editor:** The Outline Editor sports a unique outline view of the structure of a page (see Tips 85–91).

- **Layout Preview:** To see an accurate preview of what your Web pages will look in a browser, switch to this preview mode that uses the Opera browser as the rendering engine (see Tip 92).

- **PDF Preview:** GoLive includes a one-click conversion of any Web page to an Adobe PDF (Portable Document Format) file (see Tips 95–107).

TIP 30 Using the Document Window Icons

At the top of every Web page window in GoLive are document icons. The head section of a Web page (see Tip 36) is now clearly labeled at the left edge of the document (**Figure 30**). To reveal the head section, click the triangle next to the Head label.

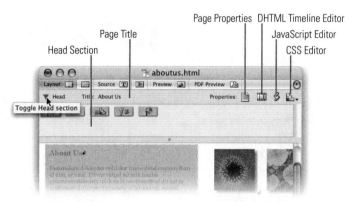

Figure 30 The icons at the top of each document window allow you to customize the page and open other editing environments.

Next is the Page Title field, which is a clearly labeled text box. The page title appears along the very top of the browser window when visitors view your site. The page title is also used when visitors add the page to their bookmarks or favorites, so it's important to give each page a useful and accurate title.

The Page Properties icon is now grouped with the JavaScript Editor, DHTML TimeLine Editor, and CSS Editor icons at the upper right end of the document window. Select the Page Properties icon to change page attributes such as page title, link colors, margins, and background image in the Page Inspector.

To open the JavaScript Editor, DHTML TimeLine Editor, or CSS Editor for the page, just click the corresponding icon at the top right of the document window. If you click and hold the icon for the CSS Editor, you'll get a list of CSS documents in your site to choose from. If you'd rather use menu commands or keyboard shortcuts for these options, you'll find a corresponding menu command for each of the buttons in the Special menu.

Changing Page Titles

Search the Web for the phrases *Welcome to Adobe GoLive* or *Untitled Page* and you'll discover hundreds of thousands of pages that Web designers forgot to give good titles. Make sure you're not guilty of this crime!

Customizing the Document Status Bar

The status bar at the bottom of a document in the Layout Editor offers single-click access to several convenient features (**Figure 31a**). Starting on the left side and working our way across, these options include:

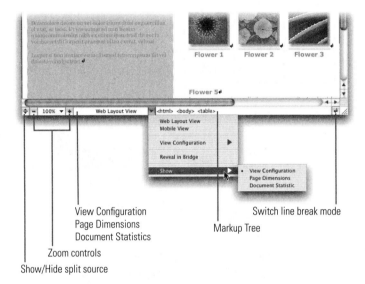

Figure 31a The status bar gives you access to several handy options.

- **Show/hide split source:** This toggles the Split Source view and is also available in the View menu (see Tip 35).

- **Zoom Out:** Zooms out on the current page to the next zoom preset (see Tip 32).

- **Zoom Value:** Select a preset zoom value from the pull-down menu (see Tip 32).

- **Zoom In:** Zooms in on the current page to the next zoom preset (see Tip 32).

- **View Configuration/Page Dimensions/Document Statistics:** Three options share this area. To select an option, click and hold the arrow and select the option from the Show menu. View Configuration lets you orient the page for Web or mobile development. Page Dimensions lets you create and choose presets for the document window dimensions (see Tip 33). Document Statistics shows the number of bytes the page uses.

- **Markup Tree:** The Markup Tree allows you to logically navigate the structure of your source code while in the Layout Editor (see Tip 34).

- **Switch line break mode:** Changes the line breaks of the current page between Mac, UNIX, and Windows formats. This setting is also available under File > Line Breaks.

You might use some of these features more then others, so GoLive lets you customize the status bar to your preference. You can toggle all these features, as well as some status bar options related to PDF preview, in the document flyout menu (**Figure 31b**).

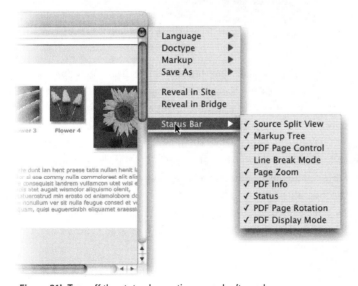

Figure 31b Turn off the status bar options you don't need.

TIP 31: Customizing the Document Status Bar

32 Zooming in Layout

The Hand Tool

GoLive CS2 now includes a Hand tool, which comes in very handy when zoomed into a page. To use it click the hand  in the Toolbox or press H on your keyboard. Once active, use it as you would in Photoshop, Illustrator, InDesign, or Acrobat by dragging the contents of a window up, down, to the right, or to the left. Remember, if all the content on the page fits into the visible area of the window, nothing will pan, so only use this feature when the content exceeds the boundaries of the document window or when you are zoomed into the page.

GoLive CS2 has an amazing zoom control in the visual authoring environment of the Layout Editor. Zooming in can be helpful for tasks such as selecting or aligning small objects, and zooming out can help you get a visual overview of a really long page. You can now zoom from 8.33% to 1600% using the Zoom Value menu in the lower left corner of the document window (**Figure 32**). Zooming has been one of the most frequent feature requests over the years, and the GoLive engineering team has pulled it off with style.

Figure 32 GoLive has the ability to zoom in and out of pages, just like the rest of the applications in the Creative Suite.

You can easily select preset zoom values in the pull-down menu or you can just click the minus (–) button to zoom out and the plus (+) button to zoom in. If you want to set a zoom value that isn't listed, select Edit at the bottom of the list and type in a number.

Click on the zoom value at the bottom of the document window to toggle back and forth between 100% and the previous setting. For example, if you need to zoom out from 100% to 50% to see the overall page composition, click the zoom value to instantly switch back to 100% again. To position the Zoom Value menu on the other side of the document window, choose Position Right from the pull-down.

TIP 33 Customizing Window Sizes

Both the Site window and documents can be resized by dragging the lower right corner, but you can also tell GoLive what page size you prefer and in what position you'd like new pages and new sites to open on your screen.

With Page Dimensions selected in the status bar (see Tip 31), you'll see a page size listed there in pixels. As you resize the page, the dimensions update. Click and hold the small down arrow to see the Window Size pull-down, which lists additional page sizes (**Figure 33a**).

Figure 33a The Window Size pull-down.

Choose Options from the pull-down list. In the dialog box that opens, you can edit the default pages sizes, delete them, or add your own (**Figure 33b**). Use the buttons in the lower right to add or delete new window configurations. Reorder the list by selecting an item and clicking the arrows on the lower left to move it up or down.

Figure 33b The Window Options dialog box.

Window Settings

Once you've got your window size options set, you may have one that you'd like to use for all new documents that are created. Set the front-most window to the desired size and then choose Settings from the Window Size pull-down list. In the dialog box that opens, enable the checkmarks for Markup Document Windows and/or Site Windows. Doing so records both the size of the windows and their position on the screen. Click OK. From then on, any new documents or sites you create will open in the size and position you set in the Window Settings.

You can always go back to the default window configuration by choosing Settings from the Window Size pull-down and then clicking the Use Default Settings button.

Removing Elements and Content

If you Control-click (Mac) or right-click (Windows) on an element in the Markup Tree, you'll see two very powerful options: Replace Element by Its Content and Remove Element's Content. These options come in very handy when you want to do some fancy maneuvering of the HTML syntax without actually touching the code. For example, if you have a piece of text enclosing in a <font> tag and want to remove the font tag, simply select the <font> tag in the Markup Tree and then choose Replace Element by Its Content from the contextual menu.

Navigating the Markup Tree

A great feature that was introduced in GoLive 6 is the Markup Tree in the bottom of the document window for documents that use structured markup, such as HTML, XHTML, and PHP pages. There are many timesaving ways to use the Markup Tree, but we focus on two particular benefits: selecting child and parents elements of the current selection.

The Markup Tree can be used to select child elements of the currently selected object. For example, select a table in the Layout Editor and then click and hold on the table tag in the Markup Tree to select a <tr> (table row) tag (**Figure 34**).

Figure 34 Drill down to child elements of a selected tag using the Markup Tree.

You can also use the Markup Tree bar to select parent elements. For example, to make sure you've selected an entire text hyperlink, select the linked text in Layout mode and then click the <a> tag in the Markup Tree bar. This Markup Tree feature is also available in the Visual Tag Editor dialog box (see Tip 63).

TIP 35 Viewing Split Source

GoLive includes several different ways to edit your pages, including a visual Layout Editor and a Source Code Editor. Different users may prefer one or the other, but a handy trick is to combine both the Layout Editor and the Source Code Editor at the same time with the Split Source view. You can work in either mode and watch the results update in real-time in the other mode.

To turn on Split Source view and edit your layout and source code simultaneously, click the show/hide icon ⬍ in the bottom left corner of the document window. You can also choose View > Show Split Source or press Command-Y (Mac) or Control-Y (Windows) to toggle Split Source view (**Figure 35**).

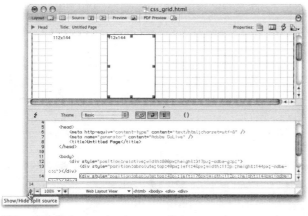

Figure 35 Split Source view lets you edit layout and source code simultaneously.

One more power tip is to open a document in Outline mode and turn on the Split Source view for a powerful editing environment coders will love. Another way to view the visual layout and source code of a page at the same time is to work in the Layout Editor and open the Source Code palette from the Window menu.

Rotating the Split Source View

Hold Option (Mac) or Alt (Windows) when you click the Split Source icon to rotate the orientation of the two views.

TIP 36 — Understanding the Head and Body of a Web Page

If you've taken the time to learn the basics of HTML, you'll remember that every page is divided into two main areas: the head and the body. The head section is at the beginning of the page and is invisible to the user unless they view the source code. The head is where you place things like meta tags for search engine optimization and certain kinds of JavaScript Actions.

Click the triangle in the upper left corner of the document window to reveal the head section (**Figure 36**). Place objects such as meta tags in the head of the page by dragging and dropping them from the head section of the Objects palette.

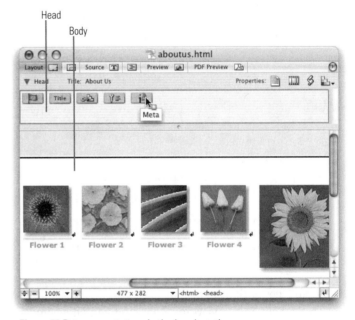

Figure 36 Put your meta tags in the head section.

The body is the visible area of the page where you place all the content your Web site visitors will see. Everything below the head section is called the body, and this is where you place tables, layers, text, images, and so on.

TIP 37 Inserting Objects in a Page

As you start to build your site in GoLive, you'll add a variety of objects such as tables, CSS layers, CSS box objects, images, and multimedia to the pages. If you can drag and drop, you can build Web pages—it's really that easy. First, select a set of objects (see Tip 4), then just drag and drop the items you need from the Objects palette into the Layout Editor or double-click the object in the Objects palette, and it will be inserted in the page at the location of your cursor.

After the object has been added to the page, you can adjust its settings in the context-sensitive Inspector palette. For example, if you select an image in the Layout Editor, the Inspector lets you control attributes such as width, height, and alignment. If you have a table selected, the Inspector lets you adjust things such as the number of rows and columns and the borders and spacing in the table (**Figure 37**).

Which Objects Should You Use?

At the lower right corner of the Objects palette is a button called Palette Options. Click that button to see both a list of object sets and a menu item called Configure. The Configure option removes any object from the palette that would create markup that does not conform to a particular DTD. To use it, choose Configure and then select a DTD from the list (for more on DTDs, see Tip 65).

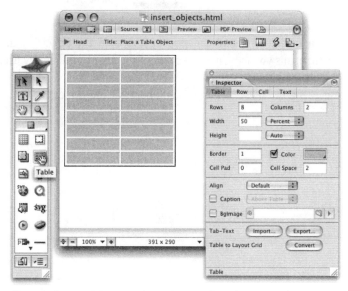

Figure 37 Drag and drop page items from the Objects palette and change their settings in the Inspector palette.

TIP 38

Inserting Objects with Menu Commands

A quick and easy method for inserting objects onto a page is to Control-click (Mac) or right-click (Windows) in the Layout Editor and choose an object from the Insert Object menu. The object will be placed at the cursor's insertion point and is automatically selected, which means you can immediately set the objects attributes in the Inspector palette (**Figure 38**).

Getting to Know Objects

Not all the objects in the Objects palette can be added to the Layout Editor. For example, Site and Diagram objects only work in the Site and Diagram windows. Similarly, the QuickTime and SMIL objects only work in the QuickTime and SMIL Editors.

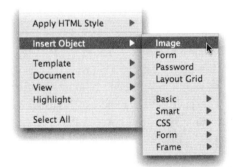

Figure 38 You can easily and quickly insert an object right where you want it using menu commands.

The Insert command can also be found in the Special menu, which means you can apply a keyboard shortcut to frequently used objects (see Tip 2). After you've used the Insert command, GoLive shows the ten most recently used objects at the top of the list.

TIP 39 Using Paste Special

Content to be used on a Web page may be given to you in a Microsoft Word document, via email, or from a number of other software applications. In the past, copying and pasting text from those sources into GoLive resulted in a loss of text styling unless you knew the hidden keyboard shortcut to use to retain the formatting. In GoLive CS2, handling this task has become much more elegant thanks to a new menu command called Paste Special.

To use Paste Special, you must first copy text from another document. Then in GoLive CS2, choose Edit > Paste Special, and a small dialog box will open (**Figure 39**).

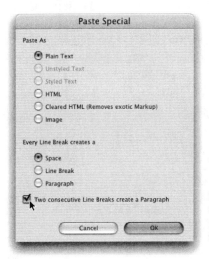

Figure 39 Paste Special offers a host of options that make it easy to bring in text from other sources.

In the top portion of the dialog box are options that let you choose to paste the text as plain text, rich text (with or without styling), HTML, cleared HTML, or even as an image, which is useful if you have fancy text whose styling you may not be able to successfully reproduce for the Web using CSS.

The lower portion of the Paste Special dialog offers options that are huge time-savers when pasting in text copied from email, which is often heavily laden with extra line breaks. Simply choose one of the three options describing how you'd like the line breaks to be handled and click OK.

No Place for a Break

At the bottom of the Paste Special dialog box is one of our favorite options—an automatic way to change multiple line breaks into paragraphs. Anyone who has ever copied and pasted text from an email knows what a timesaver this little command can be. It's a fast reliable way to clean up unwanted formatting created by email applications.

TIP
40 Using Meta Tags

In this tip we take a look at two kinds of meta tags: keywords and description. Search engines still depend on these two tags to help them determine if your site meets the criteria of a person's search. Keywords are a list of words that exemplify the content of the page or site. If the site is all about custom window treatments, for example, you might include keywords such as *fabric*, *draperies*, *sashes*, *blinds*, and so on. You could also include keywords that indicate where your business is located (*Princeton*, *Trenton*, *New Jersey*, and so on) or other pertinent information.

To create a keyword meta tag, drag and drop the Keyword object from the head portion of the Objects palette into the page.

GoLive automatically opens the head section, drops the object in, and selects it. In the Inspector palette, type a keyword into the input field and press Enter/Return to add it to the list. Repeat as needed to complete your list (**Figure 40a**).

Figure 40a Add, edit, or delete keywords via the Keyword Inspector.

The description meta tag gives the browser a bit of descriptive text to use when a search has been run and the site meets the criteria. So if a person runs a search on *"custom draperies, New Jersey,"* the search engine returns a link to the site followed by a description, if included. If there is no description, the search engine uses text on the page. To insert a description meta tag, open the head portion of the page, double-click the meta object, and then in the Meta Inspector select Description from the pull-down menu (**Figure 40b**). In the Text Input field, type the description of your Web site. If possible, include keywords in your descriptive text for best results.

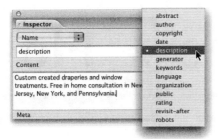

Figure 40b Choose description from the pull-down menu and enter the description.

Ruler Swooshing

When you turn the rulers on or off on a Mac, they swoosh in or out of the page as an animation with sound. On Windows they just... well, they just turn on and off.

TIP
41 Viewing Page Rulers

Here's a small but useful tip: To show rulers on your page in the Layout Editor, simply choose View > Show Rulers (**Figure 41**). To put them away, choose the command a second time. If you zoom in on the page, the rulers get larger, too (see Tip 32).

Figure 41 Page rulers help you line up objects on a page.

When an object on the page is selected, look carefully at the rulers and you'll see a darker band of gray indicating where the top and left edge of the object lines up to the ruler.

TIP 42 Creating Links

Probably the most fundamental feature of a Web page is a hyperlink, often simply called a link. Hyperlinks can be created for both text and images, and GoLive offers a number of ways to create links. Let's start with text links.

To make a link out of text, first select the text and then do one of the following:

- Type the URL into the Link field of the Inspector palette.

- Use the Fetch URL tool in the Inspector palette and point and shoot at a page in your files list or at the Page Properties icon (see Tip 30) of another open page. When the page icon is highlighted, release the mouse button and you'll have created linked text (**Figure 42a**).

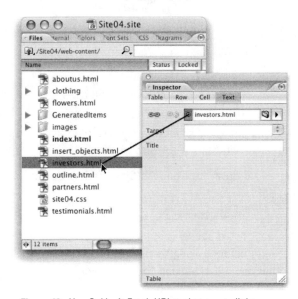

Figure 42a Use GoLive's Fetch URL tool to create links.

(continued on next page)

Linking to the Site Window

If you've ever wanted to create a link but can't see your files list because the Site window is behind the other pages, try this: Use the Fetch URL tool and point to the Select Window icon ![icon], in the toolbar. The Site window will pop to the front, and then you can finish your link. This trick works equally well for popping open folders in the files list or for bringing forward tabs in the Site window.

- Click the Browse button at the right end of the link field and navigate to a document. Select the document to create the link.

- Choose a file from the list in the pull-down menu at the right end of the link field to select from recently used files (**Figure 42b**).

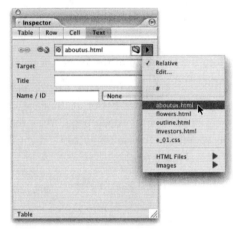

Figure 42b Use this handy list to create a link.

- Hold down the Command key (Mac) or the Control key (Windows) and point and shoot directly from the selected text to a file in the Files tab of the Site window.

- Drag and drop a file from the Site window on top of the selection.

Creating links from a selected image can be done the first three of the four ways listed above. Just remember to click the Link tab of the Inspector before making the link.

Yet another method of linking to a document is dragging and dropping a file from the Site window into an opened page. This automatically creates a link to that page using the filename as the link text. (The exception is PDF—take a look at Tip 153 to see what happens there!)

TIP 43 Autocompleting http and mailto Links

Most external hyperlinks point to Web sites or email addresses and consistently include http:// or mailto: at the beginning of the link. Did you know that GoLive automatically adds these parts of hyperlinks in the link field of the Inspector palette? For example, if you assign a link and type www.adobe.com in the Inspector, GoLive completes the address to a fully valid URL of http://www.adobe.com when you press Return/Enter (**Figure 43**).

Figure 43 GoLive intelligently autocompletes http and mailto links in the Inspector.

It's a handy little tip that'll save you unnecessary and error-prone typing time. When you need to type the address to servers using other protocols such as ftp:// or https://, GoLive is smart enough to leave those alone and not append the http:// protocol.

This works for email addresses, too. If you type email@domain.com into the link field of the Inspector palette and press Return/Enter, GoLive automatically completes the link as mailto:email@domain.com.

TIP
44 Viewing Link Warnings

If you have a bad link on a page, GoLive lets you know by putting a little red bug 🐞 in the Status column of the Files list.

To easily locate the bug on the page, use the Link Warnings icon on the toolbar. To make things super easy for you, the icon in the toolbar uses the exact same bug icon as the one in the Status column (**Figure 44a**).

Figure 44a The Link Warnings icon on the toolbar.

First, open the page with the bug and then click the Link Warning icon. The error on the page will be highlighted in red. If you don't see anything highlighted in red, remember to look in the head portion of the page. The error could be there. Select the highlighted area and re-link it via the Inspector palette (**Figure 44b**).

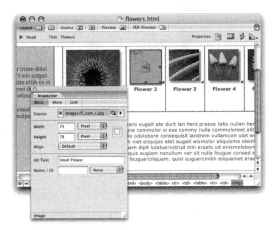

Figure 44b Link warnings highlight errors in red in the Layout Editor, the Inspector palette, and the Markup Tree at the bottom of the document window.

TIP 45 Adding Document Encodings to Pages with Errors

Document encoding is a little piece of HTML syntax that tells the browser which character set (charset) to use when displaying a Web page. *Charset* refers to the set of characters used in a particular language (English, French, and so on). If you open a page that was created without a document encoding assigned, GoLive offers options for correcting the omission. Use one of the following methods to assign a document encoding to a page.

If you open a file missing the document encoding, a dialog box opens. Selecting the first radio button and then clicking Open opens the page while temporarily using the encoding selected in the pull-down menu, but the code is not added to the page. To add the code permanently to the page, click the second radio button and choose the preferred encoding from the pull-down (**Figure 45**). GoLive writes the necessary code, and you won't get the dialog the next time you open the page.

Where's My Language?

The last option in the File > Document Encoding submenu is Edit. Edit lets you enable additional character sets such as Greek, Cryillic, Korean, and others.

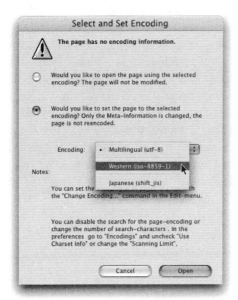

Figure 45 Select the character set from the pull-down menu and click the appropriate radio button.

Once a page is open, you can still change the character encoding by choosing File > Document Encoding and then choosing from the list in the submenu.

Using the Completely Redesigned Layout Grid

Have you ever wished there were an easy way to put images and text exactly where you want them on a Web page? Well, the all-new CSS-based GoLive Layout Grid is the answer to your prayers.

The new Layout Grid object is found in the Basic set of the Objects palette ▦. We call it new because, although previous versions of GoLive included a grid object, in the past it was a table-based object. GoLive CS2's vastly improved support for CSS reaches all the way to the Layout Grid object. Instead of writing a table tag, the Layout Grid now writes a <div> tag.

To use a grid on a page, either drag and drop it from the Objects palette or double-click to insert it at the point of your cursor (see Tip 37).

Resize the grid by dragging one of its three blue resize handles or by typing pixel dimensions into the Width and Height fields of the Layout Grid Inspector. Next, place other objects onto the grid and move them by dragging or by pressing the arrow keys to nudge right, left, up, or down.

You can drag images and movies directly onto the grid, but text needs to go inside a layout text box. If you drag and drop text onto a grid, GoLive creates a layout text box at the default size of 32x32 pixels, so you'll most likely need to resize it. You could create the layout text box first and then paste or drag text into it. Drag a layout text box from the Objects palette and drop it onto the grid, then resize as needed, or even better, use the new Grid Text Box tool ▦ to draw out text boxes wherever you need them on the grid (**Figure 46**).

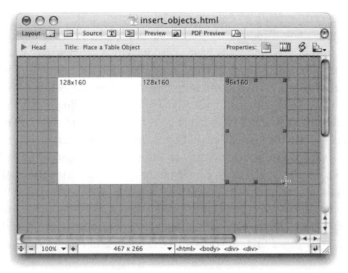

Figure 46 GoLive CS2's new Grid Text Box tool makes it a breeze to draw text boxes on a grid wherever you want them.

Select multiple objects on a Layout Grid by dragging across them or Shift-clicking them and then moving them all at once. If you want, you can use the Group and Ungroup icons on the toolbar to keep them together or break them apart, or open the Align palette from the Window menu and line them up however you'd like. Look in the Grid Inspector for additional options, such as coloring the grid or setting a background image.

Targeting Grid Locations
Click once at the intersection of two lines on the Layout Grid and look closely. You'll see a little blinking cursor indicating that you've just set a target. If you then double-click an object in the Objects palette, that object will land precisely in the spot you've targeted.

TIP 46: Using the Completely Redesigned Layout Grid

TIP 47 Converting Old Layout Grids to CSS

Previous versions of GoLive used layout grids that were actually tables when displayed by a browser. If you placed many objects onto your grid, you could have ended up with a very complex table and a copious amount of HTML code. The updated Layout Grid in GoLive CS2 is CSS-based and writes beautiful, lean <div> tags which render quickly in today's modern browsers. The cool thing is that you can convert your old table-based grids from any previous version of GoLive into the new CSS based Layout Grids very easily.

Open a document that uses an old table-based grid in GoLive CS2. In the upper right corner of the grid is a little icon that indicates whether the grid is table-based 🗔 or CSS-based 🗔. To switch from one type of grid to the other, control-click (Mac) or right-click (Windows) on the grid and then choose either Convert to Table based Grid, or Convert to CSS based Grid (**Figure 47**).

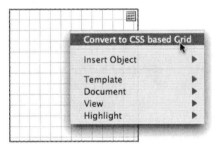

Figure 47 You can easily convert a table-based grid into the new CSS-based Layout Grid.

TIP 48 Converting Layout Grids to Tables

You can change a table-based grid into a standard HTML table. To do so, select your layout grid and then choose Layout Grid to Table from the Special menu.

If that isn't enough for you, you can also convert a table to a Layout Grid. Simply select your table and then in the Table Inspector click the Convert button next to "Table to Layout Grid" (**Figure 48**). See Tip 51 for more info on using tables.

Figure 48 One click in the Inspector palette and you can turn a table into a Layout Grid.

TIP 49 Designing with the Layer Tool

Layout Grids are fantastic for quickly designing Web pages, but a more modern approach would be to use layers. Layers offer even more flexibility than Layout Grids when it comes to placing objects on a page, because you can overlap layers, stack them, turn them on and off, and even animate them.

> **Note**
>
> *In GoLive CyberStudio 3 and Adobe GoLive 4, 5, and 6, layers were called Floating Boxes. Enough people were bewildered by that odd name that the GoLive team finally changed it.*

New in GoLive CS2 is a Layer tool that makes it easier than ever to put layers on a page where you want them. Click the Layer tool or press F on your keyboard to activate it, then click and drag in your page to draw a layer. You can draw layers that overlap, that butt up against one another, or that float anywhere on a page (**Figure 49a**).

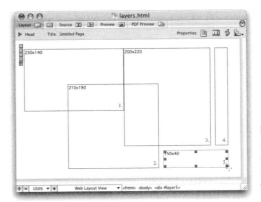

Figure 49a Layers can be adjacent, overlapping, or floating by themselves.

After drawing layers, use to the Object Selection tool to move layers around. Enable the Objects Selection tool by clicking it in the Toolbox or pressing V on the keyboard, then click and drag in a layer to move it around the page.

Notice that a layer has two parts: a black rectangle indicating the layer's border and a tiny square yellow marker. Clicking the yellow marker brings the Layer Inspector into focus; clicking the black rectangle not only focuses the Inspector, but also selects the layer itself. If you move the yellow marker, you are actually moving the syntax for the layer in the HTML source code, whereas if you move the rectangle, you are repositioning the layer on the page.

You can put other objects, such as an image, a table, text, or even a Layout Grid, into a layer. It's a good idea to give a descriptive name to your layers. Although GoLive automatically assigns a name to each layer, it's hard to tell which is which unless they are named properly. You'll also want to assign each layer a Z-index, which indicates the order in which they are stacked. Use the Inspector palette to accomplish both those tasks (**Figure 49b**).

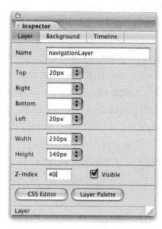

Figure 49b Set a layer's attributes, such as name and Z-index, in the Inspector palette.

Although you can move layers by dragging them, you can also position them using the fields in the Inspector. You'll also notice a checkbox for Visible in the Inspector. This turns a layer on or off in the browser and is often used in conjunction with a link or action to show and hide layers.

Go to the Background area in the Layer Inspector to assign a color or background image to a layer. The Timeline portion of the Layer Inspector has a nifty way of letting you create a quick animation. Select a layer and click the Record button, then move the layer around the page. GoLive automatically sets time markers as it records the movement. To fine-tune your animation, click the Open Timeline Editor button and work directly in the Timeline Editor itself.

(continued on next page)

Styling Layers in the CSS Editor

Layers are written as `<div>` tags with unique IDs in the HTML syntax and as such can be completely styled in the CSS Editor. Use CSS to adjust positioning or size, to add borders, padding, or margins to a layer, and much more!

TIP 49: Designing with the Layer Tool

Layers of Fun

In addition to using the Layer tool to draw layers, you can also use the Layer object in the Basic set of objects. Drag and drop a layer onto a page or double-click to insert one. You can also add new layers from the Layers palette, which can be opened from the Window menu. If you would like two layers to always move together, put the yellow marker for one inside of the other. You can zoom into and out of nested layers by using the Table & Boxes palette located in the Window menu.

Another way to select a layer is to click its name in the Layers palette. The Layers palette also sports Create New Layer and Delete Selected Layers buttons (**Figure 49c**).

Figure 49c Create or delete layers, give layers a name, or select layers in the Layers palette.

If you'd like to able to move layer names in the list, choose Hierarchic from the Layer palette menu and then simply drag the layer names up or down. The Hierarchic mode also gives a nice visual representation of nested layers. The little eyeball icon to the left of a layer in the Layer palette turns the layer on or off as you are editing, but it does not affect the visibility of the layer in the browser. For that you need to use the Visibility option in the Inspector.

TIP 50 Working with CSS Objects

New to GoLive CS2 is a set of objects called draggable CSS objects. These objects are a collection of pre-built CSS boxes, such as 3 columns with a liquid center (a center that scales as a page is made smaller or larger), navigation rows, padded boxes, and more (**Figure 50a**).

Figure 50a Creating intricate CSS-based layouts is simplified by using the new draggable CSS Objects.

These objects allow you to quickly create a complex CSS layout without hand coding. Simply drag an object from the Objects palette and drop it onto your page. You can even nest one box inside of another. When you've got your basic page layout in place, use the Inspector palette to edit the ID of the <div> tags or to change the size of a box (**Figure 50b**).

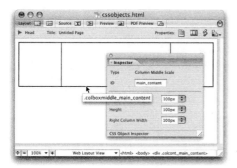

Figure 50b Select a CSS object on your page and edit its attributes, such as ID or dimensions, in the Inspector palette.

(continued on next page)

TIP 50: Working with CSS Objects

Use the CSS editor to apply styling to a box, such as padding, margin, border, background color or image, and so on (**Figure 50c**).

Figure 50c Designate a background color or image for a box in the CSS Editor.

TIP 51 — Designing with Tables

In the beginning, text on an HTML page ran clear across the window with nary a column in sight, and tables were only used as a way to cohesively present tabular data in a Web browser. Designers quickly realized that they could create more complex layouts by housing them in a table. With the recent improvements in CSS, table-less designs now are all the rage, but there are still times when tables are the best solution. GoLive handles tables very gracefully, with some unique features such as the Table & Boxes palette, so let's take a look.

GoLive has three important tools for building tables effectively: the Table object, the Table Inspector, and the Table & Boxes Palette (**Figure 51a**).

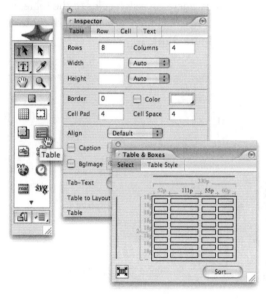

Figure 51a
Use these tools for building tables: the Table object, the Table Inspector, and the Table & Boxes Palette.

The Table object is found in the Basic set of the Objects palette. Drag and drop one onto a page or double-click to insert one and then use the Inspector to set its attributes, such as the number of rows and columns. Across the top of the Table Inspector are buttons called Table, Row, Cell, and Text, where you will find options for setting specific table attributes. What's cool is that if you select a row in your table, GoLive automatically brings the Row tools into focus. If you select a cell, the Cell tab comes forward. And so on.

(continued on next page)

TIP 51: Designing with Tables

When defining a table, row, or cell's dimensions, you can use the pull-down menu to choose Pixel, Percent, or Auto. Pixel sets a specific size in pixels, but Percent and Auto work differently. If you set your overall table size as 80 percent, then the table expands or contracts to take up 80 percent of the page it's on. If you use Auto, then the table expands or contracts according to the content inside it. When setting size options for individual cells, you can achieve various effects by combining pixels or percent in one column and auto in the adjacent column. For example, if you create a table with two columns (two cells), set the first cell at 125 pixels and the second cell to auto, the first column will always remain 125 pixels while the second expands or contracts. If you instead set the first cell at 25 percent and the second at 75 percent, the two columns always remain proportionate when the table resizes.

The Inspector is also where to set table border, cell padding, and cell spacing, as well as where to assign color to the table, row, or even an individual cell. Here's a quick explanation of these settings in the Inspector (**Figure 51b**):

Figure 51b The Table Inspector.

- **Cell Border:** Defines the size of the border around the outside of the whole table.

- **Cell Pad:** Puts padding between the contents of a cell and its border and applies to all cells in the table.

- **Cell Space:** Puts spacing in between cells and applies to all cells in the table.

- **Align Left or Right:** Allows other content to wrap around the table. **Align Center** aligns the table to the middle. **Default** puts the table on the left, but with no wrap.

- **Caption:** Puts a space either above or below the table suitable for a caption.

- **BgImage:** Allows you to define a background image for the table. Background images set this way will tile, so use CSS to define a background if you need more control.

- **Tab-Text Import:** Brings delimited text into a GoLive table, whereas **Export** extracts data from a GoLive table to a delimited text format.

- **Table to Layout Grid:** Turns a table into a GoLive Layout Grid.

  ### Note
  You can copy a range of cells from a Microsoft Excel spreadsheet and paste it directly into a GoLive table. GoLive automatically creates the correct number of rows and columns needed for the data (see Tip 53).

To add rows or columns, choose one of the following methods:

- Select a cell and then in the Table portion of the Inspector palette type in the number of rows and columns you desire.

- Select a cell and then in the Cell portion of the Inspector palette use the Add Row/Column or Delete Row/Column buttons.

- Select a cell, choose Special > Table, and insert a column or row.

- Select a cell, use the contextual menu to choose Insert or Remove, and then insert a column or row.

- Put your cursor inside the last cell of a table and press Tab to create a new bottom row.

- Press the Command key (on a Mac) and then drag the bottom or right side of the table. Sorry, there's no equivalent on Windows.

You combine cells—for example, turn a row of four cells into one wide cell—by *merging* them. To merge cells, select a range of cells, Control-click/right-click them, and choose Merge Cells or select Special > Table > Merge Cells from the menu.

A table cell can hold any content that you can put on a page, such as text, images, or even another table (see Tip 58), and data can be both imported into and exported from GoLive tables (see Tip 53).

Merging Mania

A neat trick for merging cells is to select one, hold down the Shift key, and press the right arrow key to merge right or the down arrow key to merge down. Be careful, though. While the content in the first cell is not affected, the content in the merged cells will be deleted. Move content into the first cell before merging a cell with other cells.

TIP 51: Designing with Tables

Selecting Tables

Table handling is very elegant in GoLive, and in this tip we show you a bunch of handy table-selection tricks that make daily production tasks easy. When a row, column, or cell is selected, you'll notice a thick black stroke around the selection.

- **Selecting tables with the cursor:** To select an entire table, single-click the top or left edge of the table (**Figure 52a**).

Vendor	Description	Part #	Cost
Itto	Muffler	36593	$89.00
Imagine	Upholstery	96782	$329.00
Enviro	Xeon Lamps	16677	$589.00
Moshler	LED Visor	90427	$499.00
Itto	Wheels	56341	$899.00
Enviro	Carbon Frame	18592	$1204.00
Imagine	Tinted Glass	23675	$118.00

Figure 52a Select an entire table by clicking to top or left edge.

- **Selecting tables with the Markup Tree:** If the cursor is already inserted inside the table you want to select, click the `<table>` tag in the Markup Tree at the bottom of the document window. If you have nested tables, make sure you select the correct table.

- **Selecting a table cell with the cursor:** To select an individual table cell, single-click the bottom or right edge of the cell (**Figure 52b**).

Vendor	Description	Part #	Cost
Itto	Muffler	36593	$89.00
Imagine	Upholstery	96782	$329.00
Enviro	Xeon Lamps	16677	$589.00
Moshler	LED Visor	90427	$499.00
Itto	Wheels	56341	$899.00
Enviro	Carbon Frame	18592	$1204.00
Imagine	Tinted Glass	23675	$118.00

Figure 52b Select a cell by clicking its bottom or right edge.

- **Selecting a table cell with the Markup Tree:** If the cursor is already inserted inside the table cell you want to select, click the <td> tag in the Markup Tree at the bottom of the document window.

- **Selecting table columns:** To select an entire table column, move your cursor near the top of the column and single-click with the down-facing arrow cursor (**Figure 52c**). To select multiple adjacent columns, click near the top of one column and drag horizontally. To add multiple discontiguous columns to the selection, Shift-click the tops of other columns. To subtract a column from a selection, Shift-click the top of the column.

Vendor	Description	Part #	Cost
Itto	Muffler	36593	$89.00
Imagine	Upholstery	96782	$329.00
Enviro	Xeon Lamps	16677	$589.00
Moshler	LED Visor	90427	$499.00
Itto	Wheels	56341	$899.00
Enviro	Carbon Frame	18592	$1204.00
Imagine	Tinted Glass	23675	$118.00

Figure 52c Selecting entire rows and columns is easy.

- **Selecting table rows:** To select an entire table row, move your cursor near the left edge of the row and single-click with the right-facing arrow cursor. To select multiple adjacent rows, click near the left edge of one row and drag vertically. To select multiple discontiguous rows, Shift-click the left edges of other rows. To subtract a row from a selection, Shift-click the left edge of the row.

- **Selecting multiple table cells:** To select a region of adjacent table cells, simply click and drag over the cells.

(continued on next page)

Using the Table & Boxes Palette

All these table selection tips work in the Table & Boxes palette just as they do in the Layout Editor. Open the Table & Boxes palette in the Window menu and resize it so it's easier to select tiny table cells.

- **Selecting discontiguous table cells:** To select discontiguous table cells, start with at least one cell selected and then Shift-click the other cells (**Figure 52d**). To subtract a table cell from a multi-cell selection, just Shift-click the table cells.

Vendor	Description	Part #	Cost
Itto	Muffler	36593	$89.00
Imagine	Upholstery	96782	$329.00
Enviro	Xeon Lamps	16677	$589.00
Moshler	LED Visor	90427	$499.00
Itto	Wheels	56341	$899.00
Enviro	Carbon Frame	18592	$1204.00
Imagine	Tinted Glass	23675	$118.00

Figure 52d Add and subtract cells from your selection by holding the Shift key.

- **Selecting tables and table cells with the keyboard:** Press Command-Return (Mac) or Control-Enter (Windows) to navigate up through your table structure. For example, if you have table cell content selected and you invoke this shortcut, you select the containing table cell. If you have a table cell selected and use this shortcut, you select the entire table. If you use this shortcut on a nested table, you select the parent table cell.

- **Selecting table cell contents:** When you have a table cell selected and want to edit the contents of the cell and not the cell itself, press the Enter/Return key on your keyboard or switch to the Text tab of the Table Inspector.

TIP
53 **Importing Data into Tables**

Importing text into a table works seamlessly with several applications, including Microsoft Excel, Microsoft Word, AppleWorks, Lotus 123, and Lotus Word Pro (**Figure 53**). Just follow these easy steps:

1. Select the cells and choose Edit > Copy to copy the text from the original file, such as a Microsoft Excel spreadsheet or a Microsoft Word table.

2. Switch to GoLive and choose Edit > Paste to create a table from the clipboard data. Note that GoLive automagically creates the correct number of rows and columns to accommodate the content.

If you need to import a plain text file into a table, choose Special > Table > Import Tab-Delimited Text and select the text file. You can also export tab-delimited text from HTML tables in GoLive. Just select the table in the Layout Editor and choose Special > Table > Export Tab-Delimited Text to save out a text file.

Importing Partial Tables

The cell you select in the table determines the upper-left starting point for the imported text. This means that if you already have other content in your table, such as column headers, you can select the left-most cell in the second row and you'll end up with everything intact when you paste.

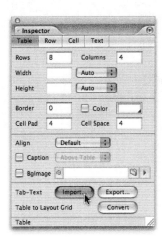

Figure 53 You can copy and paste, use the Special > Table commands, or these buttons in the Table Inspector to import and export table data.

54 Fixing Table Widths

The power of GoLive's table handling means it's typical for Web designers to experiment with several different design options when they're working with tables. One of the pitfalls of this flexibility is that you can end up with some funky math for the widths of your tables and table cells. Specifically, the sum of the table cell widths might not equal the overall width of the table.

GoLive flags the problem by displaying any mathematical errors in red in the Select tab of the Table & Boxes palette. Place your mouse pointer over these red table measurements (*220p* in **Figure 54a**) and you'll see the arrow cursor change to a checkmark.

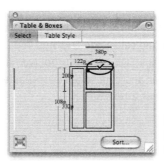

Figure 54a Click the red table measurements with the checkmark cursor to correct the table math.

Click the red numbers with the checkmark cursor, and GoLive instantly calculates the correct math and fixes your source code so that the table renders more reliably across different browsers and platforms (**Figure 54b**).

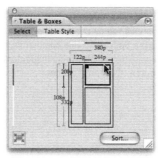

Figure 54b After fixing the math in this example, the cell width is 244 pixels instead of 220 pixels.

TIP 55 Sorting Table Data

Sometimes the data you place in an HTML table is perfectly format-ted and ordered, but sometimes you need to resort it. For example, you might need to sort a table according to part number or price. The good news is that sorting table data in GoLive is really easy.

Select the table you want to sort (see Tip 52) and open the Table & Boxes palette from the Window menu. Next, click the Sort button in the bottom right corner of the palette to see the Sort Table dialog (**Figure 55**).

Sorting Just the Selection
If you only want to sort part of a table instead of the entire table, select the cells you want to sort before you open the Sort Table dialog.

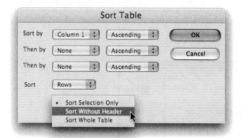

Figure 55 The Sort Table dialog offers several ways to re-order your table data.

The sort options include:

- **Sort by:** You can choose which row or column you want to sort by. You can even designate secondary and tertiary sort criteria with the **Then by** options.

- **Ascending or descending:** You can sort alphanumerically in ascending or descending order. If you want the item with the lowest price listed first, you would choose **Ascending**, and for the highest price listed first, choose **Descending.**

- **Sort Rows or Columns:** If you want to sort top to bottom, which is the most common, choose **Rows**. If you want to sort left to right, choose **Columns**.

- **Sort Selection Only:** Sorts only cells you selected when you opened the Sort Table dialog and ignores unselected cells.

- **Sort Without Header:** Sorts the entire table, except the first row or column—that is reserved as a header for text labels.

- **Sort Whole Table:** Sorts the entire table, including the header row or column, even if only part of the table is selected.

TIP
56 Rearranging Tables

Sorting table data alphabetically or numerically is a big time saver, but sometimes you just need to rearrange entire sections of a table. For example, you might want to move the price column to the far right of a table or the part number column to the far left.

To rearrange table columns or rows, select them and drag them by the small black handle in the upper left corner of the selection. The key to rearranging table content is seeing the thick black lines between rows or columns that indicates the drag location (**Figure 56**). You can also rearrange multiple rows and columns after you select them (see Tip 52). This feature even works on multiple cells as long as they are adjacent.

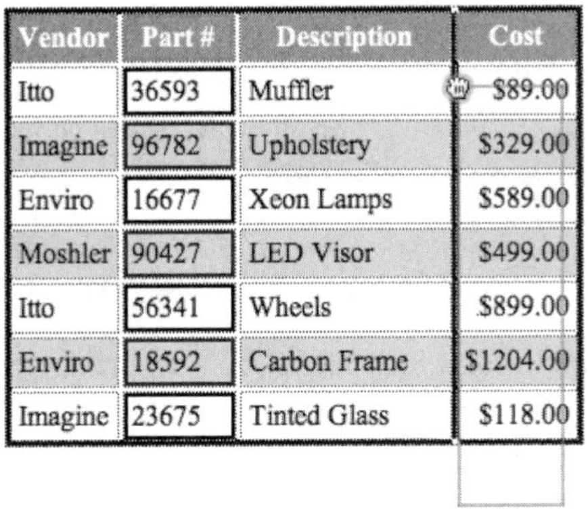

Vendor	Part #	Description	Cost
Itto	36593	Muffler	$89.00
Imagine	96782	Upholstery	$329.00
Enviro	16677	Xeon Lamps	$589.00
Moshler	90427	LED Visor	$499.00
Itto	56341	Wheels	$899.00
Enviro	18592	Carbon Frame	$1204.00
Imagine	23675	Tinted Glass	$118.00

Figure 56 Rearranging tables is as easy as drag and drop.

To make a copy of your selection, drag it to a different area of the page outside the table. This drag and drop technique works in the Table & Boxes palette like it does in the Layout Editor.

TIP 57 Styling Tables

Importing, sorting, and rearranging table data in GoLive helps you organize the content, but styling the rows and columns helps give the data the visual clarity you need to communicate effectively. Select a table, open the Table & Boxes palette from the Window menu, and switch to the Table Style tab of the palette (**Figure 57**).

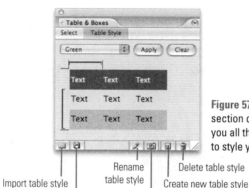

Figure 57 The Table Style section of the palette gives you all the tools you need to style your tables.

Import table style | Export table style | Rename table style | Capture table style | Create new table style | Delete table style

To style a table selected in the Layout Editor, select a table style from the pull-down menu and click Apply. If the table style doesn't look like you expected, click the Clear button in the palette and try a different style.

The default table styles give you a place to start, but you'll probably want to design your own. You can apply formatting to a table—including font, font size, font color, table color, row color, cell color, borders, padding, spacing, and alignment—and click the Create new table style icon at the bottom of the palette. Give the new table style a name and click OK. Now you can use the same style in other pages and other sites and guarantee visual consistency.

If you make some changes to a table and want to update the table style, select the table in the Layout Editor, the table style in the Table & Boxes palette, and click the Capture icon at the bottom of the palette. This updates the existing table style instead of creating a new one.

To rename a table style, select it in the pull-down menu, click the Rename icon, and give it a new name. If there are table styles you know you'll never use, you can select them in the Table & Boxes palette and click the Delete icon to permanently delete them.

Sharing Table Styles

If you create table styles you want to share with others, select Export Table Styles from the fly-out menu in the Table & Boxes palette. The table styles are saved as an XML file that you can share with others. To import table styles from another GoLive user, choose Import Table Styles from the flyout menu in the Table & Boxes palette. This is an easy way to ensure visual consistency when you have several designers contributing to the same project.

Bonus Tip

Experiment with the blue borders on the top and left edge of the table style preview in the Table & Boxes palette. This will affect how frequently the pattern repeats and will be most obvious when applied to larger tables.

TIP 57: Styling Tables

TIP
58 Zooming in Nested Tables

Selecting nested tables can be really tricky, so GoLive has a table zooming feature that makes it easy to select nested parent and child tables. It's just like zooming in and out of multiple tables but without the dizziness.

Select a table in the Layout Editor or insert your cursor in a table cell and open the Table & Boxes palette from the Window menu. To select the parent table the current table is nested inside of, click the Select parent table icon in the bottom left corner of the Table & Boxes palette (**Figure 58a**). If you have multiple nested tables, you can keep clicking this button to select the next parent table, the next parent table, and so on.

Figure 58a Click the Select parent table icon in the Table & Boxes palette to zoom out of nested tables.

To select a table nested inside another table, click the gray outline of the nested table in the Table & Boxes palette (**Figure 58b**).

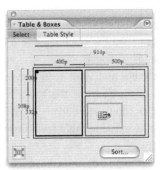

Figure 58b Click the gray outline of the nested table to zoom in.

TIP 59

Selecting Tiny Images in Tables

Many users find it challenging to select small images, such as single-pixel GIFs, inside table cells. The zooming feature can help (see Tip 32), but sometimes there are even easier ways. For example, the Markup Tree in the status bar, located at the bottom of the document window, makes this delicate task very easy.

First, select the table cell where the tiny image is positioned. Next, click and hold on the <td> tag in the Markup Tree and select the <img> tag to select the image (**Figure 59a**).

Figure 59a Select tiny images with the Markup Tree in the status bar.

When the tiny image is selected, you'll see its attributes in the Inspector palette (**Figure 59b**). Now you can change its dimensions in the Inspector or delete the image.

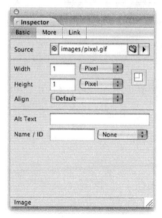

Figure 59b Change the dimensions of the tiny image in the Inspector.

Select Upper Block

GoLive has a convenient feature that allows you to easily select the element or tag that encloses your current selection in the page you are editing. Invoke the Select Upper Block command by choosing it in the Special menu or press Command-Shift-B (Mac) or Control-Shift-B (Windows).

This handy command works in Layout, Source, and Outline modes and makes page editing much easier. Some practical uses include selecting nested tables, entire paragraphs, or stylized text.

Single pixel handling

When you place a single-pixel image in the Layout Editor, the dimensions are 32x32 pixels instead of 1x1. This makes it easy to select and resize the image. If you want force the single pixel image to use its 1x1 dimensions, click the Set to original size icon ⊡ in the Inspector.

TIP 60 Designing with Smart Guides

The GoLive engineers know a good thing when they see it. That's why they thanked the Illustrator team and then proceeded to put Smart Guides, which originated in Illustrator, into GoLive. What are Smart Guides, exactly? They are guides that automatically become visible as you are moving objects around a page. When the edge of one object lines up with the edge of another object, a smart guide magically appears that gives you an easy way to line up objects with incredible precision and speed (**Figure 60**).

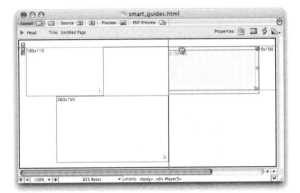

Figure 60 Smart Guides automatically appear when one object encounters the edge of another object.

Smart Guides can be found in the following areas of GoLive:

- When moving objects on a Layout Grid
- When working with multiple layers
- In the QuickTime Editor
- In the SMIL Editor

Choosing to Not Be Smart

If you prefer not to use Smart Guides, you can turn them off by deselecting Show Smart Guides from the View menu.

TIP 61 Changing View Profiles

The View palette in GoLive offers a plethora of options that many users don't know about. Using the View palette you can simulate what your page would like in a number of browsers or based on a specific profile.

Start by opening the View palette from the Window menu and opening a Web page in the Layout Editor. Notice that there are pull-down menus labeled Basic Profile and User Profiles. Nested in these lists are subcategories. Choose a browser profile from the Basic Profiles list, and your page will simulate that browser. Five recently used profiles are listed at the top of the menu (**Figure 61a**).

Figure 61a Choose from the options in the Basic Profiles menu to simulate how your page would look with various browsers, platforms, or handheld devices.

This is helpful if you want to see how a page will look in a very old browser, such as those that don't support CSS, or how the page will look on another device such as a mobile phone.

(continued on next page)

Flat Menu Option

If you prefer, you can change the way the profile menu appears by selecting Flat Menu from either the Basic or User Profiles menus. You'll get all the same options as in the Structured menu, but they'll be in one long list instead of in submenus.

Choose an option from the User Profiles list to view the page in a particular way—for instance, to see how your page would appear at a particular size or with no images. We find the Plain Text Only option valuable when we need to edit text and don't want a lot of other clutter in the way. Again, the five most recently used options will be listed at the top of the menu (**Figure 61b**). You can have multiple User Profiles enabled at the same time.

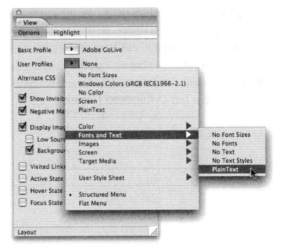

Figure 61b The User Profiles offer a number of helpful views, including a quick way to see only the text on your page.

Note

The View options are not a replacement for testing your pages with real browsers! They're great in a pinch, but don't get lazy. Test, test, test on multiple browsers and across platforms.

TIP 62 Turning Invisible Elements On and Off

GoLive has an incredible level of control when it comes to showing and hiding invisible elements such as form containers, image map areas, and table borders. Look in the General > Invisible Elements section of the application preferences and you'll see you can control visibility of a variety of invisible document markers, visual layout decorations, and a few CSS properties. In the example shown here, GoLive hides all invisible elements *except* layer and table borders, which would be helpful for hiding unnecessary elements but still seeing the layout structure of the page (**Figure 62a**).

Visibility and Template Regions

You can also hide invisible items to temporarily disable the highlighting of locked regions in a template page (see Tip 133).

Figure 62a Control invisible element settings in GoLive's preferences.

To use your custom visibility preferences, simply open a page in Layout mode and select Disable Invisible Items in the View palette (**Figure 62b**). You can also toggle invisible items with the View > Show Invisible Items command.

Figure 62b Toggle visibility in the View palette.

Syntax Tool Tip

Hold down Option-Shift (Mac) or Alt-Shift (Windows) and hover your mouse pointer over any object in the Layout Editor. After you pause for a second, you'll see a helpful Tool Tip showing you the source code for the closest object under the cursor.

Finding Attributes

If the tag or attribute you want is not visible in the list, scroll down to find it—or press its first letter on your keyboard, and GoLive will jump to the entries that begin with that letter. Descriptive information is shown in the Info field when a tag or attribute is selected in the list.

TIP 63 — Visual Tag Editor

If you've ever wanted to edit an HTML element but didn't want to switch out of Layout mode or give up part of the window to the split view, then the Visual Tag Editor is the solution for you. Using the Visual Tag Editor, you can edit a piece of code or insert a new tag.

To open the Visual Tag Editor, choose Special > Visual Tag Editor from the menu. If you select text in the page and invoke the Visual Tag Editor, the Wrap option will be enabled, meaning that the tag you add will be wrapped around your selection. If you select a tag in the Markup Tree of the document (see Tip 34) and then invoke the Visual Tag Editor, the selected tag will appear in the window, and the Edit option will be enabled so that you can edit the current tag. If you position your cursor in the Layout Editor where you'd like a new tag to be added and then invoke the Visual Tag Editor, the Insert option will be enabled.

To add a tag or attribute, either type into the field at the top of the window or double-click in the list on the left. Once a tag has been added, press the spacebar to continue. Notice that as soon as you type a space character, appropriate attributes for the tag you are editing appear in the list. You can also use the built-in Markup Tree to navigate through the code and find a particular tag to edit (**Figure 63**).

Figure 63 The Visual Tag Editor.

There are many ways that the Visual Tag Editor can come in handy, but here's an example that's pretty basic: Open the Visual Tag Editor, use its Markup Tree to select a <div> tag, and add an ID.

TIP 64 Calculating Document Statistics

Do you ever wonder how long it will take for a certain page to download over a 56K connection? An ISDN line? A T1 connection? Open a Web page in GoLive and choose Special > Document Statistics to get a helpful estimate of download times at various connection speeds (**Figure 64a**).

Figure 64a Document Statistics can help you decide whether your pages need to go on a diet.

The Document Statistics dialog shows you the size of your source code, your images, and the overall page size. Copy editors will appreciate the ability to get character and word count information for the selected page. At the bottom of the dialog is a list of estimated download times at different connection speeds. Lots of factors such as server load and Internet traffic can affect real-world performance, but these numbers should give you a good estimate.

Now you can get real-time Document Statistics on any Web page while you work. In the Status field at the bottom of the document window, choose to show Document Statistics, and now you'll see an accurate byte count of al the source code in your page (**Figure 64b**).

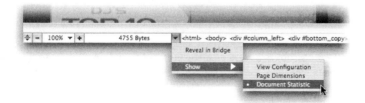

Figure 64b GoLive CS2 now shows real-time statistics.

Short vs. Long DOCTYPEs

By default, GoLive writes a short version of the DOCTYPE for HTML pages. It writes the short version because a long DOCTYPE (with the URL of the DTD) can cause problems in some browsers. Conversely, GoLive writes a long version of the DOCTYPE for XHTML pages.

To switch from one version of a DOCTYPE to another, hold the Option (Mac) or Alt (Windows) key and choose the DOCTYPE from the document flyout menu. This will switch an HTML DOCTYPE to the long version and an XHTML DOCTYPE to the short version.

Adding and Changing DOCTYPEs

A DOCTYPE—short for *document type* declaration—should be included at the beginning of every page you create (**Figure 65a**). The DOCTYPE tells your visitors' Web browsers what flavor of HTML or XHTML you used to create your page and helps render the page accurately.

Figure 65a Every page should have a DOCTYPE in the beginning of the source code.

Click the flyout menu in the upper right corner of the document window and select the appropriate DOCTYPE from the DOCTYPE menu (**Figure 65b**). If your page uses HTML, you can only select an HTML DOCTYPE; if it uses XHTML, you can only select an XHTML DOCTYPE.

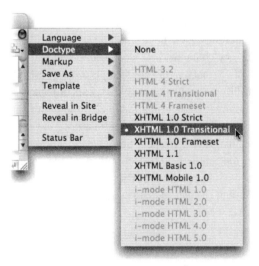

Figure 65b Choose the appropriate DOCTYPE from the document flyout menu. Notice you can also convert the markup of a page between HTML and XHTML using the document flyout menu. Choose Markup > Convert to HTML or Markup > Convert to XHTML as needed, and GoLive does the dirty work for you.

TIP 66 Managing Color with the Swatches and Color Palettes

GoLive includes a Swatches palette that is similar to the Swatches palettes you may be already familiar with in Photoshop, Illustrator, and InDesign (**Figure 66a**). This means it's that much easier to learn GoLive and work with color in familiar ways. The Swatches palette should be open by default, but if you can't find it or accidentally closed it, just open it from the Window menu.

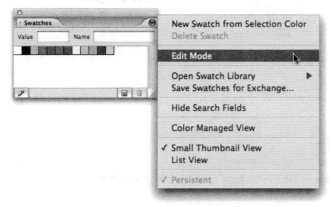

Figure 66a The Swatches palette in GoLive works like other Adobe applications.

Sharing Swatches with Photoshop, Illustrator, and InDesign

All the Creative Suite 2 applications can share a new, common swatch file format. For example, it's easy to create graphics and swatches in Photoshop and then share those swatches with GoLive to ensure consistency throughout your workflow. Just create the swatches in any CS2 application and choose the Save Swatches for Exchange command in any Swatches palette menu to save them in the new .ase format. To load custom swatch sets, choose Open Swatch Library > Other Library from any Swatch palette menu.

To open different swatch sets, use the palette menu in the upper right corner and select the one you want to use. The Visi-Bone swatch layouts are some of our favorites. If there's a set of swatches you really like and want to use all the time, enable the Persistent option in the palette menu of that swatch. Now your favorite Swatch palettes will always be open, even after you quit and relaunch GoLive. To create a new swatch, mix a new color in the Color palette and click the New swatch icon 🔲 at the bottom of the Swatches palette.

If you use other Adobe applications, you might prefer the list view for your swatches so you can see a color swatch and a text description of the swatch. The good news is that GoLive offers you this same familiar way to manage your swatches for Web design. Just use the Swatches palette menu and select List View instead of Small Thumbnail View.

(continued on next page)

TIP 66: Managing Color with the Swatches and Color Palettes

Searching Swatches

Searching for specific values or names of swatches is easy in GoLive. Just turn on the Show Search Fields option in the Swatches palette menu, and color value and color name fields will appear at the top of the Swatches palette. Now to locate a specific color within your active swatches, just enter a search value and hit Return/Enter. Note that this handy features works in both thumbnail and list view.

The Color palette in GoLive also works like other Adobe applications and includes color pickers for grayscale, RGB, CMYK, HSB, and HSV. Switch between the different color pickers by clicking the icons at the top of the Color palette or choose from the flyout menu. Select a color field in any palette or toolbar and mix the color in the Color palette to see the changes in real-time (**Figure 66b**).

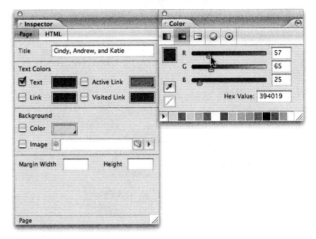

Figure 66b Use the Color palette to create swatches and mix new colors.

TIP 67
Editing Swatches with the Color Picker

For the first time ever, GoLive CS2 allows you to edit color swatches with the standard Adobe color picker. This is the same color picker from Adobe Photoshop and Adobe Illustrator that users have loved for years, and it's a welcome addition. Create a new swatch by clicking the new icon 🔲 at the bottom of the Swatches palette. Then click the Pencil icon 🖉 in the bottom left corner of the Swatches palettes to enable Edit mode and double-click on any of the swatches to open the color picker (**Figure 67a**).

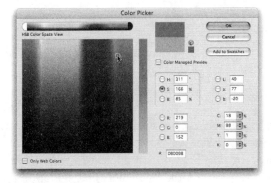

Figure 67a
Double-click a swatch in Edit mode to access the color picker.

Inside the color picker dialog you can mix color with the HSB, RGB, or Lab color models and you can even mix in CMYK if you're trying to match a Web site to a printed piece. If you want to limit the colors to the 216-color Web Safe palette (see Tip 68), just click the Only Web Colors option in the bottom left corner of the dialog. If you want to mix several swatches in this dialog, click the Add to Swatches button for each new color so you can leave the color picker open as long as you want.

Figure 67b Give your swatches custom names and they'll be easier to find.

When you're done mixing your colors with the color picker, click OK. Before you move on, make sure to notice that you can also give your new swatches custom names. While you're still in Edit mode, you can select a swatch in the Swatches palette and assign a name in the Name field (**Figure 67b**).

Are Web Safe Colors Necessary?

In the early days of the Web, most computer monitors could only display 256 colors. This meant Web designers tried to limit their color usage to the 216 Web safe colors so they wouldn't have any unexpected dithering in their graphics. Computer monitors and graphics cards have come a long way over the years and now usually display thousands or millions of colors. This means it's probably not necessary to limit your color palette to Web safe colors anymore.

TIP 68 Picking Web Safe Colors

If picking Web safe colors is important to you, GoLive makes it very easy to do just that. The easiest way is to choose colors from the VisiBone, VisiBone2, Web Hues, Web Safe, or Web Spectrum swatch sets in the Swatches palette (**Figure 68a**).

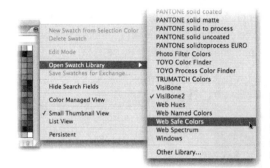

Figure 68a
Several of the swatch sets show only Web safe colors.

Another way to make sure you select a Web safe color swatch is to turn on the Small List View option in the Swatches palette and only select colors with the small cube icon next to them (**Figure 68b**). Lastly, you can turn on the Web Colors Only option in the Color palette menu and you can mix colors with any of the familiar color mixers and be confident you'll only get Web safe colors.

Figure 68b Swatches that have the cube icon next to them in the list view are Web safe.

TIP 69 Using the Eyedropper Tool

The Eyedropper tool in the Color palette ✎ allows you to quickly sample color from anywhere on your monitor. It even works in other windows and other applications that might be open in the background. For example, the Eyedropper allows you to match the color of text selected in your Web page with a color in an open Photoshop document or Illustrator logo.

Select the Eyedropper tool in the Color palette and place your mouse pointer over the color you want to sample (**Figure 69**). When you see a preview of the sampled color in the top left corner of the Color palette, click to sample the color to apply it to your selection.

Figure 69 Use the Eyedropper to sample color anywhere on your screen.

Removing Color

We've shown you several ways to manage and apply color, but what about removing it? Select the text or color field you want to change and click the Remove color icon (empty white box with a red line through it) on the left edge of the Color palette. You can achieve the same result by selecting the Type > Remove Color command for selected text.

Using Color Shortcut Menus

Places to Use Color Shortcut Menus

Color fields exist in many different parts of GoLive, including the toolbar, the CSS Editor, the Highlight section of the View palette, and several Inspectors.

Shortcut to Adobe Color Picker

If you don't want to choose a color from a Swatch palette, a quick way to access the Adobe color picker from any color field is to simply double-click on it! Select a color from the color picker and then choose OK. The color you chose will appear in the color field.

Normally, you apply a color to something by selecting the object, selecting the color field that corresponds to the selected object, and then picking a swatch from the Swatches palette or mixing a color in the Color palette. This works fine, but you might have noticed that there's a small black triangle in the bottom right corner of every color field throughout GoLive. When you click and hold on the black corner triangles, you get access to a convenient popup swatch picker where you can make instant color changes (**Figure 70a**). You can also Control-click (Mac) or right-click (Windows) anywhere in the color field to open the swatch shortcut menus.

Figure 70a Pick colors quickly from the swatch shortcut menus in every color field.

Figure 70b You can customize the swatch set that is available in the color fields.

That's handy, but what makes these hidden menus really powerful is that you can choose which set of swatches is shown when you open them. You can select any of the installed color swatches, including the popular Visi-Bone swatches, from the bottom of the pull-down menu (**Figure 70b**).

Working with Pages

TIP 71 Remembering Recently Used Colors

When you plan a site or start designing a Web page, a major consideration is the consistent use of color. If you mix a color you want to remember, just click the small triangle in the bottom left corner of the Color palette to add it to the list of recently used colors (**Figure 71a**). Colors you apply to objects are added automatically to the small row of swatches at the bottom of the palette. This is a really easy way to store colors and compare your options. If you don't see the row of recent color swatches at the bottom of the Color palette, make sure the Show Recent Colors Option is checked in the palette menu.

Figure 71a The bottom row of the Color palette stores recently used colors for easy access.

To see more of your recently used colors, make the Color palette wider. For an exhaustive history of colors you've used, choose Window > Swatch Libraries > Recent Colors. Set the view to Small List in the palette menu and you can see GoLive keeps track of all the colors you use and even records the date and time the swatch was recorded (**Figure 71b**).

Value	000000	Name	1/26/05 12:21 AM
	#5656AF	2/2/05 1:49 PM	
	#304D29	2/2/05 1:49 PM	
	#2D334D	2/2/05 1:49 PM	
	#8B825B	1/26/05 1:34 AM	
	#000000	1/26/05 12:21 AM	
	#000055	1/3/05 12:12 PM	

Figure 71b GoLive automatically keeps track of all the colors you've used.

(continued on next page)

After you've decided which colors you're going to use through-out a site, you'll probably want to keep them consistent. Let's say you've created a specific set of colors in the Colors tab of your Site window and you want to make sure that you don't stray from those standards on the rest of the pages in the site. Choose Window > Swatch Libraries > Site Colors and you'll see this swatch set matches exactly with the Colors tab of the Site window (**Figure 71c**). Now you don't have to worry about accidentally using six different shades of the same green.

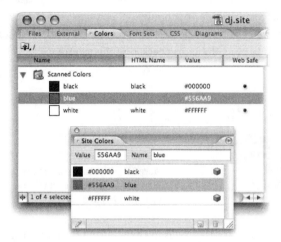

Figure 71c If you always pick from the Site Colors swatches in the Swatches palette, you can ensure consistent color usage across all the pages in the site.

TIP 72
Leveraging Common Adobe Color Management

Like the rest of the applications in Adobe Creative Suite, GoLive offers a consistent interface for color management of your images and artwork (**Figure 72**). Open the Color Settings dialog from the bottom of the Edit menu.

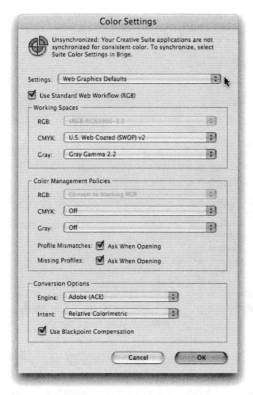

Figure 72 All the Creative Suite applications share the same color management technology.

Manage Color in The Bridge

If you are using the Adobe Creative Suite 2, then use the Bridge application to manage your color settings. Doing so assures that your color settings are the same across all the suite applications.

It's beyond us to explain all the details of color management in one short tip, but the good news is that whether you use one of the default settings or create your own custom settings, you can share these settings with all the Creative Suite applications. The color management in GoLive kicks in when you're converting native source files such as Photoshop and Illustrator to Web formats such as GIF and JPEG with the Smart Objects feature (see Tip 141).

TIP 73 Troubleshooting Pages with Highlights

The Highlight feature is an incredibly powerful feature that can help you in so many different ways it's impossible to list them all here. Open a Web page, open the View palette, and switch to the Highlight section (**Figure 73**). You can also enable many of the Highlight options from the View > Highlight submenus.

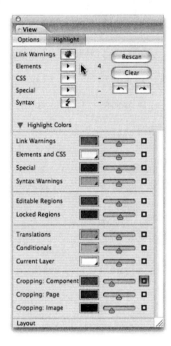

Figure 73 The Highlight feature is a great way to locate and troubleshoot different items on a page.

Highlight is an easy way to toggle Link Warnings and run the Syntax Checker , but it does so much more than that. For example, the Elements pull-down menu shows you an alphabetical list of every element used in the page. Select an element, and all instances of that tag are highlighted in your page. You can even select multiple elements and get a complete count of all occurrences.

Another great way to use Highlight is to quickly and easily locate CSS usage in a page. Open a page in GoLive and select a CSS class or ID from the CSS pull-down menu to instantly highlight the styled objects.

Highlight also has a pull-down menu labeled Special that includes a variety of helpful items you might want to highlight in a page. One of our favorite options in this menu is JavaScript Actions, which quickly shows how many GoLive actions are in a page and where they are located.

Twirl down the Colors section of the palette and you can adjust the highlight color, opacity, and style for anything from link and syntax warnings to locked and editable regions. Check out the other options, and you'll find all sorts of cool uses for highlighting.

TIP 74 Using OS X Services

We want to say up front that this tip is only for Mac users, but it's so cool we just had to put it in the book. If you're not familiar with OS X Services, they are system-wide features available in the application menu of most OS X software. To use a service, select some text in the Layout Editor or a file in the Site window and choose a service from the GoLive > Services menu (**Figure 74**).

Figure 74 Manipulate your selection with a variety of OS X Services.

There are a variety of services available, but some of the most practical uses include:

- **Open URL:** Select a Web site address in the Layout Editor and open the URL in your default Web browser.

- **Search with Google:** Use the selected text as a search at the world's most popular search engine.

- **Send File to Bluetooth Device:** Select a file in the Site window, such as a SMIL presentation, an MPEG movie, or a JPEG, and transfer it to a wireless device. This only works if your Mac and device are Bluetooth-compatible.

- **Speech:** Select text and let your Mac read it aloud to you. This is a fun way to "proofread" your writing.

- **Summarize:** Select all the text in a page or paragraph and let your Mac summarize the text for you. This might be an easier way to write description meta tags.

- **Translate:** Download the Translation Service from www. kavasoft.com/TranslationService/ and translate text back and forth among more than a dozen languages.

CHAPTER FOUR

Advanced Page Editing

In Chapters 2 and 3 we give you the basics you need to get started building a site in GoLive CS2. In this chapter, we go beyond the basics to introduce features in the intermediate to advanced categories. It doesn't take long to become familiar with GoLive's page-building tools, and before you know it you'll probably feel compelled to dive in deeper and become familiar with the other editing modes available to you: the Frames Editor, Source Editor, and Outline Editor.

In this chapter we not only demonstrate additional editing possibilities, we also show how to fix errors on your pages, validate your code, add DOCTYPEs, and do much more.

Once you've been totally immersed in syntax handling, we illustrate how to use GoLive's previewing tools so that you can check the work you've completed. The options for previewing in GoLive CS2 include Page Preview, Live Rendering, Preview in Browser, and the exceptional PDF Preview—each of which has unique features. We also journey into exciting new territory: GoLive's amazing ability to create and edit PDFs, including managing the links contained in them.

75 Designing with Frames

With frames you can split up a browser window into sections, each of which can display a separate HTML page. Once a very common method of designing a Web site, frames have lost popularity somewhat due to issues that search engine spiders sometimes encounter when attempting to index framed pages. At times, though, frames can be useful, and GoLive handles them quite nicely.

Many of the common configurations can be found in the Frame section of the Objects palette. To access them, choose the Frame objects from the Object sets pull-down in the Objects palette ▣.

To use one of the frame objects, click the Frame Editor button ▤ at the top of a document window to enter the frames editing mode and then drag and drop a Frame object into the page. With the Frame object in place, the Inspector palette shows two tabs: Frame and Frameset. The attributes in the Frame tab are applied to the individual sections within the frameset, whereas the attributes in the Frameset tab are applied to the border and separators between the frames. You can also edit the frameset attributes if you click directly on one of the borders of the frameset (**Figure 75a**).

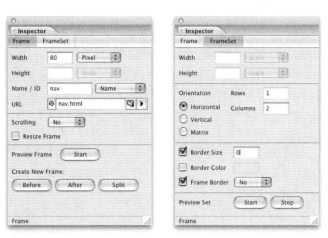

Figure 75a The Frame Inspector and the Frameset Inspector offer easy ways to set the attributes for both the individual frames and the frameset itself.

To change the size of a frame, enter pixel dimensions into the Height and Width fields of the Inspector or drag the frame separators to be larger or smaller. To add additional frames to your configuration, simply drag another Frame object into the page or use the Create New Frame button in the Inspector. Select whether or not you'd like a scrollbar to appear by choosing an option from the Scroll popup and give the user the ability to resize the frame by enabling the Resize checkbox.

If you don't want a border to show between the sections, enable the checkbox next to Border in the Frameset Inspector and press 0; you'll also need to check the Frame Border checkbox and select No from the pull-down menu. You can set border color in the Frameset Inspector, but expect wide-ranging results in different Web browsers.

The last step is to designate which pages will be shown in the sections of the frameset. To assign the pages to the frames, click in a frame and then use the URL field in the Inspector palette to link to a page in your Site window. Or drag a page from the Site window and drop it onto a frame to make the link.

Give each frame in a frameset a unique name in the Name field of the Frame Inspector. Later, when you create links on pages within a frameset, use the target pull-down to select a frame name or type the frame name into the Target field in the Inspector to indicate which of the frames the link should load into (**Figure 75b**).

Auto DOCTYPE Correction

If you drop a Frame object into a page that does not contain the appropriate DOCTYPE (see Tip 65) for frames, GoLive intelligently puts up a dialog box showing the current DOCTYPE and the suggested one. To accept the change, click OK, and to leave the DOCTYPE untouched, click Cancel.

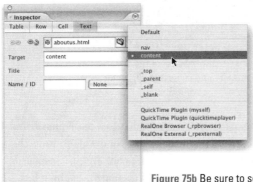

Figure 75b Be sure to select a target frame when creating links within framesets.

When you've got everything set up as you want it, you can get a temporary preview by clicking the Start button next to Preview Frame in the Frame Inspector or Preview Frameset in the Frameset Inspector. Once enabled, the button will read Stop. Click it to stop the temporary preview.

TIP 75: Designing with Frames

76 Creating iFrames

iFrame or iDon't frame

Some older browsers do not support iFrames, so be sure to know your audience and test pages using iFrames in target browsers.

What is the first object in the Frame set of Objects 📓, and why can't you drag it into your frameset? That, friends, is no ordinary frame. It's an *inline* frame, better known as an iFrame, and it's not used in a frameset, but to create a frame right inside a regular HTML page. iFrames are neat because they can be placed anywhere on your page, giving the effect of a virtual window.

To create an iFrame, open a page in Layout mode and drag the iFrame object in. An iFrame can be placed into a layer, a table cell, or anywhere else in a page (**Figure 76**).

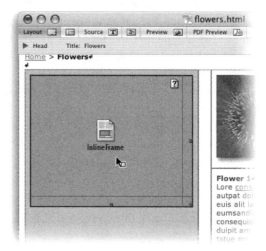

Figure 76 Postion an iFrame on a page by placing it into a layer, table cell, or Layout Grid.

Designate the page that will load into the iFrame using the Source field of the Inspector or by dragging a page from the Site window and dropping it onto the iFrame. In the Inspector, set options such as the height, width, or alignment of the iFrame. Add a margin if desired by entering pixel dimensions into the Margin fields or enable the Border checkbox if you'd like a border to show around the iFrame.

TIP 77 Customizing Source Code Formatting (Themes)

GoLive CS2 has the ability to customize the formatting of your source code by creating code themes. Themes are available in the Source Editor, the Split Source view, the JavaScript Editor, and the Source tab of the CSS Editor and are accessible by choosing an option from the Theme pull-down menu (**Figure 77a**).

Figure 77a Choose a theme from the Theme pull-down in the Source Editor.

Although GoLive has a number of useful themes already configured, you can create your own or edit any of the default themes in the GoLive preferences. On a Mac, choose GoLive > Preferences; on Windows, choose Edit > Preferences. Next, open the Source pane of the preferences and click Themes.

Pick the type of syntax you want to create or edit a theme from the Syntax pull-down menu and then select a theme name from the Theme pull-down menu. Select the font face and size and the text and background colors for the theme in the upper portion of the Preference dialog. To set specific colors and font styles for text, tags, attributes, and so on, choose an option in the text list on the left and set the styling for that option using the Color field, font face buttons, and Size pull-down menu on the right (**Figure 77b**).

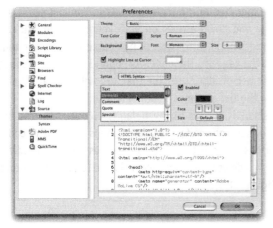

Figure 77b Edit themes in the Themes portion of the GoLive preferences.

Theme Manager Extension

GoLive CS2 ships with an extension called Theme Manager that allows you to duplicate, delete, rename, reorder, import, or export themes. See Tip 236 to learn more about extensions. To turn on the extension, open GoLive's preferences and in the Modules section enable the checkmark next to Theme Manager. After restarting GoLive, you'll find a menu item named Theme Manager in the Special menu. Select it to manage your source code themes.

Themes Are Not for Browsers

Themes only affect how the code looks when you edit in GoLive. It has no effect on how your pages look or work in a Web browser.

Setting the Default Theme

To set the default theme as a preference, use the pull-down menu in the Source portion of the preferences. You can specify both a default theme (for viewing on screen) and a print theme, which will be used when a page of code is printed from GoLive.

TIP 77: Customizing Source Code Formatting (Themes)

Automating Code Completion and Adjusting Settings

Any Flavor Will Do

The code-completion feature is context sensitive, so if you're working in PHP it will display the appropriate list of elements for PHP, and likewise for JavaScript.

We have, on occasion, made a typo or two when editing source code and then spent ages trying to find what we'd done wrong. Not to worry—code completion in GoLive CS2 allows even the most abysmal typists to turn out perfect pages.

In GoLive's Source Editor, type an opening bracket. As you do so a list pops up, displaying a full set of tags appropriate for the type of syntax you're working with (**Figure 78a**).

Figure 78a With code completion enabled, a list of tags you can pick from appears as you type source code.

If you type the first letter of the tag you want to use, the list will jump to the tags beginning with that letter. You can scroll the list using the up and down arrows on your keyboard and you can select a tag by pressing Return/Enter or by double-clicking the tag. Doing so writes the tag into the code. As soon as you type a space to continue, the list of attributes for that tag will appear. Again, simply navigate the list and make your selection.

Code-completion is turned on by default, but you can disable it if you'd like or set options for how it responds. To set the code-completion options, choose GoLive > Preferences on Mac or Edit > Preferences on Windows and then select Syntax under the Source preferences (**Figure 78b**).

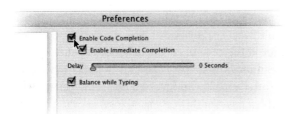

Figure 78b Disable or customize the code-completion features in the application preferences.

Choosing Enable Immediate Completion will insert the necessary end tags into the code. Selecting Balance While Typing automatically jumps you to the next open bracket as soon as you type a closing bracket. You can also decrease the delay of the pop-up list by dragging the slider toward zero.

Disabling Code Colorization

To turn off code colorization, click the Colorize Code button ⬛ in the Source Editor. This is a sticky setting, meaning that if you turn it off on one page, it will be turned off on all pages, including the Source view in the CSS Editor, the Split Source view, and the JavaScript Editor.

What Are Web Settings?

In the pull-down for General Markup Options in the Rewrite Source Code dialog, you'll find a selection called Web Settings. By accessing these settings, advanced users can get very granular about how they want their code to be written by GoLive. Choose GoLive > Web Settings on Mac or Edit > Web Settings on Windows. A word of caution, though: If you don't know what you are doing, stay away! You could end up wreaking havoc with your source code.

TIP 79 Rewriting Your Source Code

Call us picky, but we prefer our source code written in a particular way, thank you very much. Sometimes, though, if we've been mucking around a lot in the code or cutting and pasting code from here to there, we end up with source code that is formatted inconsistently. When that happens, we invoke a command called Rewrite Source Code. Don't mistake this command for one that fixes poorly written code. Instead, it restores the formatting of your code to your specifications, including line breaks, indents, uppercase or lowercase, and CSS formatting.

You'll find the command under Special > Source Code > Rewrite Source Code. Once you invoke the command, a dialog appears offering choices on how the source code should be rewritten. There are four sections in the dialog: HTML Options, CSS Options, General Markup Options, and Text Options. To set preferences for any of these options, choose from the options in the pull-down menus. When you are happy with the settings, choose which files are to be rewritten by selecting from the Work On pull-down list (**Figure 79**).

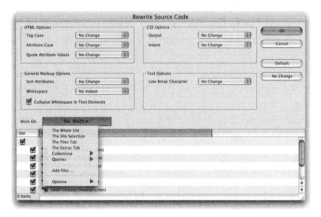

Figure 79 The Rewrite Source Code dialog offers several choices on how to format the code as well as an easy way to choose which files to rewrite.

Bonus Tip

You can assign a keyboard shortcut to the Rewrite Source Code command so that you can run it very simply by pressing a key combination on your keyboard.

TIP 80
Selecting Tags Easily in the Source Editor

Here is a small but handy-dandy tip: While in the source code, double-click on the opening bracket of any tag to select the entire block of code between the opening and closing tags. For instance, to select a block of code between the opening and closing <table> tags, including the opening and closing tags themselves, double-click on left bracket of the opening <table> tag. If you double-click on the right bracket of the <table> tag, you'll select the contents of the tag but not the tag itself (**Figure 80**).

Figure 80 Double-click the left bracket of a tag to select the whole tag. Double-click the right bracket to select just the contents of the opening and closing tags.

In the same manner, you can select an attribute and its value by double-clicking the equal sign (=) that comes after the attribute. If you only want to select the value of an attribute, but not the attribute itself, double-click on either of the quotation marks surrounding the value. Last but not least, to select both a CSS property and its value, double-click on the colon in front of the value.

Once you've memorized these selection techniques, you'll find working in source code a lot less time consuming.

TIP
81

Navigating Your Source Code

There's one spot in your source code that you always seem to edit. But to find that particular spot, you've got to remember the line number, right? Well, no. GoLive CS2 does have line numbers and even has a sweet feature that makes using them a snap, but it also has something that makes finding a certain spot in source code easy as pie.

Figure 81a Type in a line number and press Return/ Enter to jump directly to that line of code.

Figure 81b The Go To Line... command makes it simple to jump through your code.

To jump to a precise line number, type the number into the small input field in the lower left corner of the page and press Return/Enter (**Figure 81a**). GoLive instantly places the cursor right at the beginning of the desired line.

Special > Source Code > Go To Line... brings up a teeny box where you type the line number and press Return/Enter (**Figure 81b**). Add a keyboard shortcut to that menu item for a mouse-less way to quickly navigate your code.

To simplify matters even more, though, use the handy new Navigate Through Code button in the Source, CSS, and JavaScript Editors, and in the Split Source View { }. This button is automatically populated with any tags in your HTML page that have the name attribute assigned (see Tip 91). In the JavaScript editor, it's auto-populated with the functions in the page, whether you are working in JavaScript, VBScript, ASP, or Perl. In the CSS Editor, it's populated with the definitions themselves. Just select an item in the list to jump directly to that spot in the code.

But what to do if the spot you want to jump to happens to be a tag that does not have the name attribute? In that case, set your own marker. Simply put your cursor in the spot you want to mark and then click the Navigate Through Code button and choose New Marker. Give the marker a name and click OK. Next time you click the button, your new marker name will be in the list.

TIP 82 Creating New Objects in the Source Editor

Back in Chapter 3, we explained how to take objects from the Objects palette and drag them into the Layout Editor (see Tip 37). But did you know that you could use those very same objects in the Source Editor, too? To test it out, open a new blank HTML page in GoLive and switch to the Source Editor. Next, drag a Table object from the Objects palette and drop it into the page between the opening and closing <body> tags (**Figure 82**). Ta-da! Instant table. Go to the Head objects and drag a meta object into the head portion of the page. Ta-da! Instant meta tag. Double-click the word *generic* to select it and type the value you want to use. Combine use of the Objects palette with code completion and you'll be zipping through source code at high speed.

Outline Editor

So, you can use objects from the Objects palette in both the Layout and Source Editors. Wouldn't it be nice if you could use those objects in the Outline Editor, too? You can! Just drag and drop. See Tips 85–91 to learn more about the Outline Editor.

Figure 82 You can use the Objects palette to write markup in the Source Editor. Just drag and drop an object into the page. The first image shows the Table object being dragged; the second shows the code that is written when the object is dropped.

TIP 83
Keeping Selections in Different Editors

The different editing environments in GoLive add up to a really potent combination, and we expect you'll want to use different modes for different tasks. Fortunately, the different editors work together smoothly as you switch from one to the other. For example, if you select an object such as an image, table, or text in the Layout Editor and switch to the Source Code Editor, the code for that object is still selected and cued up (**Figure 83**).

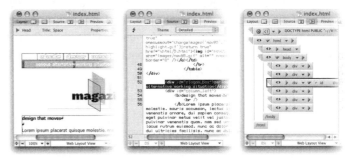

Figure 83 Selection Cueing works between the Layout, Source Code, and Outline Editors.

Now if you switch modes one more time to the Outline Editor, the same object is still selected and cued up in the Outline Editor. And now if you select a specific attribute in the Outline Editor and switch back to the Source Code Editor, just the code for that attribute will be selected. The integration of all the different Editors (Layout, Frame, Source, and Outline) is just amazing.

Selecting Cueing makes it easy to switch between the different editing modes for a quick edit, because you don't have to find your place in the page over and over again. It's also a great way to learn more about HTML, because you can immediately see the source that corresponds to your selection in a different editing mode.

TIP 84
Validating Your Source Code Syntax

You spend precious time creating pages that look good and navigate properly. To that end, it behooves you to make sure your pages are free from errors and that they use valid syntax to ensure that they behave as expected in a Web browser.

Using GoLive's built-in Syntax Checker, you can see whether your pages are compliant with a particular DTD (see Tip 65) or whether your code is well formed (meaning all tag pairs are complete and so on). To use the Syntax Checker, choose Edit > Check Syntax, click the Check Syntax button in the Highlight tab of the View palette, or control-click (right-click on Windows) on a page in the Files tab of the Site window and choose Check Syntax (**Figure 84a**).

Figure 84a There's a Check Syntax menu item in the Edit menu, a Check Syntax command in the contextual menu, and a Check Syntax button in the Highlight tab of the View palette as shown here.

Once invoked, a modal dialog will open. In the Comply With portion in the upper left, choose one or more DTDs to check against by enabling the checkbox next to them. Alternatively, you could check for well-formedness only.

The Additionally Allowed portion in the lower left lets GoLive-specific tags and attributes go through the checker without being flagged (**Figure 84b**). If you intend to strip out the GoLive-specific code while uploading (see Tip 222), then enable these checkboxes.

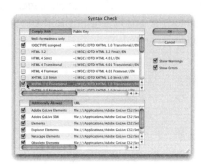

Figure 84b Choose the DTD to check against and whether to allow additional elements.

(continued on next page)

TIP 84: Validating Your Source Code Syntax

By default, the Warnings and Errors checkboxes in the upper right are enabled. For the best results, leave them on. When you're done making your selections, click OK. The syntax checker proceeds, and a list of results is shown (**Figure 84c**). If errors or warnings are found, the problems are highlighted on the page.

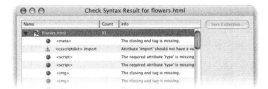

Figure 84c After running the Syntax Checker, a results list is shown.

Double-clicking on a warning or error in the results list causes the page to pop forward with the problem area in view, ready for you to fix. Using the Outline Editor is the easiest way to fix errors because it not only highlights the errors on the page but also gives a brief description of the problem. If a required attribute of a tag is missing, the Outline Editor even puts a bullet next to it in the tag's attributes list, making it a snap to fix (**Figure 84d**).

Figure 84d The Outline Editor is the best choice for fixing syntax errors.

You can run the Syntax Checker on a single open page, on selected pages in the Site window, or on the entire site if the Site window is in focus with no pages selected.

TIP 85 Working with the Outline Editor

The Outline Editor in GoLive is a unique and powerful feature that makes tedious Web-authoring tasks a breeze and helps ensure better quality code. There are lots of cool things you can do in the Outline Editor, but the essence of this mode is that it displays a fast and easy-to-use structural view of the markup of a document (**Figure 85**).

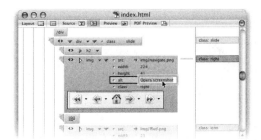

Figure 85 The Outline Editor makes newbies more comfortable and experts more efficient.

However, the Outline Editor isn't just a pretty way to look at your code. It's also a great way to edit and add to your pages. If you ever need to troubleshoot a complex page or streamline some deeply nested tables, you'll love the Outline Editor. To add to pages in the Outline Editor, just drag and drop items from the Objects palette to the appropriate location in the outline.

The Outline Editor is also a great way to learn about source code within a structured editing environment, which minimizes the tedium and mistakes of hand coding. You can study anything from the structure of tables to the attributes of images. This is a powerful tool for trainers teaching HTML basics and Web-design fundamentals.

TIP 86 Working with Elements and Attributes in the Outline Editor

It's easy to add attributes to elements correctly even if you don't remember the attribute names or proper syntax. Simply select the new attribute for the selected element from the pull-down menu in the Outline Editor (**Figure 86a**).

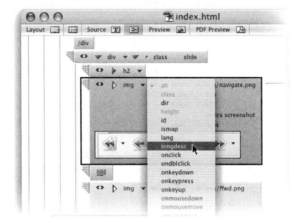

Figure 86a Adding attributes is easy in the Outline Editor.

It's just as easy to edit attributes in the Outline Editor as it is to add them. For example, the LONGDESC attribute can be used to add extended accessibility features to images, but there is no corresponding field in the Image Inspector when you use the Layout Editor. Outline mode makes it easy to add and edit attributes that are used less frequently and are not available in the Inspector (**Figure 86b**).

Figure 86b You can edit obscure attributes as easily as you can add them.

TIP 87 Finding Elusive Page Errors with the Outline Editor

If there's a red bug icon ![bug] in the Status column for a page in your Site window, you probably have a broken link or missing image that needs to be fixed. Open the page with the error, make sure Link Warnings is enabled in the toolbar, and the obvious errors should appear with a red highlight.

However, there are times when the errors aren't as easy to locate. You might have a broken link to a deleted style sheet, an old component, or a missing single-pixel GIF that's very hard to see in the Layout Editor.

Switch to the Outline Editor and toggle the Link Warnings icon in the toolbar, and obscure errors such as missing single-pixel GIFs are instantly revealed and highlighted in the outline (**Figure 87**).

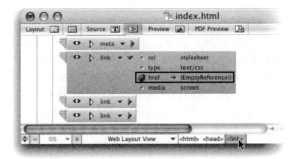

Figure 87 Toggle Link Warnings in the Outline Editor to instantly reveal and highlight obscure errors.

After you've found the error, you can fix it in the Outline Editor or select it and switch to the Layout or Source Code Editors and make the correction there.

TIP 88
Adding Missing End Tags with the Outline Editor

When you run the Syntax Checker (see Tip 84) to validate your source code, you might get an occasional warning that the closing end tag for an element is missing (**Figure 88a**). This means the opening tag of a pair such as a table, multimedia object, or layer is missing the required end tag. There are some elements such as <img> and <meta> that don't need a closing tag, but these are exceptions to the rule.

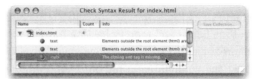

Figure 88a
The Syntax Checker warns you of missing end tags.

If you need to fix a missing end tag error, switch to the Outline Editor instead of wading through lines of lines of source code trying to locate the problem. You can easily toggle an element in the Outline Editor from unary (no closing tag) to binary (closing tag) by Control-clicking (Mac) or right-clicking (Windows) on the element and choosing Binary from the contextual menu (**Figure 88b**).

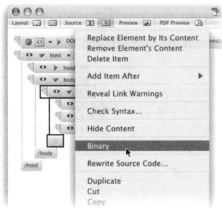

Figure 88b Add the closing tag by choosing Binary from the contextual menu.

You can also toggle from unary to binary with the Toggle Binary icon </> in the toolbar. GoLive is smart enough to determine where the closing tag of a binary pair should be placed in the page and creates it in the correct location.

TIP 89 Viewing Images in the Outline Editor

The Outline Editor is a great way to navigate and edit your Source Code, but it can also be really helpful to see your images in this editing mode. If you're trying to select and edit a certain image or a specific button in a navigation bar, an accurate preview of the image in the Outline Editor helps you make sure you've selected the right file.

By default, images are disabled in the Outline Editor to keep things simple, but you can turn them on with a single click. Switch to the Outline Editor and open the View palette from the Window menu if it's not open already. Then check the Images option in the View palette and you'll be able to see all images at their natural size right in the Outline Editor (**Figure 89a**).

Choose Another Picture

What if you want to use a different image? Toggle open the `<img>` attributes and click the little arrow to the right of the `<src>` attribute. A dialog box opens allowing you to browse through your drives and select another image (**Figure 89b**).

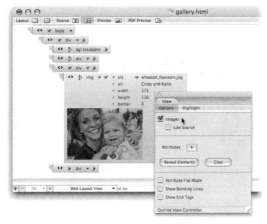

Figure 89a Use the View palette to enable images in the Outline Editor.

Figure 89b Click this little arrow in the Outline Editor to open a dialog box that lets you browse to an image (see sidebar).

TIP 90 Expanding and Collapsing the Outline Editor

The Outline Editor is really one of our favorite features in GoLive, but if you use it a lot you'll find it can require a lot of mousing around the screen. You can navigate most of the features with the keyboard, and here are a few of the most helpful shortcuts:

- **Unfold/Collapse Selected Element:** Select the element and press Return/ Enter to toggle the unfolding or collapsing of an element (**Figure 90a**).

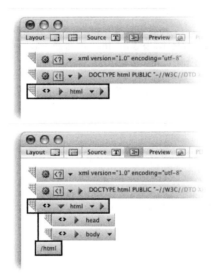

Figure 90a Collapsed element (top), unfolded element (bottom).

- **Unfold/Collapse Selected Element Recursively:** Select the element and press Option-Return (Mac) or Shift-Enter (Windows) (**Figure 90b**).

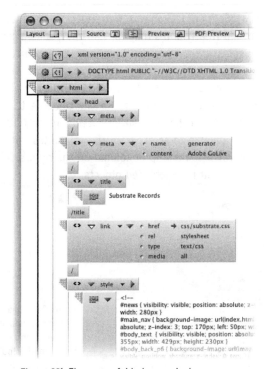

Figure 90b Element unfolded recursively.

- **Unfold/Collapse Attributes of Selected Element:** Select the element and press Return (Mac) or the Enter key in the numeric keypad (Windows).

- **Unfold/Collapse Attributes of Selected Element Recursively:** Select the element and press Option-Return (Mac) or Shift-Enter key in the numeric keypad (Windows).

You can also navigate from one element to another using the keyboard. Use the arrow keys to navigate up and down the outline tree and press Tab to jump to the next text box.

The Markup Palette

A new addition to GoLive CS2 is the Markup palette. This little palette lets you apply attributes such as ID, Class, Title, and Language to an element. It also offers a quick way to add JavaScript to an element and works in both the Outline and Layout Editors.

<table>
<tr><td>TIP
91</td><td># Showing Name and ID
Information in the Outline</td></tr>
</table>

If you use much JavaScript or CSS on your Web pages, you'll be familiar with the Name and ID attributes that you can apply to objects in the page. When you assign a Name or ID attribute to an object, it makes it easy to access with a JavaScript action or style with a CSS rule. When in the Layout or Outline Editor, use the Basic tab of the Inspector palette to add these attributes to a selected object.

To see the Name, ID or other attribute of items in the Outline Editor, use the View palette to select from the Attributes options (**Figure 91a**). Now you'll see a helpful column on the right side of the outline that shows all the identified objects.

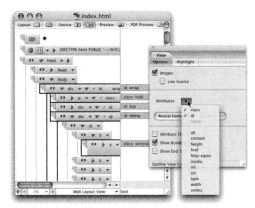

Figure 91a IDs and other attributes are enabled in the View palette and listed on the right side of the Outline Editor.

Most objects can have a Name or ID assigned to them, but a few of the most common uses include forms, form elements, images, and DIVs for CSS layers. If you have a hard time locating all the named objects, click the Reveal Elements button in the View palettes (**Figure 91b**) to reveal and highlight any objects with an assigned name or ID in the outline.

Another option is to switch on Attribute Flat Mode. This option switches the display of the attributes to a horizontal rather than vertical orientation.

Figure 91b One click on Reveal Elements and you can see all the named objects.

TIP 92 Previewing Web Pages in GoLive

When building a site in GoLive, you might like to quickly preview a page without actually leaving the application. GoLive's Preview tab allows you to do just that. The Preview uses an embedded version of the Opera browser, and because it is an actual Web browser that powers the Preview mode, you not only can preview a page, you can test out its links and JavaScript, too (**Figure 92**).

Figure 92 Use the Preview mode to test links and JavaScripts.

To Preview a page, simply click the Preview button at the top of the document window. Even if you navigate away from the page as you are testing links, you are returned to the original page when you switch back to one of the editing modes. If you use the Preview mode frequently, you might like to add a keyboard shortcut to its menu command found under View > Document Mode > Preview.

Updating the Rendering Engine

Newer versions of Opera may be released, and GoLive has a nifty way of allowing the embedded browser to be updated. Simply add the new version to the list found in the Browser Preferences (see Tip 3), and the rendering engine is automatically updated. To select which version of Opera is used for the rendering engine, click the radio button on the right of the browser name.

Sometimes new software combinations can also result in new incompatibilities, though. If adding a new embedded browser causes any problems, just remove it from the list of preview browsers.

TIP 93 — Live Rendering with Live Update

If you've ever wished that you could edit a page in one mode and see it update in real-time in another window, then the Live Rendering window is the answer. To open the Live Rendering window, choose File > Preview in > Live Rendering or press Command-T on Mac (Control-T on Windows). The page you have open will load into the Live Rendering window.

Like Preview mode, the Live Rendering window is an embedded Web browser, so you can use it to test page links, navigation, and JavaScript. There are four commands in the Live Rendering window flyout menu which execute the following tasks:

- **Load:** Invokes the Browse dialog to select a page from your hard drive. Clicking the Browse button that looks like a folder in the upper right accomplishes the same task as Load.

- **Reload:** When AutoUpdate is off, Reload updates the page.

- **AutoUpdate:** Updates changes by clicking on the Live Rendering window.

- **Bound:** Binds an open page to the Live Rendering window.

You can have more than one Live Rendering window open at a time, so if you've got multiple monitors, knock yourself out. Another sweet feature is that by using the Fetch URL tool from the upper left of the Live Rendering window, you can quickly bind the window to a page in the Files tab of the Site window.

A new addition to the Live Rendering window is the Small Screen Rendering (SSR) button. Clicking it renders your page as it would look on a small screen such as those used for mobile devices. To exit SSR, click the button again. You can also open SSR from the menu by choosing File > Preview in > Small Screen Rendering (**Figure 93**).

What's In There?

Want to preview pages, but don't want to open each one to do so? No problem. Bring the site window into focus, select a page in the Files list and then open the Live Rendering window. Load a different page by selecting another file in the Files list. You can even preview your templates and components this way.

Figure 93 Shown here are the Live Rendering window and the Small Screen Rendering window (front), both with the same page loaded.

Surfing the Web and Previewing Files

If you type a URL into the Address field at the top of the Live Rendering window, you can access the Web just like a regular browser. Control or right-click in the window to get options for Back, Forward, Stop, Home, Copy Address, and Send Link in Email.

TIP 93: Live Rendering with Live Update

Previewing Pages in Web Browsers

A very important step toward getting the best results from your Web site is to test the pages in multiple Web browsers. In Tip 3 we outline how to set the browser preview preferences, and in this tip we explain how to invoke the Preview in Browser feature.

A button called Preview in Browser resides in the main toolbar and is easily accessible at any time . To preview a page in a browser, open a page and then click the Preview in Browser button. The browser specified as the default (in the Browser Preferences) for previewing is the one that will launch. If you have additional browsers listed in the preferences, you could launch one of them by choosing one from the pull-down list that appears by clicking and holding the Preview in Browser button (**Figure 94**).

Figure 94 The Preview in Browser button has a submenu that appears when you hold the button down for a moment.

Note

The first time you click the Preview in Browser button, GoLive prompts you to select a default browser if you have not already assigned the Browser Preferences. The default browser is assigned by enabling the checkbox next to the preferred browser name in the Browser Preferences. If more than one browser has a checkmark next to it, clicking the Preview in Browser button will launch the page into each of them simultaneously.

An alternate method of launching the default browser is to press the keyboard shortcut Shift-Command-T on Mac (Shift-Control-T on Windows) or choose File > Preview In > Default Browser.

Preview in Browser without Opening in GoLive

To launch a page into a Web browser directly from the Site window without first opening the page in GoLive, select the page in the Files list and then click the Preview in Browser button in the toolbar.

95 Exporting Web Pages to PDF

The PDF Preview mode lets you convert any Web page to a PDF with one click, and it becomes more powerful with every new version of GoLive. If you're not accustomed to converting Web pages to PDF, you might wonder why you would want to do it. Some of the most common uses include:

- **Preparing a page for review by a client, co-worker, or art director:** It's so much easer to email a single PDF than to upload to a staging server or explain how to unpack a compressed .sit or .zip archive. Anybody with a computer and a pulse can view a PDF with the free Adobe Reader (www.adobe.com/reader).

- **Generating a print version:** If you want to offer your visitors a print-ready version of a page without having to surrender yourself to the whims of browsers and printers, just use a PDF.

- **Archiving a page design:** We always do this before handing over a site to clients who want to do their own updates. Your great design will probably never look the same again, and PDF is a great way to preserve it.

It's easy to convert Web pages to PDF files with GoLive. Just switch to PDF Preview mode and click the Export as Adobe PDF icon in the toolbar (**Figure 95**).

Figure 95 Export or email any page as an Adobe PDF with a single click.

Printing a PDF

It's easy and convenient to print PDF files right inside GoLive without launching Adobe Acrobat or Adobe Reader. Double-click a PDF file in the Site window to open it in GoLive and click the Print PDF icon in the toolbar.

Handy Icons

Use the icons at the bottom of the PDF Preview to change the page, view, rotation, and zoom of the file.

TIP
96

Customizing PDF Preferences

If you use the PDF Preview frequently to convert Web pages to PDF, you might find yourself adjusting the same settings over and over again. To save yourself time and ensure consistent quality, you can change the application preferences for how PDF files are created. Select GoLive > Preferences (Mac) or Edit > Preferences (Windows) and choose the Adobe PDF section on the left side. Click the triangle (Mac) or the plus sign (Windows) next to the Adobe PDF item to reveal all the categories of related preferences (**Figure 96**).

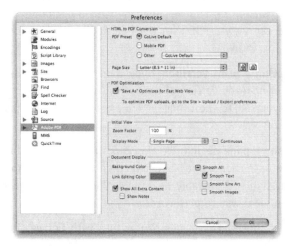

Figure 96 Adjust these preferences to customize how GoLive converts and opens PDF files.

Customize the settings here, and they will affect all new PDF files you create and open with GoLive. The most common settings you should adjust are at the top and include the default PDF Preset used for conversion, the default page size, and whether or not to optimize for Fast Web View (like streaming PDF from a Web server).

You can also control the initial zoom view and display settings for any PDF you open with GoLive. Notice the ability to smooth text, line art, and images, but remember that this only affects how the file is viewed in GoLive and doesn't actually change the PDF.

TIP 97 Saving Time with PDF Presets

All PDFs are not created equal. There are so many different options and settings for generating PDFs for different purposes, and GoLive puts all these controls at your fingertips with PDF Presets. To examine existing presets and to create new ones, choose Edit > Adobe PDF Presets and you'll see the Adobe PDF Presets dialog (**Figure 97a**).

Figure 97a Create and edit PDF conversion presets in the Adobe PDF Presets dialog.

Click New to create a new preset and give it a descriptive name. Choose the PDF compatibility you need in the upper right corner of the dialog and then adjust your settings as desired from the General, Compression, HTML Conversion, and Advanced categories on the left (**Figure 97b**).

Figure 97b Use the Tool Tips for the various options to help you adjust the appropriate settings.

(continued on next page)

TIP 97: Saving Time with PDF Presets

Recreating a PDF with New Settings

When you switch between different PDF Presets in the Inspector, you might notice that nothing changes automatically. To force the PDF to update based on a new preset or any custom changes, make sure you click the Refresh PDF Preview button in the Inspector palette.

It could take an entire book to discuss all the settings for PDF conversion, so in lieu of that, let us recommend the Tool Tips to you. That's right, hover your cursor over many of the controls in the Adobe PDF Preset dialog for a helpful description of what the option affects. Click OK and Done when you're done editing your PDF Presets.

Now to use one of your PDF Presets, open a Web page in GoLive, switch to PDF Preview mode, and choose the preset in the PDF Creation Inspector (**Figure 97c**). The size of the PDF file is shown in the bottom left corner of the Inspector, so you can decide if you've used the best settings or if you need to do some more tweaking.

Figure 97c Use the Tool Tips for the various options to help you adjust the appropriate settings.

If you want to override some aspect of the selected PDF Preset, such as page margins or removing background images and colors, you can make those adjustments in the Inspector and click the Refresh PDF Preview button. When you're ready to export the final PDF, choose File > Export > HTML as Adobe PDF or click the Save as PDF button ⬛ in the toolbar.

TIP 98 Controlling PDF Page Size and Margins

Converting Web pages to PDF documents can get tricky when the proportions of your pages don't match your intended paper size. The PDF Creation Inspector (**Figure 98**) lets you control several options related to page orientation, document dimensions, and margins, which will help you solve these problems:

Figure 98 Adjust page size settings for PDF creation in the Inspector or as part of a PDF Preset.

- **Paper Size:** You'll probably want to select Letter, but you can choose from several defaults.

- **Orientation:** Switch between Portrait and Landscape depending on the layout of the page.

- **Margin:** Adjust all four margins of the PDF here or click the Link All Margins icon to automatically use the same margin on all four sides.

- **Shrink Content to Paper Width:** If the content of your page doesn't fit in the paper size, trying to print can result in unexpected page tiling. We recommend you enable this option. When you do so, GoLive shrinks the page to fit your paper width and even accounts for custom page margins.

If you find yourself entering the same settings over and over again, see Tip 97 to learn how to set these once and for all just how you like them.

TIP 99 Adding Metadata to a PDF

Metadata such as author information, description, and keywords makes a better PDF because:

- Search engines can more easily find the PDF.

- The PDF can be better managed by an asset-management system or database.

- The metadata is embedded in the PDF so readers know who created it and what the document is about.

Using metadata in a PDF essentially makes the file more valuable, and it's really easy to add with GoLive. Switch to PDF Preview and choose File > Export > HTML as Adobe PDF. Choose the appropriate PDF settings for the file and then select the Advanced section on the left side of the Export Adobe PDF dialog.

If the Web page already has a good title, check the Use HTML Page Title option. If the page title isn't that descriptive, or if you want to customize the title, uncheck this option and type a better one in the Title field. You can also enter custom metadata for the Author, Subject, and Keywords fields (**Figure 99**).

Figure 99 Customize metadata in the Advanced section of the Export Adobe PDF dialog.

TIP 100 Hiding Page Backgrounds in a PDF

Web pages with background images usually don't print very well, and the readability of text is often diminished, especially with black and white printers. To minimize ink waste and maximize readability of printed PDFs, you can check the Remove Backgrounds option in the Inspector when you create PDF files (**Figure 100**).

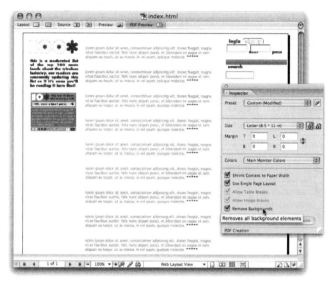

Figure 100 Hide backgrounds when you convert Web pages to PDF to enhance readability, improve printability, and minimize file size.

Checking the Remove Backgrounds option ignores background images and colors for tables, table cells, layers, and entire pages. It even affects background images and colors defined with CSS. The backgrounds are replaced with white to highlight the content and remove distractions. Just imagine how much ink you'll save by not making your printer print out your colored page backgrounds.

TIP 102 Creating Secure Adobe PDFs

One of the greatest aspects of Adobe's PDF technology is that it can be viewed by anybody anywhere on almost any device. However, sometimes you want to keep a tight lid on sensitive documents and you want to limit who is allowed to see certain files. For the first time ever, you can export secured PDFs directly from GoLive CS2 so you can control who views your documents.

Start by opening the Web page you want to convert, switch to PDF Preview mode, and choose File > Export > HTML as Adobe PDF. Customize all the other PDF export settings you need and then select the Security section. To prevent users from opening the PDF unless they have the special password, check the option labeled Require a Password to Open the Document and enter the password twice for verification (**Figure 102**). Nobody, including you, can open this PDF without the assigned password. If you're not confident you'll remember the password, you should write it down in a discreet location or create a non-secure version of the same PDF for your backups.

Figure 102 Customize the security settings of a PDF in the Export dialog.

Another interesting way to secure a PDF is to allow anybody to open the file, but restrict certain kinds of access. For example, you can assign a Permissions password that allows viewers to read the PDF but prohibits printing the document. You can also adjust the permissions security so that viewers can open the PDF and make comments, but not extract any content from the PDF. Experiment with the various options and you'll find several interesting possibilities.

Working with Links in PDF

GoLive gives you powerful control over all aspects of hyperlinks in PDF files. The links can be checked, created, and edited in GoLive whether the PDF was generated with GoLive or another application.

Checking Links in a PDF

When you convert a Web page into a PDF with GoLive, all the hyperlinks are retained. Open the PDF in GoLive and you can click the hyperlinks in PDF Preview mode (**Figure 103a**). A link to a local PDF file or Web page will open the file in GoLive; a link to an external URL will open your Web browser to that address; a link to a PDF page number or bookmark will change to that PDF view; and a link to an email address will open a properly configured email client.

Figure 103a Open a PDF in GoLive to verify the links.

Creating Links in a PDF

It's easy to create a new link in a PDF because the tools work just like the rest of GoLive. Open the PDF in GoLive and click the PDF Link Editing tab at the top of the document window. Select the New Link Tool in the toolbar 🔳 and click and drag in the PDF to define the region of the new link. Now define the link destination in the Inspector palette as usual (**Figure 103b**).

(continued on next page)

Tool Tip Tip

If you patiently hover your cursor over a hyperlink for a moment, you'll see the link destination in the Tool Tip.

Embedding Movies and Multimedia in PDF

When Adobe released Acrobat 6, it included the amazing ability to embed interactive multimedia content such as QuickTime movies and Flash files right inside the PDF. This means Adobe PDF files can now be robust containers for compelling interactive presentations that include a variety of file formats. It can all be stored in one file that can be viewed by anybody with the free Adobe Reader (www.adobe.com/reader).

If your Web pages include movies, they can be embedded inside a PDF you create with the PDF Export feature in GoLive. There are two important options you must enable in the General section of the Export Adobe PDF dialog (**Figure 104**) for the conversion to work correctly:

Figure 104 Adjust the settings so the multimedia is embedded in a PDF 1.5 or 1.6 file.

- **Compatibility:** Make sure this is set to at least PDF 1.5, because only Acrobat 6 and Acrobat 7 viewers support the new embedded multimedia content.

- **Multimedia:** Choose Embed All to embed multimedia files such as QuickTime and SWF in the exported PDF. If you don't check this option, the multimedia might still work, but you'll need to always keep the PDF and multimedia files together.

Advanced Page Editing

TIP 105
Working with PDF Comments

You can add, edit, and delete PDF comments that interchange seamlessly with other GoLive, Acrobat, and Adobe Reader users. PDF comments are a great way to document a process, give feedback, and share ideas right inside the PDF.

Adding Comments

Open a PDF in GoLive and select the Comment tool 💬 in the toolbar. Click in the PDF with the Comment tool to create a new comment anywhere in the document. Make sure the comment is selected and write a note in the Inspector palette (**Figure 105**). Notice that GoLive automatically records the date and time of the comment so it's easy to keep track of the feedback. When you save the file, the comments are added to the PDF for others to read and review.

Figure 105
Click with the Comment tool and add a note in the Inspector.

Missing Comments?

Are you missing comments you know are there? Open the PDF in GoLive and make sure Show Annotations and Show Text Annotations are enabled in the View palette.

Editing Comments

You can view just about any kind of PDF comment in GoLive and you can edit Note comments using the Inspector palette. Select the comment in the PDF and edit the note in the Inspector. Notice how the time and date are updated to reflect your changes.

Deleting Comments

To delete a note comment, just select it in GoLive and press the Delete key. If you make a mistake, you can always use the Multiple Undo feature by pressing Command-Z (Mac) or Control-Z (Windows).

TIP
106 Converting Single Pages

If you see something on the Web that you really want to keep in a format that's easy to store, search, print, and share, then PDF is a great option. If you own Acrobat Standard or Acrobat Professional you can use the Web Capture feature in those applications to convert any Web page or Web site to PDF, but if you only have GoLive this trick is for you.

First choose File > Server > Download Page and type in the URL of the page you want to capture (**Figure 106a**). Click Save As, and GoLive will download all the files used by the page and reassemble the design for you right inside GoLive.

Figure 106a First download the page you want to convert to a PDF.

When you have the page you want in GoLive, switch to PDF Preview (**Figure 106b**) and click the Save as PDF button in the toolbar. Voila, there's your PDF.

Figure 106b Then export the page as a PDF with GoLive.

TIP 107 Converting Entire Sites to PDF

For years, Adobe Acrobat has had the ability to turn a Web page or an entire Web site into a PDF. Now in GoLive CS2 you can create a PDF of your entire Web site in just a few clicks without leaving your favorite Web-authoring application. Make sure the Site window is open and active and choose File > Export > HTML as Adobe PDF. The Export dialog looks the same as the one we've explained in the rest of this chapter with one exception: the Site Creation section (**Figure 107**).

Figure 107 The Site Creation section of the Export Adobe PDF dialog allows you to create one linked PDF from your entire Web site.

Adjust the rest of your PDF settings as you prefer them and select Site Creation on the left side of the Export dialog. From the top, choose whether you want to create one multipage PDF of all the selected files or separate PDF files for each individual HTML page. If you're trying to create archives or print-only versions of several individual Web pages, the second option might help, but we almost always choose the Single PDF option. Also make sure you keep the Resolve Links option enabled.

(continued on next page)

Web Capture with Adobe Acrobat

If you want to convert a site to PDF but don't have the files on your local hard drive, the Web Capture feature in Adobe Acrobat is the fastest option. In Acrobat, choose File > Create PDF > From Web Page, choose Get Entire Site, and click Create. If you're sure you really want to download and convert the entire site to PDF, just click Yes when you see the Potentially Large Download Confirmation dialog and grab a cup of coffee while Acrobat gets the site for you.

The only other decision you have to make is exactly which files you want to convert with the Work On menu in the middle of the dialog. If you had some files selected in the Site window before choosing the Export command, you can choose to convert just those selected files. Otherwise, you'll probably want to convert everything in the Files tab or the Whole site (including templates, stationery, and so on). When you've made your choices, click Export and watch as GoLive does all the hard work for you.

CHAPTER FIVE

Working with Cascading Style Sheets

If you have time to pay attention to current trends, you've certainly seen the impact that Cascading Style Sheets (CSS) is having on the Web-design industry. CSS is changing how designers approach everything from text styling to layout to accessibility. It's saving people time, making site redesigns easier, and "future-proofing" code.

GoLive has always been on the leading edge of Web technologies, and its use of CSS is no exception. Although GoLive has supported CSS for several years, GoLive CS2 received a complete makeover in the CSS department this time around. The engineers worked really hard to consolidate the interface, streamline the workflow, and support all the latest CSS technologies. We're sure you'll be impressed.

If you're still not convinced that learning CSS is worth your time, read the internationally acclaimed CSS presentation at www.hotdesign.com/seybold/. Adam co-presented this material with CSS guru and Web standards evangelist Bill Merikallio at Seybold Seminars. When you're done, we're confident you'll be convinced, and if so, be sure to come back and read this chapter.

TIP 108 Exploring the CSS Editor

The CSS Editor in GoLive CS2 adds several impressive new features. To open the CSS Editor for the internal CSS in a Web page, click the CSS Editor icon in the top right corner of the page in Layout mode, or click and hold to reveal a list of linked external CSS files. If you'd rather work with a new external CSS file, you can create a new one by choosing File > New and then selecting a Basic CSS file from the Favorites category, or use one of the CSS templates in the Web > CSS category.

When the CSS Editor opens you see existing rules on the left, and on the right are icons and menus that help you create new rules, including powerful, advanced features such as @import statements. To create the various types of CSS rules, click the appropriate icon on the right side of the window (**Figure 108a**).

Figure 108a
The default view of the new and improved CSS Editor with the advanced options revealed.

When you select one of the items on the left (called a *selector* in CSS terminology) the CSS Editor changes to show eight different editing tabs on the right. Use the style properties in these eight tabs to customize the CSS rules you select on the left.

In the lower left corner are two buttons that split the editor horizontally. Click the eyeball icon to show the Style Preview pane so you don't have to guess what the changes will look like (**Figure 108b**). That's right—no saving, no updating, and no reloading. Just make your CSS edits and see an accurate preview immediately!

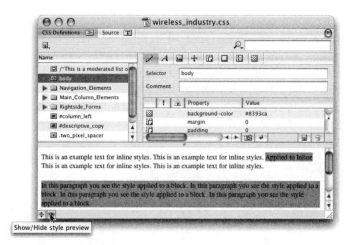

Show/Hide style preview

Figure 108b Toggle open the Style Preview using the eyeball button in the lower left.

Customizing the Preview

If you want to make the preview area larger, just resize the window or drag the divider that separates the top and bottom portions of the CSS Editor.

Click the double-facing arrow to show or hide the source code for the CSS (**Figure 108c**). All of the cool Source Code Editor features you learned about in tips 77–83 work the same here because it's the same source-editing environment throughout GoLive.

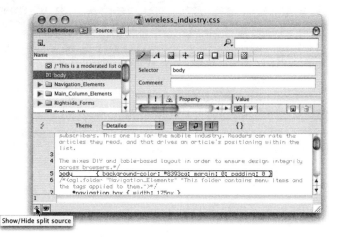

Show/Hide split source

Figure 108c GoLive's powerful Source Code Editor is also helpful when working with CSS.

TIP 108: Exploring the CSS Editor

TIP
109 Enabling the CSS Button Bar

Where's the Default View?

Once you've clicked out of the default view of the CSS Editor, you may not know how to go back to it. Do so by clicking into any unused space on the left side of the CSS editor, where the names of the styles are listed.

The default view of the CSS Editor includes an option labeled Show These Buttons at Top (**Figure 109**). Enabling the checkbox replicates the buttons from the default view by placing them neatly across the top of the window, making them easily accessible at all times. You'll use the buttons to create new styles, to add folders for organizing styles, and much more. We find this option quite handy and recommend turning it on.

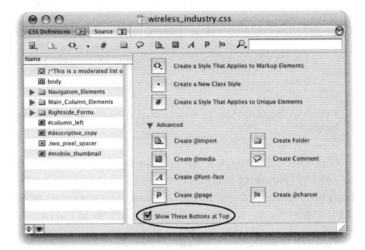

Figure 109 The buttons that appear at the top of the CSS Editor with this option enabled are exactly the same as those that appear in the right half of the CSS Editor in its default view, as shown here.

You can click on a button to create a new element, class, ID style or to create an "at" (@) statement, or even to create a folder in which to organize your styles. In the next tip we show another way to use the buttons.

Saving Time with Pull-down Menus

Whether you're a CSS beginner who needs help getting started or an experienced coder hoping to save time, you'll love the pull-down menus throughout the CSS Editor (**Figure 110**). Some of the new style icons in the default view of the CSS Editor, or in the buttons on top if you've turned them on as described in Tip 109, have small black triangles on them. These triangles indicate that if you click and hold on the icons you'll see an automatically populated list of options to choose from.

For example, if you click and hold on external or @import icons, those menus are auto-populated with all the .css files from the active site. The Elements pull-down menu is also populated with several of the most common elements you'll want to create CSS rules for.

Customizing the Elements Menu

From the bottom of the Elements menu, choose Edit Styles Example to open the settings file. If there's an obscure element or style property you always want to use, edit it here, and it will be added to the pull-down menu.

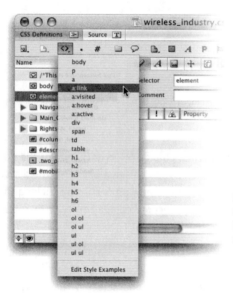

Figure 110 The pull-down menus in the CSS Editor help you learn and save time when editing CSS.

Understanding the CSS Editor Tabs

You can edit dozens of different CSS style properties and attributes, and they are broken into several logical categories in the different sections of the CSS Editor (**Figure 111**). Let's start on the left side and work our way across.

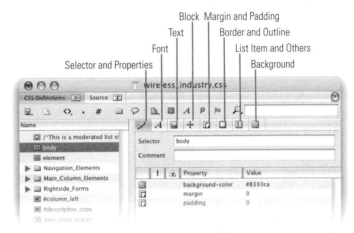

Figure 111 The CSS Editor includes eight different categories of properties you can edit for a CSS rule.

Selector and Properties: Change selector (name) of the rule and add a comment here. You can see a list of all the active style properties and even add new properties by clicking the New Property icon. This ensures compatibility with future releases of the CSS specification.

A **Font:** Customize the font family, size, color, and line height (like leading in print design) in this section. Remember, site visitors will only see the fonts you select if they have the same ones installed on their computer. It's a good idea to stick to the font families included here.

Text: Adjust text spacing, alignment, and indenting in this section. You can also make text uppercase and lowercase and use small caps in this section, but not all properties will render accurately in the Layout Editor. Make sure to use Preview mode for a more accurate rendering.

✛ **Block:** You can edit the size, position, and visibility of an item here. Advanced users will want to use the float and clear properties.

🗗 **Margin and Padding:** The margin is the space between the item and other items, and padding is the space between the item outline and any interior content. When you edit these properties, decide whether you want to have the same value on all sides or edit the top, right, bottom, and left independently.

▢ **Border and Outline:** Change the thickness, color, and style of borders for items in this section.

▤ **List Item and Others:** List bullets can be customized and even rendered from images using the properties in this section.

▨ **Background:** Customize the background color or image of an item, such as the body element, in this section. You can also control the tiling behavior of background images.

Editing Multiple Rules
Select multiple rules on the left to change common properties at the same time.

TIP 111: Understanding the CSS Editor Tabs

TIP 112 Using the CSS Editor Properties List

All the style properties for the selected rule are listed in the first tab of the CSS Editor so you can quickly see an overview of the rule. If you're comfortable with CSS, you can add any existing or future property by clicking the New Property icon, naming the property, and assigning it attributes. An advanced user can add and edit all the style properties in this list instead of switching to all the different tabs. Even if you're used to hand coding, the Properties list will save you time and minimize typing errors.

If you click and hold on the New Property icon, you can choose from an extensive list of all possible CSS properties. The list is so long it can't all fit in the screenshot, as seen in **Figure 112**.

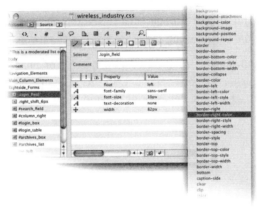

Figure 112
The New Property is preloaded with all the possible CSS properties.

To delete a property in a CSS rule, select the property in this list and click the trashcan icon. This method is much easier than trying to find all the properties in the appropriate tabs. To delete several contiguous properties, Shift-click them all then delete them all together.

Another slick new feature found in the Properties list is the ability to store and reuse property collections. Say, for example, you have an element that has many properties applied to it and you want to style another element the same way. Select the element and then click the Store Property Collection button 🔳 to store its properties as a collection. To apply the collection to another element, select the element, click the Apply Property Collection button 🔳 and choose the collection name from the list.

TIP 113 Sorting Styles

You may find that in short order your style sheet document has grown into a very long list. To help you quickly locate styles in the list, you can use the Sort Statements command found in both the CSS Editor flyout menu and the contextual menu. Choose the command to sort your statements alphabetically by groups: first elements, then classes, and finally IDs (**Figure 113**).

Figure 113 If you'd like to sort the statements in your style sheet, use the Sort Statements command. Here you can see the list before (left) and after (right) it has been sorted.

TIP 114 Find CSS Rules with Quicksearch

The CSS Editor, like the Site window, sports a fabulous new tool called Quicksearch. Located in the upper right corner of the CSS Editor, Quicksearch is extremely handy for quickly locating statements, selectors, or declarations in the CSS document.

To find an item, begin typing its name into the Quicksearch input field. As GoLive identifies items that begin with the letters you type, they will be isolated in the CSS Editor window. To clear the input field, click the ⊠ to its right. (Don't fret if you don't see it; it will appear once you type something into the input field.)

Quicksearch in the CSS Editor also has a pull-down menu (**Figure 114**) that gives you a handy way to isolate a number of items you may use in a style sheet (Figure 114).

Figure 114 Isolating statements or selectors in a complicated style sheet is simple when you use Quicksearch.

TIP 115 Jumping to CSS Properties

If you have styles defined that use a number of properties, it can be challenging to remember which tab of the CSS Editor contains which definitions. That means that if you want to change the style definition, you often end up clicking through all the tabs until you find the property you want to edit. There's an excellent new feature in GoLive CS2 that takes the guesswork out of finding the correct tab.

To the right of each style name in the list in the column marked Info are icons representing the tabs in the CSS Editor where properties are currently defined. If you don't see them, drag the lower right corner of the CSS Editor a bit larger until they appear (**Figure 115a**).

Show Properties in the List

From the CSS Editor flyout menu, select the option called Show Properties in List to have access to the defined properties directly in the styles list. To see the properties, click the gray triangle to the left of the style name on Mac (the plus sign on Windows). You can also jump to a property's tab by clicking the icon next to the property name in the list.

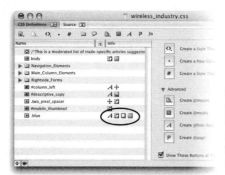

Figure 115a When you enlarge the CSS Editor, you'll see icons representing the areas where properties are defined.

Now, to go to an area, simply click one of those icons. The CSS Editor will jump to the tab for those properties (**Figure 115b**).

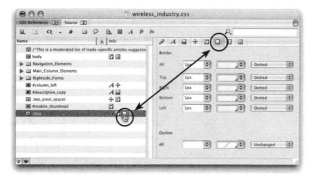

Figure 115b Click an icon to jump to that tab of the CSS Editor.

116 Creating CSS Comments and Folders

When you create complex CSS files, you'll want to organize the rules in a way that makes the rules easy to remember, manage, and share with others. The advanced comments and folders options in the CSS Editor make these challenges a breeze (**Figure 116**).

Dragging to Resort Statements

To change the order of CSS rules and move rules in and out of folders, just select the rules and drag them into their new location in the list on the left of the CSS Editor window.

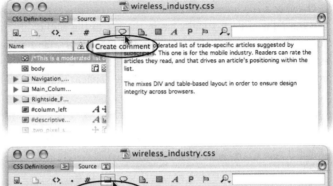

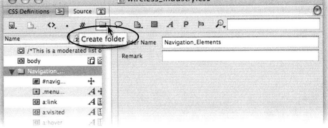

Figure 116 Comments and folders make it easy to organize and document complex CSS files.

Create a comment in your CSS source code to leave yourself a reminder, document your work, or communicate style standards to coworkers. Just click the Create Comment button on the right side or top of the CSS Editor. Type the text of your comment in the right side of the window and you're done. You can go back to edit or delete your comments at any time.

You can also create folders to organize complex style sheets. Folders in the GoLive CSS Editor are really just comments in the source code that look like folders in the list of CSS definitions, so there's nothing wrong with the code and it's a really nice editing convenience. Create a new folder by clicking the New Folder icon on the right or top of the CSS Editor. Remember that the order of the folders does affect the cascade of the CSS.

TIP 117 Using the CSS Tab in the Site Window

As the use of CSS becomes more common among Web designers, it becomes more important to manage all the external CSS files and the various CSS rules. GoLive CS2 introduces a groundbreaking new way to manage all these aspects of CSS usage in one centralized location: the new CSS tab in the Site window (**Figure 117**).

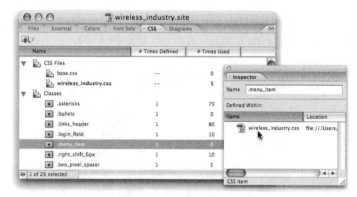

Figure 117 Manage all your CSS from the new CSS tab of the Site window.

Keepin' It Fresh

If you've been doing some heavy CSS editing, make sure you click the Refresh button in the toolbar to ensure you're looking at the most current CSS style information.

Inside the new CSS tab you can see a centralized listing of all the external .css files and every Class and ID style that is defined or used in every page of the site. You might notice that Element styles are not listed, and that is because they are applied automatically and you don't have any control over them other than editing the rules in the CSS Editor.

You can even see how many times a style is defined and how many times it's been used throughout the pages of your site. This CSS inventory will help you avoid unnecessary duplicates and improve the efficiency of your styles.

If you need to make some changes to a CSS rule, select it in the CSS tab of the Site window and look in the Inspector palette to see where the rule is defined. Remember that it's possible for one style to be defined in multiple locations, but in most cases you'll have just one source location. Double-click the file where the style is defined to open it, and the selected rule is automatically selected in the source document. Now all you have to do is edit the CSS rule and save the file.

TIP 118
Tracking CSS Usage with In & Out Links

The ability to observe all the CSS definitions in the CSS tab of the Site window is a cool addition, but what makes this a truly awesome feature is that you can actually manage and update the CSS all in one place. For example, select an external CSS file in the CSS tab of the Site window and open the In & Out Links palette from the Window menu. The pages that reference the selected CSS file are listed on the left, and the Class and ID styles that are contained within the selected CSS file are listed on the right (**Figure 118a**).

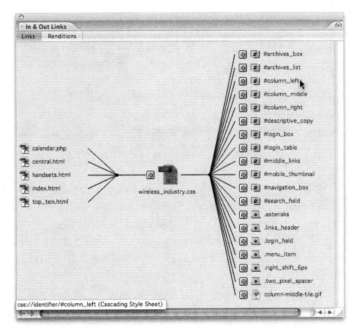

Figure 118a Select a .css file and open the In & Out Links palette to get an overview of the style usage in the site.

For even more detail, select one of the Class or ID styles on the right. On the left side of the In & Out Links palette you'll see where the style is defined and on the right you can see all the files that use the selected style (**Figure 118b**).

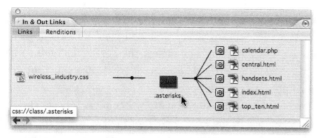

Figure 118b Select a single style to see all the places it's defined and used.

At this point, you might want to replace one class with a different one. The old way of making an update such as this involved editing each page by hand or performing tedious Find and Replace operations. Now with GoLive CS2, you just have to select the page you want to update and use the Pick Whip tool from the In & Out Links palette (**Figure 118c**). Find the style on the right that you want to replace and redirect the reference to the new style in the CSS tab of the Site window.

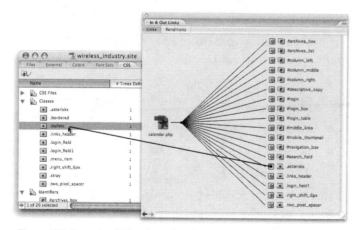

Figure 118c Reassign CSS styles using the In & Out Links palette.

TIP 118: Tracking CSS Usage with In & Out Links

Assigning a Default CSS File for a Web Site

Speedy Shortcut

You can also Control-click (Mac) or right-click (Windows) and choose the Default CSS command to define the default CSS file for a site.

One of the greatest benefits of CSS is the consistency of design and text formatting it can bring to a Web site. All these benefits are easy to achieve, assuming one thing: that you remember to use the same CSS file for all your pages.

To help you with this mundane detail, GoLive CS2 has a new feature that lets you define an external CSS file for each Web site you work on. This means every time you create a new page in a site, GoLive will automagically attach the default CSS file to that page. It's thoughtful little timesaving features like this that make GoLive so pleasant to use.

In the Files tab of the Site window, select a .css file and click the Default CSS option in the Page section of the File Inspector (**Figure 119**). Notice that the default CSS file is now listed in bold in the Files tab, just as the default home page of a site is listed in bold.

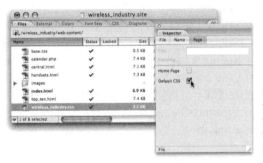

Figure 119 Define the default CSS file for a site with the File Inspector.

There are three ways to create a new page in a site that will take advantage of the default CSS file:

- Control-click (Mac) or right-click (Windows) in the Files tab of the Site window and choose New > Document....

- Click the New Page button in the toolbar.

- Drag in a Generic Page object from the Site section of the Objects palette.

This makes it impossible to forget to assign a CSS file to a page in your site. It also saves you time and guarantees consistency across your site.

TIP
120   Applying CSS Styles

Element styles such as <body>, <td>, and <h1> are applied automatically at every instance of the styled element, but class and ID styles must be applied by hand.

You can apply CSS classes with the Type > CSS Span, Type > CSS Paragraph, or Type > CSS Div commands, but select Type > CSS Style... for the easiest method. When you invoke this menu command, a small floating window appears by your selection in the Layout Editor, and with one click you can apply the class as an inline style, block, style, or to the active HTML element (**Figure 120a**).

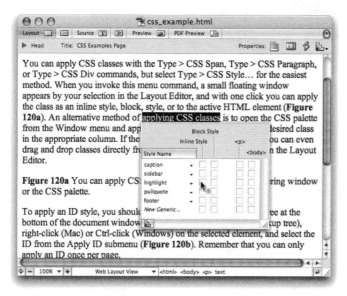

Figure 120a You can apply CSS classes with one click in this hovering window of the CSS palette.

An alternative method of applying CSS classes is to open the CSS palette from the Window menu and apply the class by clicking next to the desired class in the appropriate column. If the CSS Editor window is still open, you can even drag and drop classes directly from the CSS Editor into a selection in the Layout Editor.

(continued on next page)

To apply an ID style, select the element in the Markup Tree at the bottom of the document window (see Tip 34 to learn about the Markup Tree), Control-click (Mac) or right-click (Windows) on the selected element, and select the ID from the Apply ID submenu (**Figure 120b**). Remember that you can only apply an ID once per page.

Figure 120b You can apply ID rules with the Markup Tree and contextual menus.

TIP 121 Previewing CSS Styles

Before you apply a class with the Type menu or the CSS palette, you can get a quick preview to help you make the right text styling decisions (**Figure 121**). For example, when you place your cursor over the Inline Style and Block Style checkboxes for a moment, a small preview window will pop up and show you an accurate preview of how the style will appear when applied in different ways.

Opening the CSS Editor

If you decide your CSS rules need a few tweaks, just click the shortcut icon in the bottom left corner to make some last-minute changes.

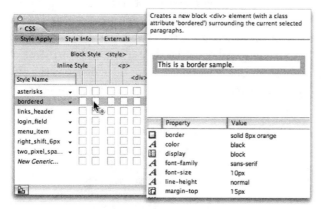

Figure 121 This preview takes the guesswork out of applying CSS styles.

At the top of the preview is a nicely written description of how the style will be applied. In the middle is a visual preview of how the style will appear when applied as an inline style, block style, or when applied to a specific HTML element. The comprehensive list of properties at the bottom shows an accurate cascade of all the styling information that will make the CSS gurus drool.

TIP
122

Viewing the Cascaded Style Info

Changing the Active Element

To evaluate the cascaded style info of other items on the page, select a different element or style from the menu in the top right corner of the CSS Palette.

Cascading Style Sheets (CSS) are an amazing technology that can make life much easier for a Web designer. Then again, they can make you pull your hair out with frustration and confusion. When you're dealing with multiple complex style sheets, it can be hard to keep track of how all the style properties cascade and inherit to render the final results.

To help you keep everything straight, the CSS palette includes an innovative new feature that shows you the complete CSS style information of your selection in the Layout Editor. Make a selection in the Layout editor and open the Style Info tab of the CSS palette (**Figure 122**). This information will help you understand the effect of the inheritance and cascade of the styles on your selection.

Figure 122 The Style Info section of the CSS palette shows the complete final cascade and inheritance of the selection in the Layout Editor.

For example, the cascade rules of CSS determine that if an external style sheet says captions are red, but an internal style says captions are blue, then the internal definition "wins," and the captions will be blue.

TIP 123
Shortcut to CSS Editor from CSS Palette

When you have multiple pages and multiple CSS files, keeping track of which styles are defined where can be challenging. GoLive makes this tedious task a piece of cake with a secret little shortcut in the CSS palette (**Figure 123**). Click and hold the small black triangle next to any of the class names in the CSS palette and select the Edit In command to open the file where the class is defined. If the rule is defined in multiple locations, GoLive lets you pick from all the appropriate options.

Figure 123 Double-click a class in the CSS palette to open the corresponding style sheet.

You can also double-click a class in the CSS palette to open the correct style sheet automatically. If the selected rule is defined in multiple files, the last reference in the source code is the one that is opened when you double-click the class name.

For example, if you have two external style sheets applied to one page, GoLive is smart enough to open the correct .css file and even select the rule you want to edit. Because it's automatically selected for you, all you have to do is make your edits, evaluate the results with the Live Preview, and save when you're done.

Applying External CSS to Multiple Pages

Point and Shoot Power

You can also use the Point and Shoot tool in the CSS palette to attach an external CSS file to multiple pages. Select multiple pages, grab the Pick Whip tool in the CSS palette, and point to the .css file in the Files tab of the Site window.

If you're creating a new site with CSS, you'll probably assign an external CSS file to your template pages or create a default CSS file for the site (see Tip 119). But if you have an old site that isn't based on templates, the prospect of retrofitting it with CSS can be pretty daunting. Fortunately, GoLive makes it really easy to apply an external style sheet to multiple pages at one time with the CSS palette. Follow these three easy steps:

1. Select the Web pages in the Files tab of the Site window. You can even select files in multiple and nested folders (see Tip 23 about selecting files).

2. Open the CSS palette from the Window menu if it's not already available.

3. Click and hold the New Link button 🔲 in the CSS palette to choose the .css file you want to attach to all the selected pages (**Figure 124**). This pull-down menu is automatically populated with all the .css files in the active Site window.

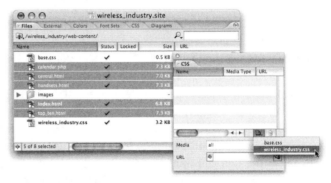

Figure 124 It's easy to assign an external .css file to multiple pages with the pull-down menu or the Point and Shoot tool in the CSS palette.

TIP 125 Exporting Internal Styles

Sometimes you'll create some really nice internal styles that you decide would work well on other pages. You could copy and paste the source code from page to page, but there must be an easier way, right? It's easy to export an internal style sheet with the CSS Editor.

Follow these steps to learn how to export an internal style sheet:

1. Open the page with the internal style sheet.

2. Select File > Export > Internal Style Sheet....

3. Name and save the new .css file. If you intend to use it in the site you are currently working in, click Root folder from the Site pull-down menu in the Save dialog. This will automatically choose the root folder of your site.

Another way to export an internal style sheet to a separate file is to select Export Internal CSS from the flyout menu of an internal style sheet, as seen in **Figure 125**.

Importing External Styles

Using the same menus, you can import external styles just like you export internal styles. It's a two-way street.

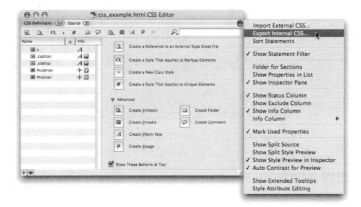

Figure 125 Exporting an internal sheet and using the results with Tip 124 is a great way to retrofit an old site with new technology.

TIP
126 Using the CSS Samples

It can be intimidating to get started with a new technology you're not familiar with. Sometimes the best way to learn a new Web-design technique is to dissect somebody else's work. With this in mind, GoLive CS2 includes dozens of pre-built style sheets to use and learn from. Here's a good way to do that:

1. Choose File > New, then select Web on the left side, and then select the CSS category in the middle (**Figure 126a**). In the bottom right corner of the New dialog is a nice preview of how the selected CSS sample will affect a typical Web page. When you find one you like, select it in the list and click OK.

Figure 126a Dozens of CSS examples are waiting for you in the New dialog.

2. GoLive creates a new untitled .css file based on the sample you selected in the New dialog box (**Figure 126b**). Now choose File > Save As... to save it into the root folder of the Web site you're working on.

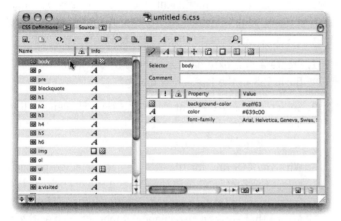

Figure 126b GoLive makes a new CSS file from the sample you choose.

3. Now you can make your new CSS file the default for your site (see Tip 119) or attach the external CSS file to existing pages in your site (see Tip 124). Now that you've found a style sheet you want to use, you might want to customize it further or learn from the example file. Open the .css file from the Site window and examine the various rules in the CSS Editor window.

TIP 126: Using the CSS Samples

TIP 127 Removing Link Underlines

One of the most common requests in any Web design forum is: "How do I remove the underlines from all my text links?" You've probably figured it out by now, but you'll need to use CSS to achieve this common effect. You *can* remove link underlines with internal style sheets, but that's very inefficient because it means opening and editing every page individually. Instead, here's an easier solution that uses an external style sheet. Just follow these steps:

1. Create a new external style sheet by selecting Web > CSS > Basic CSS in the File > New dialog.

2. Select the <a> element from the New Element pull-down menu on the right to create a new style sheet rule that affects how hyperlinks are displayed in your Web pages.

3. With the CSS rule for the <a> element selected on the left, select the Font tab 𝐴 in the CSS editor and click the No Text Decoration button to remove the underlines (**Figure 127**). Notice that you can also change properties such as the color, size, and background color of your hyperlinks in the same tab of the CSS Editor.

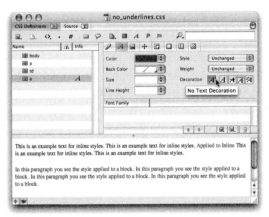

Figure 127
You're not stuck with underlined links if you follow these steps.

After you save this external .css file into your Web site, follow the steps in Tip 124 to apply this effect to all the pages in your site. Isn't it amazing how much time GoLive is saving you? Now you can take an extra week of summer vacation.

TIP 128 Creating CSS Text Rollovers

You know the effect where you mouse over a text link and the text changes color, or even the background of the link changes color? If you guessed this is done with CSS, you're on the road to great Web wisdom and success. Be aware that this CSS rollover effect may not work in older browsers, but the links themselves will work just fine.

Follow these steps to create CSS text rollovers:

1. Open your style sheet (internal or external) in the CSS Editor.

2. Add an element style for the *a:hover* element by selecting it from the New Element pull-down menu on the right side of the CSS Editor window, as seen in **Figure 128a**.

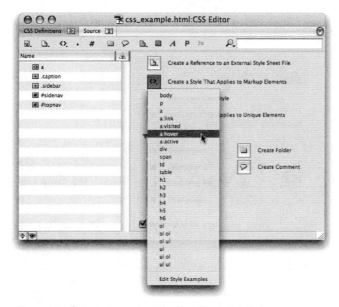

Figure 128a Select a:hover from the New Element pull-down menu.

(continued on next page)

3. With the *a:hover* rule selected on the left side of the window, change the text color in the Font Properties tab of the CSS Editor, as seen in **Figure 128b**. This will be the color of the text when you hover your cursor over the text link.

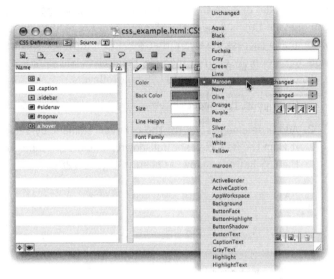

Figure 128b Change the color of the rollover text in the Font Properties tab of the CSS Editor.

4. If you also want to change the background color of the text link, edit the Back(ground) Color field in the same tab of the CSS Editor.

Now all pages that use this style sheet will have this new rollover effect on text links. To test the effect, switch to Preview mode (see Tips 92–94 for more about previewing) and hover your cursor over the text links in your page (**Figure 128c**). Voila!

Figure 128c This simple navigation bar shows the CSS rollover effect in Preview mode.

CHAPTER SIX

Automating Repetitive Tasks

Copy and Paste are lovely things, and years ago they were practically the only way to reuse elements when building a Web site. But back in 1998, a feature was introduced into GoLive (at that time called GoLive CyberStudio 3) that allowed you to save part of a page as a *component* and then reuse it on other pages. The coolest thing about a component was that if you changed the original component, all the pages where it was used were automatically updated to reflect the change.

Well, that was only the beginning. Since then, every release of GoLive has added new features to help you quickly build and maintain Web sites and to automate time-consuming repetitive tasks.

In this chapter, we concentrate on four features that we rely on daily to automate our design process: snippets, components, stationery, and page templates, all of which are neatly tucked into the Library palette and some of which are accessible via the New dialog box. (Although Smart Objects are stored in the Library palette, too, they are covered in Chapter Seven.) We also discuss the process for checking the spelling on your pages prior to making it live for the world to see.

TIP 129
Navigating the Library Palette

Start by opening the Library palette from the Window menu. This little palette is multi-talented. It stores items that are available for use application-wide as well as items specific to any open Web site projects.

Across the top of the Library palette are six buttons: Snippets, Components, Smart Objects, Stationery, Templates, and Documents. To see what's in the Snippets area, click the Snippets button, and so on (**Figure 129a**).

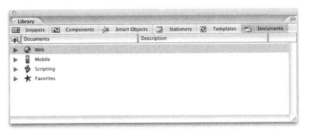

Figure 129a The Library palette.

In the area below the buttons is a folder called Application-wide along with folders representing any sites you have open. These folders work like the folders in the Files tab of the Site window. They can be toggled open or closed by clicking the gray arrow to the left of the folder name (click the plus (+) sign in Windows), or you can drill down into a folder by double-clicking it. Use the up arrow in the upper left corner to move back up a level.

In the Library palette's flyout menu are options to turn preview on and off and to have the preview appear at the right instead of the bottom. This choice comes in handy when previewing a template or component (**Figure 129b**).

Figure 129b
Viewing one of the included page templates in the Library palette with preview enabled and on the right.

TIP 130 — Using Snippets

Snippets are, very simply, pieces of a page that you can use over and over again. A few examples would be an address, a table of data, or a piece of JavaScript. If you find that you are using one element on lots of pages, turn it into a snippet for drag and drop ease of use:

1. Choose File > New, click Web, then choose Pages in the center pane and HTML in the right pane to start with a new, blank page.

2. Type your name and address onto the page.

3. Select everything you typed and drag it into the Application-wide folder in the Snippets area of the Library palette.

The folder will automatically pop open, and you'll see a new file there called snippet.agls. If the filename isn't highlighted for renaming, press Return/Enter. Call it address.agls (**Figure 130**).

Figure 130
When you create a new snippet, give it a descriptive name.

Now follow these steps to complete the process:

1. Choose File > New Page to get another new blank page.

2. Drag the snippet you named address.agls onto the new page.

Tada! You have successfully created and used a snippet. You can create a snippet out of grids, tables, text, images, and more. If you have a styled table with an image and text, surrounded by additional text, grab the whole kaboodle and save it as one snippet.

To modify a snippet, double-click the file in the Library palette, make the changes, and then save the document. The changes will affect only the snippet you've edited, not the pages on which the snippet was already used.

Try the Samples

There are some very handy samples included in the Snippets area of the Library palette. Go through and drag some of them onto a page to see what's there. Note that some of the included snippets are for use in the body of a page, whereas others, such as the meta snippets, are for the head portion of the page. Likewise, some snippets are easily used in the Source Editor, and others are perfect for the Layout Editor. Play around, and you'll see how flexible snippets can be.

TIP 131 Using Components

There is one major difference between snippets and components. If you create a snippet, use it on ten pages, and then change the snippet file, no change is made to the pages that already use that snippet. Not so with components. If you create a component, use it on ten pages, and then change the component file, every page that uses the component will be updated to reflect the change.

Some examples of when components are perfect: navigation bars, copyright notices, or any item that is used on multiple pages but needs occasional updating.

The process for creating a component is a little different than for creating a snippet. Instead of dragging items off a page and into the Components section of the Library palette, you need to save the whole page as a component. To do so, either choose File > Save as and then choose Components from the Site Folder pop-up in the Save dialog box, or choose Save as > Component from the document's flyout menu (**Figure 131a**). Use a descriptive name when you save the file so that you know which component is which when you later go to use one on a page.

Figure 131a Use the handy Site Folder pop-up to save directly into the site's component folder or save the file as a component via its flyout menu.

When the component is saved, it will appear both in the Components folder of the Site Extras and in the Components section of the Library palette. To use it, drag it from the Library palette onto a page.

To edit a component, double-click it in the Library palette, make your changes, and then save the file. When you save the component, any pages using that component will be automatically updated (**Figure 131b**). A dialog box will inform you when the update has been completed. Click OK.

Figure 131b GoLive shows you which pages reference the component and will therefore be updated.

Note

After you change a component that is used on other pages, remember to upload the changed pages to the Web server.

TIP 131: Using Components

Using Stationery

Stationery vs. Templates

Stationery pages are great for those times when modifying the original should not affect pages that had been created from it—for example, a newsletter or archive. However, when you want to update multiple pages with ease, template pages are the best choice because any page created from a template will be updated to reflect changes made to the original file.

Anyone who has seen a stack of company letterhead will be familiar with the term *stationery*. If you take a piece of letterhead, type a letter on it, send it to your mom, and then subsequently redesign the letterhead, your mom's letter would remain unchanged. GoLive's stationery pages work precisely the same way.

Design a stationery page as you would any other page, but instead of saving it into the Files tab of the Site window, save it into the Stationery folder. There are two easy ways to do this: Choose File > Save as and then choose Stationery from the Site Folder pop-up in the Save dialog box, or choose Save as > Stationery from the document's flyout menu.

Your new stationery file will appear in both the Stationery folder of the Extras tab in the Site window and in the Stationery section of the Library palette. To create a new page from stationery, do one of the following:

- Drag the stationery file from the Stationery folder in the Extras tab or from the Stationery section of the Library palette and drop it into the Files tab of the Site window. A dialog box will ask if you want to move the file or create a new file. Choose Create, and a new page will be created and opened, ready for you to work on.

- Double-click the stationery file in the Stationery folder of the Extras tab or from the Stationery section of the Library palette. A dialog box appears asking if you want to Create a new page or Modify the Stationery page. Click Create, and a new page based on the stationery opens. Be sure to name and save the page into your site (**Figure 132**).

Figure 132 Choose Create to make a new page based on the stationery, or choose Modify to change the stationery file itself.

If you would like to change the stationery file, double-click it and choose Modify. Make your changes and then save the file. None of the pages that were created from the stationery page will be affected by the modification of the original.

TIP 133 Creating a Template

Of the four brethren, snippets, components, stationery, and templates, templates are by far the most powerful. By building a template-based site, you can update the entire look of your Web site quickly and easily. Templates require a little more setup than stationery pages, so we devote the next several tips exclusively to the topic of templates.

Note
Another powerful way of making site-wide visual changes is to employ Cascading Style Sheets (see Chapter 5).

The idea behind a template is that certain areas of the page are locked and unchangeable, while other areas are editable. Locked areas typically include the parts of the page that repeat throughout the site, such as navigation bars, while editable regions contain elements that will vary on each page, such as the text.

As you create your template page, you specify which areas of the page are editable via the Template Regions palette, found in the Window menu. To create an editable region, make a selection on the page and then click the Create New Editable Region button in the Template Regions palette. GoLive automatically names text regions according to the first few words in the selection. Other objects are simply named Object or Region. You can rename any region by clicking on its name in the Template Regions palette and pressing Return/Enter, or by clicking a second time (**Figure 133a**).

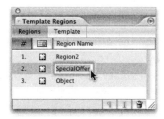

Figure 133a GoLive automatically gives newly created regions a name, but they are easily edited in the Template Regions palette.

(continued on next page)

Editable CSS in the Template Head

Here's a nifty trick: If you have CSS written into a template page, when you make new pages from the template the CSS will be locked. You can't use the Template Regions palette to assign editable regions in the head, but you can go into the source code and add the necessary syntax yourself. Just add `<!-- InstanceBeginEditable name="CSS" -->` right before the `<style>` tag and `<!-- TemplateEndEditable -->` right after the closing `</style>` tag. Although these regions won't show up in the Template Regions palette, when you create a page from the template you will be able to edit the CSS by double-clicking the CSS head tag in the page.

Templates in the New Dialog

When you choose File > New... the resulting dialog has five categories on the left. When you have a site open that includes template or stationery files, those files will be found in the Favorites section.

You can turn off the automatic naming of regions by disabling Selection Defines Region Name in the Template Regions flyout menu. By turning it off, all new regions will simply be called Region2, Region3, and so on. Editable regions are highlighted on the page in dark green, making them very easy to identify. You can determine a region's location on the page by double-clicking its name in the Template Regions palette, which will show the region with a lighter green highlight (**Figure 133b**).

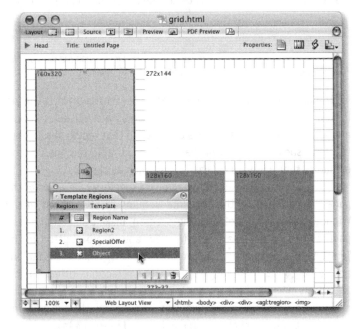

Figure 133b Editable regions that appear light gray here are highlighted in green on your template page.

Create as many editable regions on the page as you need and then save the page as a template by choosing File > Save as and then clicking Templates from the Site Folder pop-up in the Save dialog box, or choose Save as > Template, from the document's flyout menu. The new template page will appear in both the Templates folder of the Extras tab in the Site window and in the Templates portion of the Library palette.

Note

You must specify at least one editable region on a page before the template will perform like a template. When no editable regions are indicated, GoLive treats the page as a normal page, and you won't be able to create new pages from it.

TIP 134 Creating Pages from a Template

When your template page is complete, the next step is to build additional pages from it. Choose one of the following methods to create a new page based on your template:

- Choose File > New and then select Web > Templates to see all the templates for the active site. Choose the template you want to build off of and click OK (**Figure 134a**).

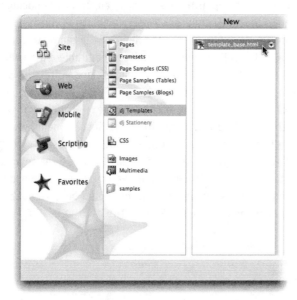

Figure 134a Create pages based on templates using the New dialog or directly from the Site window.

- Control-click (Mac) or right-click (Windows) in the Files tab of the Site window and choose New > Page from Template. From that submenu choose from the list of page templates already saved into your site.

- Double-click the template file in the Templates folder of the Extras tab of the Site window or in the Templates portion of the Library palette. A dialog box will ask if you want to modify the file or create a new file. Click Create, and a new page based on the template is created.

(continued on next page)

TIP 134: Creating Pages from a Template

Highlight Color

You can change both the color and the type of highlighting used to indicate editable regions in the Highlight section of the View palette. Move the sliders to make the editable region's highlight color more or less opaque or click the "Show Border Only" button on the right of the opacity slider to highlight only the region's border. To change the color entirely, click the color well and choose a new color from the Color or Swatches palette.

All the editable regions show in their normal color, whereas the locked regions (any area *not* designated as editable) are highlighted in purple. You can try to select or edit a highlighted area, but you won't be able to because those areas are protected and, hence, not editable. You can, however, modify any editable region. When you're done, save the page into your site.

Applying Templates

What if you have an existing page that already has content on it and you want to drop that content into a template? Here's how.

One method is to open the page and then, from the document flyout menu, choose Template > Apply Template > *yourtemplate. html*, where *yourtemplate.html* is the name of the template you are applying. A dialog will ask you to specify the editable region where the page's content will go. Make your choice, and voila! The page assumes the look of the template page.

An optional method is to open the page to which you want to apply the template and then, from the Special menu, choose Template > Apply Template. The Open dialog box appears with the Templates folder for your site already loaded. Choose the template you want to use and click Open. Again, you're asked to choose the editable region where the pages' content should be placed. Select the region name and click OK (**Figure 134b**).

Figure 134b When applying a template to an existing page, select the region where the page's content will be placed.

TIP 135 Creating Nested Templates

New in GoLive CS 2 is the ability to have *nested* templates. This is a very valuable feature that allows you to base one template on another, which is useful, for example, when a site follows a basic design but has sections that vary slightly.

To create a nested template, you must first create the *master* template, the one that the subsequent templates will be based on. Using the instructions in Tip 133, create the first template. Next, double-click the template in the Library palette or select it in the File > New... dialog, under the Web category. When asked if you want to create a new page from the template or modify it, choose Create.

Add additional editable regions into the newly created page and then choose Save As > Template, from the page's flyout menu. Be sure to give the new template a unique name. You can now create new pages from the second template. If the first template is updated, not only will all the pages based on it will be updated, but all the pages based on the second template will be updated, too. Switch to Icon View in the Site window (see Tip 20) to see the additional marking on the lower left corner of the template's icon that indicates it is a nested template (**Figure 135**).

A Regular Template
template1.html

A Nested Template
template2.html

Figure 135 In Icon View, you can clearly recognize the marking on a nested template.

TIP 136 Redefining Templates

Let's say you've based your site entirely on templates. Well done. Now maybe you get in a creative mood one day and come up with a completely new design. How do you take all those pages built upon one template and port them over to a new template? It's simple, really.

First save the new design as a template, making sure that you define its editable regions. To make upgrading pages to a new template a snap, it is important that you *use the same editable region names* in the new template that you used in the original. Using the same region names allows the content to flow seamlessly from the old template to the new one.

Let's first explore how to redefine a single page and then we'll see how to redefine multiple pages at once.

To redefine which template a page uses, employ one of the following methods:

- Open the page and then from the document flyout menu choose Template > Apply Other Template > *newtemplate. html*, where *newtemplate.html* is the filename of your new template (**Figure 136a**).

Figure 136a Choose a different template to base the page on from the document flyout menu.

- Open the page and then click the Template button in the Template Regions palette. Use the Fetch URL tool to point and shoot to a new template file in the templates folder of the Extras tab of the Site window (**Figure 136b**).

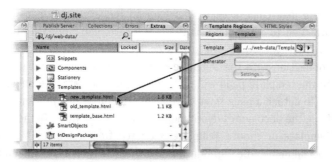

Figure 136b Use the Fetch URL tool from the Template Regions palette to redefine a page's template.

Redefining Components

You can use the In & Out Links palette to redefine components as well as templates. Follow the steps outlined for redefining page templates site-wide, but select the original component inside the Components folder found in the Extras tab of the Site window and then point and shoot to the replacement component.

In both cases, if the editable region names match, the new template is automatically applied. If you don't use the same region names in both templates, you get a dialog box asking you to choose an editable region from the list. This can be tricky because you can only select one region from the list.

To redefine the template used on multiple pages, use the In & Out Links palette as follows:

1. Open the In & Out Links palette from the Window menu.

2. Select the original template file by clicking it once. You should find it in the Templates folder in the Extras tab of the Site window. The In & Out Links palette will show all the pages connected to the old template.

3. Use the Fetch URL tool next to the template name to point and shoot to the new template in the Templates folder (**Figure 136c**).

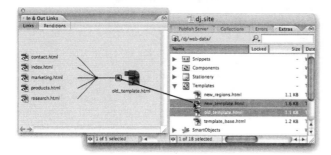

Figure 136c Easily redefine the template used on multiple pages by using the In & Out Links palette.

TIP 136: Redefining Templates

Detaching Templates
Detaching Templates

There may come a time when you no longer want a page to be attached to a template. If that's the case, you can easily detach it. When you do so, the page's design remains the same, but the connection with the template is broken. Any subsequent updates to the template page will no longer affect the detached page.

To detach a page from its template, begin by opening the page. From the document's flyout menu, choose Templates > Detach from Template or choose Template > Detach from Template from the Special menu. The highlighting of locked areas is removed, and the entire page becomes editable (**Figure 137**).

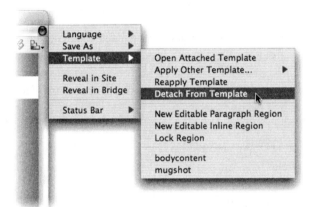

Figure 137 A page detached from its template becomes fully editable again.

Detaching Components

Not only can you detach a page template from its source document, you can detach a component as well, thereby breaking the link back to its original version. Simply Control-click/right-click on a component in a page and choose Components > Detach Selected Component. You can also choose Detach All Components or Detach Single Component and then select the component's name from the list. From then on, changes made to the original component are not updated in the detached version.

TIP 138 Using Sample Templates

You might have noticed in the New dialog that there are dozens of page templates to give you a jumpstart on your Web projects. Let's take a look at what's there and how you can make use of them.

First choose File > New and select Web on the left side and then one of the Page Samples categories in the middle. Select any of the templates to see a preview thumbnail of the page on the right (**Figure 138**). When you find a template page you want to work with, click OK and then save it into the Templates folder for your site (see Tip 133). You can now create new pages from the template, as explained earlier in this chapter, or modify the template to better suit your needs. Notice that the sample templates already have editable regions defined, so you're ready to add your content right away.

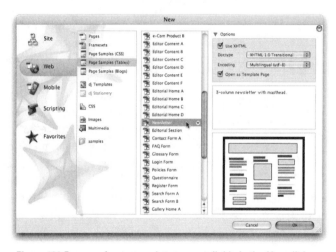

Figure 138 Dozens of page templates are available in the New dialog.

You may need to unlock the page to make modifications, but you can lock it again when you are done. To unlock the page, choose Special > Template > Unlock Page. Replace the image placeholders with images of your own, substitute the placeholder text with your own text, and resave the template. You can now use it as you would any other template in your site.

The fun part comes when you combine the page templates with one of the included CSS samples. You can change the entire look of a page (or site) by attaching an external style sheet to a template (see Tip 126).

TIP 138: Using Sample Templates

TIP
139 Spellchecking

An interesting thing about the two authors of this book is that Adam is a better speller than Lynn, but Lynn is a better typist than Adam. Either way, we both make plenty of errors, and having the ability to run a spelling check on one page, a series of pages, or an entire site is immensely helpful and a huge time-saver.

Figure 139 Adjust your settings and choose the files to process from the Work On pull-down menu.

Start by opening the Check Spelling window from the Edit menu. A spellcheck begins at the position of the cursor on an open page. To run the spellcheck from the top of the page, enable the From Top check box. To spellcheck more than the top document, you can use the Work On menu to control how much of the site will be checked (**Figure 139**).

Choose your preferred language from the pop-up menu and select the appropriate options for your spelling check. Then click Start to begin the spellcheck. As the check proceeds, you'll choose from several options:

- **Delete** removes the word from the page.
- **Replace** replaces the questionable word with the selected suggestion.
- **Ignore** skips over the word with no modification.
- **Ignore All** skips all instances of the unknown word.
- **Learn** adds the word to your personal dictionary.
- **Next File** moves to the next document in the site.

Changing Documents Site-wide

There may be times when you need to make site-wide changes, such as updating the DOCTYPE of every page. GoLive CS2 offers an easy method for making this kind of change quickly and accurately.

There are several site-wide document content changes that you can make, including: Convert Styles, Convert Encoding, Convert to HTML, Convert to XHTML, Change Doctype, Convert to XHTML Mobile, and Rewrite Source Code. Choose Edit > Document Content and then select one of the five options from the submenu (**Figure 140a**).

Figure 140a You can select a conversion option from the Special > Convert submenu. Find the Rewrite Source Code command under Special > Source Code.

Here's a brief description of what each option does:

- **Convert Styles** inventories text styles and converts them to structural markup and CSS.

- **Change Encoding** changes the charset (character set) meta tag and re-encodes all the text in the page (see Tip 45).

- **Convert to HTML** converts XHTML syntax to HTML.

- **Convert to XHTML** converts HTML syntax to XHTML.

(continued on next page)

- **Change DOCTYPE** allows you to assign a different DOCTYPE (see Tip 65) to the pages.

- **Convert to XHTML Mobile** converts Web pages for wireless publishing by converting the markup to XHTML, downsizing the images, and stripping unnecessary code and graphics.

- **Rewrite Source Code** is found under Special > Source Code and cleans up the way the source code is formatted.

Regardless of which conversion command you choose, you'll be greeted with a dialog box that acts as both a safety net (what if you really didn't want to convert your whole site from XHMTL to HTML?) and as an opportunity to fine-tune the changes that will be made. Adjust the settings as you like and then use the Work On menu near the bottom of the dialog to decide which pages will be affected (**Figure 140b**).

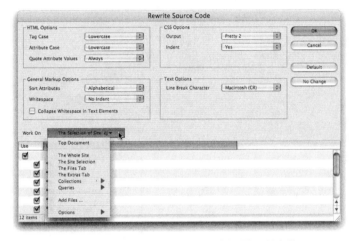

Figure 140b Adjust the conversion settings and decide which files to process before you click OK.

CHAPTER SEVEN

Creative Suite Integration

Can we see a show of hands from people here who use Photoshop? That's what we thought. Virtually everybody uses Photoshop. And most designers also use Illustrator. Everybody deals with Adobe PDF files. All this is important for GoLive users because using files and designs from other Creative Suite applications in GoLive CS2 is easier than ever before.

Whether you're using Web layouts from ImageReady, digital photos from Photoshop, logos from Illustrator, or Adobe PDF files from Acrobat, GoLive makes it as easy as drag and drop to use all that content in your Web site. GoLive's unique Smart Objects feature makes it easy to use all these native Adobe source files in your site. We're confident that by the end of this chapter you'll agree the Creative Suite really is greater than the sum of its parts.

TIP 141 Introducing Smart Objects

You use GIF and JPEG images on your Web pages, right? Well, Adobe makes it as easy as drag and drop to convert a variety of source files, such as layered Photoshop documents or high-resolution TIFF images, into Web-friendly GIFs and JPEGs right inside GoLive.

You can store your Smart Objects source files in the SmartObjects directory in the Extras tab of the Site window. This method of storage makes it easy to use the files, and GoLive can keep track of them if you move them. To place a Smart Object, select a source file in the SmartObjects directory and drag and drop it into your Web page layout, as seen in **Figure 141**.

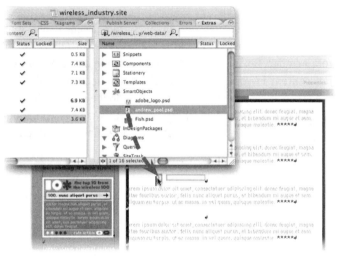

Figure 141 Drag and drop native source files to the Layout Editor to place a Smart Object.

After you place a Smart Object, choose the image optimization settings in the Save For Web dialog (see Tip 142 for more details about Save For Web) and save the target file in your Site Root folder.

Here's a complete list of the file formats supported by Smart Objects:

CMYK Conversions for Print-to-Web Workflows

Smart Object source files that are high resolution are automatically converted to 72 dpi, and CMYK images are instantly and seamlessly converted to RGB. This makes print-to-Web publishing a reality!

RGB file formats

- Adobe Illustrator (.ai and .aisvg)
- Adobe Photoshop (.psd)
- BMP
- Clipboard
- EPS
- GIF
- JPEG
- JPEG2000
- PICT
- PCX
- PDF
- PDF with security
- Pixar
- PNG
- SVG
- SVGZ (compressed)
- Targa
- TIFF, flat
- TIFF, layered
- TIFF, JPEG compression

CMYK file formats

- Adobe Illustrator (.ai and .aisvg)
- Adobe Photoshop (.psd)
- EPS
- JPEG
- JPEG2000
- PDF
- PDF with security
- SVG
- SVGZ (compressed)
- TIFF, flat
- TIFF, layered
- TIFF, JPEG compression

TIP 141: Introducing Smart Objects

TIP 142
Optimizing Images with Save For Web

The Save For Web dialog appears every time you create a Smart Object (see Tip 141) in GoLive. Whether you create a Web graphic in Photoshop, ImageReady, Illustrator, or GoLive, it's essentially the same interface. Using Save for Web in GoLive (**Figure 142**) lets you quickly and easily optimize your source files to image formats such as GIF, JPEG, and PNG. The powerful optimization algorithms let you maximize quality and minimize download times all in one dialog. Let's take a quick tour through the major features.

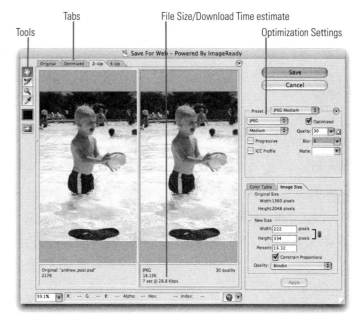

Figure 142 The Save For Web dialog optimizes all your Smart Object source files into Web-friendly target files.

Across the top of the Save For Web window are four tabs that show you (in order from left to right) the Original uncompressed image, an Optimized view with real-time compression preview, a 2-Up view, and a 4-Up view to compare multiple compression settings side by side.

On the right side you can select an optimization preset from the pull-down menu or create your own settings with the available options. You can choose from JPEG, GIF, PNG-8, PNG-24, and WBMP—but JPEG and GIF will be your most likely choices.

As you adjust your optimization settings, you can see a real-time compression preview in the image previews on the left and estimated file size and download time at the bottom of the dialog. Use the preview and the download estimates to decide which optimization settings work best for each image.

On the left side there's a small toolbar with four tools. Use the Hand tool to pan around the image; double-click the Hand tool to fit the entire image in the window. Also notice that as you pan in 2-Up and 4-Up modes, all the images pan together so you can compare areas of detail with different optimization settings. Click with the Zoom tool to zoom in and Option/Alt-click to zoom out.

Adjusting Image Size in Save For Web

To change the dimensions of the target file without affecting the source image, enter the new image dimensions in the Image Size tab in the bottom right corner of the Save for Web window. Make sure you click the Apply button instead of hitting Return or Enter because Return/ Enter confirms *all* the changes, not just the image size changes.

TIP 142: Optimizing Images with Save For Web

Using Large JPEGs as Smart Objects

Ask any Web designer if you should ever recompress a JPEG image and they're likely to roll their eyes, stomp their feet, and snort out something like, "Absolutely not!" Well, that was true a few years ago, but modern digital cameras store very high-quality photographs in the JPEG format. The fact that a JPEG image can be high-quality contradicts most designer's expectations, but the fact is that JPEG doesn't necessarily mean it's had all the quality squeezed out of it.

All of this means it's perfectly reasonable to use a high-quality JPEG image as a Smart Object source file even though, technically speaking, the image will be compressed twice: first by the camera and then by GoLive. To make it easier for GoLive to use large JPEGs as Smart Object sources, there's a new application preference that controls how Smart Objects are handled. Choose GoLive > Preferences (Mac) or Edit > Preferences (Windows) and choose the Smart Objects section of the Images preferences (**Figure 143**).

Figure 143 Control the size threshold of JPEG Smart Objects in the application preferences.

The setting that automatically converts large, Web-friendly images to Smart Objects is enabled by default. The feature kicks in when the source image has a dimension larger than 1,000 pixels. If you want to increase or decrease the limit you can, but 1,000 is a good default because it lets you use images less then 1,000 pixels wide as full-size gallery images but will convert anything larger to a Smart Object. To see the feature in action, drag a JPEG with a dimension greater than 1,000 pixels (such as a JPEG from a 4-megapixel digital camera) into the Layout Editor.

TIP 144 Working with Source and Target Files

Being able to compress native source files into Web graphics right inside GoLive is cool, but it's just the beginning when it comes to Smart Objects. The real powers of Smart Objects are the amazing ways the source and target images work together (**Figure 144**).

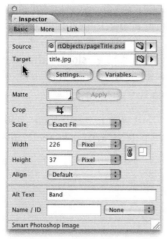

Figure 144 The smart connection between the source and target files makes the magic of Smart Objects happen.

For example, if you resize a Smart Object in the Layout Editor (hold Shift to constrain proportions), GoLive automatically generates a fresh target file using the same optimization settings. The new target file is saved over the previous version with the same name in the same place so you don't end up with cluttered files. This makes it really easy to make last-minute tweaks without any hassles.

To change the optimization settings for a Smart Object, click the Settings button in the Inspector palette and adjust the compression options. Click Save, and a new target file is saved into your site for you. The most important thing to note about all these changes is that they're completely non-destructive to the original Source file. This means you can change the size and compression of a Smart Object a hundred times, yet the source file is never altered, and the target file is always regenerated based on the original so you'll never see any generational quality loss or recompression.

To really blow your mind, try double-clicking on the Smart Object in the Layout Editor. Instead of opening the JPEG or GIF target file, the source file is opened in its creator application such as Photoshop or Illustrator. Make any changes you want to the source file, such as adding layers, deleting layers, editing text, and adding adjustment layers, and save it when you're done. When you switch back to GoLive, the program instantly recognizes the changes you've made in the other Creative Suite applications and automatically updates all your dependent target images.

TIP 145 Sharing Smart Objects Site-wide

In previous versions of GoLive, it was required that you drag or place your source file (see Tip 141 for the list of supported source file types) onto a page in order to invoke the Save for Web window, where the Web-ready target file (the .gif or .jpg) would be generated. GoLive CS2 goes one step further, allowing for simple creation of Web-ready images from the source files directly in the Site window.

The benefit is that you can create a Web version of the image even if you don't yet have a page for it to go on. The process is simple. Choose one of the following two methods:

- Select the source file in the Site window and then choose the Smart tab of the Inspector palette and click Create Smart Object... (**Figure 145**).

Figure 145 You can create a Web-ready image directly from the source file using the Create Smart Object button in the Inspector palette.

- Drag the source file from the right pane of the Site window into the Files tab in the left pane of the Site window.

Both of these methods invoke the Save for Web window, where you can set the compression for the image, name it, and save it (see Tip 142 for more on optimization). The newly created target file can be used on any number of pages, and as with all Smart Objects, will be updated if the original source file is edited in the original application.

TIP 146 Integrating with Photoshop or ImageReady CS2

You can easily place native Photoshop documents by dragging the .psd file from the SmartObjects folder (or from anywhere on your drive or network) and dropping it directly onto the GoLive page. When the Save For Web window opens, compress the image in the format of your choice and then save it into your site.

If you prefer, you can put a Photoshop Smart Object placeholder on the page first and size it to fit your layout. Drag the placeholder from the Smart section of the Objects palette onto the page and then use the Inspector palette to locate the source file by clicking the Browse button, the small folder icon to the right of the Source field (**Figure 146**).

Editing Original Source Files

Double-click to open the PSD in Photoshop and makes changes, such as adding layers, deleting layers, editing text layers, using the healing brush, changing colors, running filters, adding adjustments, and extracting the background.

Figure 146 You can use a Smart Object placeholder and browse to the Photoshop document from the Inspector.

Works in Illustrator, Too!

Just as you can place your source PSD documents into GoLive pages, you can place Adobe Illustrator documents, your .ai files, too. And it's just as simple to update the target file by double-clicking it in the Layout Editor to open the source file in Illustrator.

When you select the source file, the Save For Web window opens and displays a version of the image that fits the dimensions of your placeholder exactly. Choose your compression settings and save the Web-ready version of the file into your site. Using this method, you can also choose file types other than PSD to use as the source, such as EPS or TIF. (See Tip 141 for a list of useable file formats.)

TIP 147 Optimizing Photoshop Layouts

Most users place normal Photoshop files, but you can also place entire page comps complete with slices. Create your layout in Photoshop, slice it as desired, and then use either of the two methods outlined in Tip 146 to place the sliced PSD file onto your GoLive page. As expected, the Save For Web window opens and displays the entire document, including the slices. To set the compression for a slice, select it with the Slice Select tool on the left side of the Save For Web window and then adjust the settings using the options on the right (see Tip 142 for more on Save For Web).

Note
If you've used ImageReady to create the sliced layout and have already set your compression settings there, those settings will be honored when you use the PSD in GoLive.

When you're done fine-tuning your settings, click Save to save the resulting files into your site. You'll notice in the Save dialog box that the file extension is .data. Upon saving the .data file you'll see that GoLive has created a folder whose contents include a settings.opt file and images created from the slices in the PSD (**Figure 147**).

Figure 147 GoLive automatically generates a folder with a .data extension that holds a settings file and images.

If later you want to adjust the design, you can simply double-click on the edge of the SmartObject you placed into your page, and the original PSD file will open in Photoshop or ImageReady for you to edit. When you save the PSD file, GoLive will update the SmartObject, including its slices. In GoLive, you can adjust the size of the entire image, crop it, or change the matte color as you can with any other SmartObject. However, you cannot adjust the table, add text to any of its cells, or add functionality such as Actions to the slices. This method works best if you prefer to edit the design in Photoshop.

TIP 148 Customizing Text Variables

If you have ever used a layered PSD file as a Smart Object and had a text layer as the topmost layer in the Photoshop file, then you'll probably have seen a dialog like the one here (**Figure 148**). The Variable Settings dialog box lets you customize some part of a Smart Object without the original authoring application.

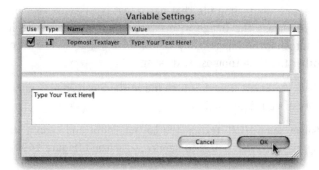

Figure 148 The Variable Settings dialog box.

Use this simple dialog box to easily change the text string in the PSD file. Simply enable the check box next to the words Topmost Textlayer and then, in the input field that appears, type in the new text. When you click OK, the Save for Web window opens, and you can save a Web-ready version of the image that uses the new text string instead of the original. This is handy for creating multiple headings, buttons, or other repetitive items that need the same styling with different wording. It's also a good solution for those times when the font you want to use is not a typical Web font.

Using Photoshop Type on a Path

Photoshop CS2 includes the ability to create type on a path. As long as the type on a path is the topmost text layer or is assigned as a variable, then even type on a path can be customized as a variable.

TIP 149 Converting Text to Images

GoLive includes the ability to convert HTML text to a Web graphic by combining Adobe's incredible Smart Object and Variables technologies. This is an easy way to create consistent and visually compelling navigation buttons, graphical subheads, and banner ads.

Here are the steps:

1. Create a Photoshop file that has a text layer as its topmost layer or use the Image > Variables > Define... command in Photoshop or ImageReady to assign a variable to a layer other than the topmost text layer.

2. Save the Smart Object Source file in the SmartObjects directory of your Site window.

3. Select some HTML text in the Layout Editor and choose the Special > Convert > Text to Banner... command (**Figure 149a**).

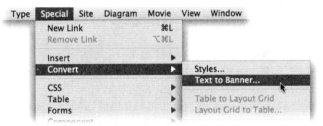

Figure 149a Select text in the Layout Editor and choose Special > Convert > Text to Banner.

4. In the Open dialog, select the Smart Object Source file you want to use and click OK.

5. Notice that the Variables Settings dialog automatically copies your selected HTML text and applies it to your Topmost Textlayer variable. Change the text variable if you need to and click OK.

Bonus Tip
See the little red 1 character next to the T icon? That helps you differentiate the topmost text layer from other variable text objects.

6. Compress the new target file using Save For Web (**Figure 149b**) and save the graphic in your Site Root folder.

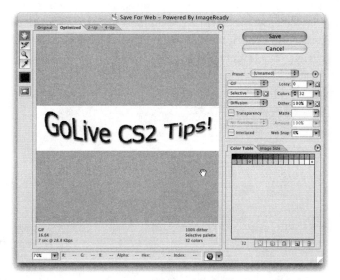

Figure 149b Your HTML will be saved as a beautiful graphic using all the type and layer effects that can't be created with HTML and CSS.

Bonus Tip
GoLive intelligently names the target file using your variable text data.

7. Your Text-to-Banner conversion is complete. If you need to alter the variable values, just select the image in the Layout Editor and click on the Variables button in the Inspector. Now whenever you need to change the graphic headers or navigation buttons on your Web site, all you have to do is change one Photoshop file (change a color, choose a different font, add a drop shadow, and so on), and all the Smart Objects in your site will be updated automatically.

Stripping GoLive Data from Media Files

Optimization and variables settings data is stored inside the target files (GIF, JPEG, PNG, SWF, and SVG) that you view in a Web browser. That makes the target files a little larger (typically 100 to 300 bytes per image) but doesn't affect their display at all. To get rid of the unwanted size overhead, you can strip out that data on site export/upload/publish by checking the "Strip GoLive data from media files" option. This setting is found under Site > Settings in the Upload/Export category.

TIP 149: Converting Text to Images

TIP 150 Using ImageReady CS2 Output

Tip 147 explains how to drop a complete sliced layout into a GoLive page, but there is another method that we use even more. With a Web design open in ImageReady, choose File > Save Optimized As. A Save dialog will open. Near the bottom, a pop-up list labeled Format offers the options of saving HTML and Images, Images only, or HTML only (**Figure 150**).

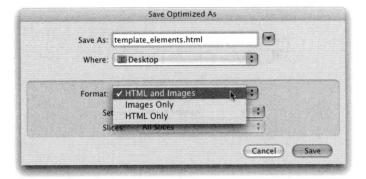

Figure 150 Click Save Optimized As from the File menu to get options for saving the HTML, the images, or both.

You can fine-tune your settings from the Settings pop-up and select which slices you want to save by choosing from the Slices pop-up. When you've made your selections, click Save and save directly into the Site Root folder of GoLive.

Note
If you have slices selected when you invoke the Save Optimized As command, you will see the Selected Slices option in the Slices pop-up.

The assets you saved will appear in the Files tab of the Site window after you click the Refresh button (see Tip 18). If you've saved HTML and images, simply double-click the HTML page to open it in GoLive. If you've saved images only, you can now drag and drop the images as you would any other images in your site.

This can be an effective way to work if you don't expect to make frequent changes to the design (see Tip 147 if you do plan to edit the design frequently). Combine this with the ability to export just slice selection sets from ImageReady for a great way to build navigation bars that you'll save as reusable components in GoLive.

TIP 151 Customizing ImageReady SWF Variables

Using Adobe ImageReady CS2, you can include a text variable in a SWF animation (Flash animation) and edit that text after you place it in your GoLive page. This comes in very handy when, for example, you have an ad banner whose design remains constant, but whose text must change. Using a text variable, you can change "This week's special, 4 days in Florida, only $399!" to "This week's special, 5 days in New York, only $699!" and use the same SWF both times.

To accomplish this, create the animation complete with text variables in ImageReady and then choose File > Export > Macromedia Flash SWF. When the Export dialog box appears, select Enable Dynamic Text and choose which fonts to embed (**Figure 151a**).

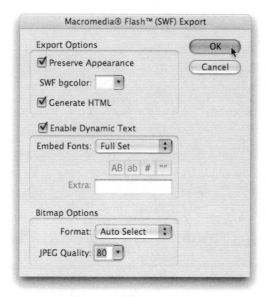

Figure 151a Choose Enable Dynamic Text when importing to SWF to make the text variables accessible in GoLive.

(continued on next page)

When placed in a GoLive page, edit the text by following these simple steps:

1. Select the SWF on the page.

2. Click the right-facing arrow at the far right end of the File field in the Inspector.

3. Choose Edit from the list.

4. In the Edit URL dialog box, select a Query Parameter from the list.

5. Edit the text value (**Figure 151b**).

6. Click the Update button.

7. Click OK.

Figure 151b Change the dynamic SWF text variable from within GoLive using the Edit URL dialog.

Now, go back to your page and preview the animation. The original text will be replaced by the new text you just entered.

TIP 152 Creating Favicons

Have you ever wondered how to create custom Web site icons like the ones in **Figure 152**?

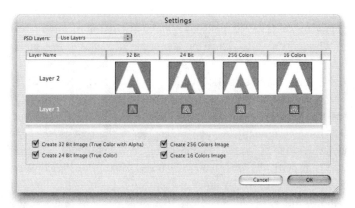

Figure 152 You can create custom browser icons, or *favicons*, with GoLive CS2.

Due to recent developments in the Web browser market, more and more Web designers want to create these custom favorites icons called *favicons*. GoLive CS2 makes it easy to create and manage these custom icons that are used in the address bar and bookmarks of most modern Web browsers.

Start by creating a 16x16-pixel image in a graphics application such as Photoshop or Illustrator. When your mini-masterpiece is complete, add the image to the SmartObjects folder in the Extras tab of the Site window. Note that you can't just put a GIF or JPEG in your site and call it favicon.ico. It might work in some cases, but in many instances it fails. Believe us, we tried. Now select the source image and choose Site > Smart Objects > Create Smart Favorite Icon so GoLive can convert your source image into the .ico format.

(continued on next page)

The Settings dialog opens when you create the icon file, and you can control a few different options. The .ico file is an interesting format that supports multiple image sizes and multiple bit depths all in one file. Given these capabilities, you can choose the bit depths you want to create, and if your Photoshop source file has layers or layer sets, you can even create different sizes for your icon. If your source image only has one layer, just choose Use Single Image from the pull-down menu at the top of the dialog.

When you're done adjusting the settings, save the file, making sure you call it favicon.ico, and save it into the root level of your Web site. Remember that your favicon.ico file is a Smart Object, which means that if you update the source file, GoLive will update the favicon.ico file for you.

After you upload the favicon.ico file to the root level of your Web server (see Chapter 11), most Web browsers should pick up the icon automatically when you visit or bookmark the site. However, be aware that even the browsers that do support it handle it differently. For example, Microsoft IE 6.x for Windows will not show the favicon in the address bar until that URL has been added to the favorites, and Apple Safari will not show an updated favicon until the browser cache has been cleared.

TIP 153 Creating PDF Thumbnail Galleries

Lots of folks make PDF files available on their Web sites. If you have multiple PDFs, you've probably thought about the best way to present the links.

One of our favorite tricks is to create a little thumbnail version of the PDF in GoLive and then add a link to the original PDF so that users can quickly see what they're getting. The process for creating thumbnails of your PDFs is easy. Drag and drop a PDF file into the Layout Editor. If the PDF has more than one page, you get a dialog box called PDF Options (**Figure 153**), asking you to choose which page you want to use to create the image.

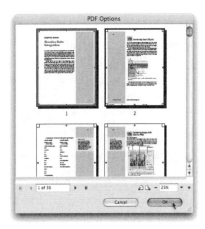

Figure 153 Select which page of the PDF you want to use to create a thumbnail preview image.

Make your selection and click OK. When the Save For Web window appears, compress the image as a GIF or JPEG and resize it so that it's tiny.

Note
Be sure to click the Apply button in the Image Size area before pressing Return/Enter on your keyboard, or the resize will be dismissed before it has been applied.

When you are all done with the settings, click Save and save the image into your site. Now visitors don't have to guess what's inside the PDF file they're about to download because they'll see a nice thumbnail preview. Using this method on a page with several PDFs, you can quickly and easily create a very attractive PDF gallery.

Linking to the Original PDF

Once your PDF thumbnail is on the page, simply select it, click the Link tab in the Image Inspector, and then point and shoot to the original PDF to create the link.

TIP 154 Cropping Smart Objects

After a Smart Object is placed on a page, you may decide you don't want to use the entire image on the Web. A perfect example of this would be when you use a Photoshop image for a print piece in Adobe InDesign, but then want to use just a portion of that image on your Web site. Instead of creating and managing two versions of the same Photoshop file, just use GoLive's crop feature to customize the target file for appropriate Web use.

Select the Smart Object in the Layout Editor and choose the Crop tool in the Inspector palette. When you select the Crop tool, a new set of options appears in the toolbar at the top of the screen (**Figure 154**).

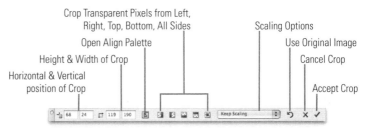

Figure 154 When cropping a Smart Object, you can use the tools in the toolbar to achieve various results, such as trimming transparent pixels from one or more sides.

Click and drag over the Smart Object you want to crop just as you would in Photoshop. As you drag, the parts of the image that will be cropped out are dimmed. Click one of the buttons in the toolbar to crop transparent pixels from any or all edges of the image. If you want to align the crop to the image itself, click the Open Align palette button in the toolbar and use the Align palette to line up the edges perfectly. The Scaling pop-up gives some neat options. For example, choose Keep Scaling if you simply want to crop off parts of the image. Select Keep Object Size, and you can then use the Crop tool to select an area that fills the image at its current size. Choose Scale to Source Size to select an area with the crop tool and have only that area render at the image's original size.

Confirm a crop with the checkmark icon in the toolbar, cancel a crop with the X icon in the toolbar, and revert a crop with the circle arrow icon in the toolbar. Remember that any crop you make here only affects the target file and never the source file.

TIP 155 Scaling Smart Objects

When you scale Smart Objects, hold the Shift key to constrain the proportions of the image (**Figure 155a**). Holding Shift to constrain proportions is pretty typical in just about every graphics and layout application in the world and will probably give you the results you expect.

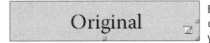

Figure 155a Hold Shift to constrain proportions when you scale a Smart Object.

However, when you scale the bounding box of a Smart Object non-proportionally, GoLive gives you three unique ways to scale the results. The option you choose will depend on the composition of the image and how it fits with the other objects on the page. The three scaling options in the Basic section of the Image Inspector are as follows:

- **Exact Fit (default option):** This option forces the image to fill the entire bounding box of the image. If the Smart Object is resized non-proportionally, the image will be distorted (**Figure 155b**).

Figure 155b Resize a Smart Object non-proportionally with Exact Fit, and the image will be distorted.

(continued on next page)

- **No Border:** If you scale a Smart Object proportionally with this option, nothing peculiar happens, and the image just scales. It gets interesting when you scale the Smart Object non-proportionally (from an edge or the corner without the Shift key). The No Border option maintains the proportions of the image and fills the entire image's bounding box with image data. If the proportions are uneven, then any extra pixels are cropped off (**Figure 155c**). This setting is great if you want to use text variables in Smart Objects for navigation buttons but want the images to be different sizes.

Figure 155c
The No Border option crops image data but preserves the proportions of the image.

- **Show All:** This option scales the image proportionally as large as possible within the image's bounding box and adds transparent or matte-colored borders to whichever sides need the padding (**Figure 155d**). This setting is particularly helpful if you have a Smart Object that needs to be resized to fill a table cell or a template region but you don't want to crop off any of the image data.

Figure 155d
The Show All option maintains image proportions, crops nothing, and adds padding as needed.

TIP 156 Matting Smart Objects

Have you ever tried to eliminate the amateur-looking white fringe around transparent images? It's normally a pain in the you-know-what, but with GoLive Smart Objects it's a piece of cake.

Place a source file that has a transparent background. Then select the Matte field in the Inspector palette and select the appropriate matte (fringe) color with the Eyedropper tool from the Color palette or a swatch from the Swatches palette. When you have the right matte color selected, click the Apply button in the Inspector to matte the image.

Figure 156 shows a good before-and-after comparison of the benefits of using a custom matte color to eliminate the anti-aliased fringe. See the yucky white halo in the image on the left and the perfect anti-aliasing on the image on the right?

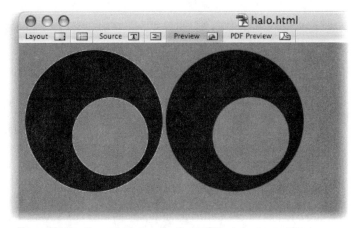

Figure 156 Use the matte feature for Smart Objects to remove the amateur-looking white fringe on transparent images.

Adjusting matte works with Adobe Photoshop, Illustrator, and PDF files and even works with target file formats that don't support transparency, such as JPEG.

Note
Smart Illustrator objects that use the SVG or SWF format for the target file do not support a matte color.

TIP 156: Matting Smart Objects

TIP
157 Tracing Images

You can use a design comp from an application such as Photoshop or Illustrator as a quick way to start a new page design. Just as you can place a sheet of tracing paper over a printed design and trace over parts of it, you can place an image in the background of a GoLive page and trace parts as well. Such an image is called a *tracing image*. Open the Tracing Image palette from the Window menu, click the Source checkmark, and then point and shoot to the tracing image you want to use as the basis for your design. You can change the position of the tracing image as required by using the Hand tool in the palette (not the one in the toolbar, which moves the entire page) and you can change the opacity depending on how much visibility you need (**Figure 157**).

Cropped Images Are Smart Objects

All the images that are cut out of a tracing image behave like Smart Objects. This means if you go make changes in the tracing image file, all the cutouts update automatically. This is a really interesting way to prototype new page designs quickly.

Figure 157 Use the Tracing Image palette to place an image in the background of a page and then cut out the parts you want to use.

Next, start cropping. Select the Crop tool in the Tracing Image palette, drag over the part you want to use, and click the Cut Out button to use that piece. When you cut out a part of the tracing image, the Save For Web window opens—this is where you set the compression options and save the resulting image into your site. The cut-out pieces are automatically placed into CSS Layers, and you can easily rearrange the Layers to experiment with the layout. When you're done cutting out pieces, turn off the tracing image by disabling the Source checkbox in the Tracing Image palette.

TIP 158 Organizing Smart Objects

We're convinced that Smart Objects will save you so much time you'll want to use them as often as possible. Managing lots of files in the SmartObjects folder could get unwieldy, though, so to manage them more effectively, create subfolders in the SmartObjects directory in the Extras tab of the Site window.

Select the SmartObjects folder in the Extras tab of the Site window and click the New Folder icon in the toolbar to create a subfolder (**Figure 158**). Notice that you can even create subfolders inside subfolders. Give the new subfolders logical names and organize them however you want.

Figure 158 Use subfolders to organize your Smart Object Source files.

By storing your Source files in the GoLive Site window, you leverage the powerful site management of GoLive and gain an extra level of control over how your files are organized. For example, you can create subfolders for different file types such as Photoshop, Illustrator, and PDF. Another option would be to organize the files according to the different phases of the design cycle, such as originals, retouched, and final.

TIP 159 Updating Pages Based on Smart Objects

GoLive generally does a great job of automatically updating pages that use library items such as templates and components, but sometimes it needs a little nudge. For example, if you repackage an InDesign layout or make changes to a Smart Object on a closed page, you can force GoLive to update all the dependent pages with a quick menu command.

Open the Site window and select Site > Update > Files Dependent on Site Extras. GoLive checks all the Site Extras (templates, components, snippets, Smart Objects, and InDesign Packages) and updates all the pages in your site as necessary (**Figure 159**). You can also click the corresponding button in the toolbar.

Figure 159 Force pages with Smart Objects and other site extras to update in the Site window.

To force pages to update based on a specific Smart Object, select the file in the Extras tab of the Site window and choose Site > Update > Files Dependent On Selection.

CHAPTER EIGHT

Print to Web Workflow with InDesign and GoLive

Those amongst us who wear more than one hat are always looking for ways to reuse our work, to take chunks of data and repurpose them, or use imagery in more than one place. From small shops to large agencies, designers are being asked to do more than ever before, to deliver their designs in formats appropriate for print, Web, PDF, email and even mobile devices.

Creative Suite 2 offers a unique way to take a document created in InDesign CS2 and reuse bits from a page, a whole page, multiple pages or even the entire document in your GoLive Web site. New in GoLive CS2 is the ability to take the package created in InDesign, open it and export directly to HTML. While using a page layout application for Web design can never be quite the same as designing explicitly for the Web, this chapter will get you pretty darn close.

160 From InDesign to GoLive

InDesign CS and GoLive CS offer a radically new approach to repurposing print content for the Web called Package for GoLive and Import from InDesign. Design the print piece in InDesign CS however you want to, for example, and the Package for GoLive feature takes care of converting it for use in GoLive. This means you don't have to do anything special, such as tagging or structuring the content in special ways.

When the print piece is done and ready to be repurposed for the Web, click File > Package for GoLive in InDesign CS (**Figure 160a**). The Package for GoLive dialog box will open and give you options on which parts of the InDesign file to package. The top portion of the dialog allows you to choose to package the entire document or particular pages (see Tip 162). The lower portion allows you to select whether to include images and multimedia files. When you've made your selections, click Package to have InDesign export the text stories to XML files, save the images and multimedia files into subfolders, and include a visually accurate PDF of the original print layout.

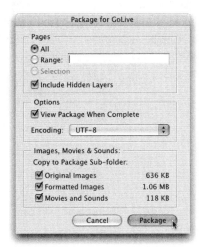

Figure 160a The Package for GoLive dialog box is the place to choose how much of your InDesign document will be brought into GoLive.

In the middle portion of the Package dialog is an option to have the Package automatically open when the export is complete. However, if you didn't enable that option when you packaged your document, you can still open the Package from the GoLive menu. Choose File > Import > From InDesign and locate the InDesign Package folder you generated. Inside it will be a file with the extension .idpk. Double-click that file to import the Package into GoLive.

When you're asked if you want the Package copied into the site, click Yes. GoLive will copy the Package to the InDesignPackages folder in the Extras tab of the Site window and open the default view of the Package window. You can change the zoom value and page number with the buttons at the lower right (**Figure 160b**).

Figure 160b
The Package window shows a PDF preview of the original InDesign layout.

Customizing the Package with Layers

In the CS versions of InDesign and GoLive, hidden layers were not exported to the GoLive Package. In the CS2 versions you can enable the checkbox in the Package for GoLive window to include hidden layers. Once you open the Package in GoLive, you can toggle the Package layers in the Layers palette in GoLive.

If you plan to reuse individual elements of the InDesign document rather than whole pages, then design a Web page in GoLive with the look and feel and navigation you need for your site and leave room for any text, image, or video content you want to use from the InDesign Package. You can even use GoLive templates to make long-term site updates easier.

Notice that stories and images in the Package window are highlighted when you place your mouse pointer over them. The highlight is an indication that you can drag and drop that item into your Web page. (See Tips 167 and 168 for details.)

TIP 160: From InDesign to GoLive

TIP 161 Selectively Packaging from InDesign

As mentioned in Tip 160, you are not required to package your entire InDesign document if you don't intend to repurpose it all. After choosing Package for GoLive from the File menu in InDesign, you can choose to export a range of pages, or only the items that are currently selected on a page. To choose a range of pages, such as pages three through six, you would type **3-6** in the Range field. To choose pages that are discontiguous, separate the pages with commas, such as **3, 5, 7**. If you need to choose both a range of pages and individual pages, you can use both methods (**Figure 161a**).

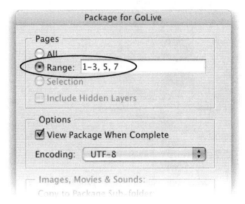

Figure 161a You can select an individual page, a range of pages, or both here in the Package for GoLive dialog.

If you merely want to package a single story or a few elements on a page, select those elements in the InDesign document and then choose File > Package for GoLive. In this scenario, InDesign will automatically enable the Selected option in the Package for GoLive dialog. However, if you change your mind and want to package the entire document or page, you can still choose different options before pressing the Package button (**Figure 161b**).

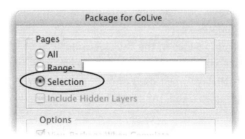

Figure 161b If you have elements on a page selected prior to invoking Package for GoLive, InDesign will choose the Selected option in the Package for GoLive dialog.

TIP 162 Exporting Pages as HTML

GoLive CS2 now includes the ability to take an InDesign publication into GoLive and then export it directly to HTML. You can choose whether to export the entire document as a series of pages or select individual pages from the package. If you want a basic conversion simply choose Export to HTML from the package menu (**Figure 162a**), which will invoke the export dialog box.

Figure 162a Export pages as HTML from the flyout menu.

However, if you'd like to adjust and preview the pages before you export them, click the HTML preview tab of the Package window. When in HTML Preview mode, you'll notice a new set of page optimization tools in the toolbar at the top of the screen (**Figure 162b**).

Figure 162b Customize the HTML Export results with the toolbar.

On the left is the Layout Scale slider. Moving this slider rearranges the flow of the objects on the page. This gives you a visual idea of how the page will look when rendered into HTML. Different scale values will yield widely varying results in how the page displays. The Optimize button lets GoLive try to pick a percentage, and Apply to All Pages uses the same percentage on each page in the document. In our experience we've found that we always came up with the best-looking page by using the slider and viewing each of the pages individually.

When you're finished with your optimization settings, click the Export to HTML button on the right side of the toolbar (see Tip 163).

163 Customizing HTML Export

Clicking the Export to HTML button in the toolbar or choosing Export to HTML from the Package menu as described in Tip 162 opens an Export dialog box. In this dialog box you can choose to export the current page, the entire document, or a selection of pages. In the first two options, click the appropriate radio button. To export a selection of pages, type in the page numbers of the pages you want to export, such as pages **3-5** or **2, 5, 7** (**Figure 163a**). If you would like to link the pages together, you can also enable the checkbox next to Use Template. This will drop the pages into a pre-made template that includes Previous and Next links so that it's easy to navigate through the exported pages (see sidebar).

Figure 163a Choose whether to export single or multiple pages in the Export as HTML dialog box.

When you click OK, a Save dialog will appear allowing you to choose the location for the folder which will contain the exported pages. GoLive helpfully names the folder based on the name of the InDesign package. Save the folder into your site's root folder. GoLive exports the pages and shows the status of the process in the Exporting Pages dialog (**Figure 163b**). When the process is complete, click OK.

Figure 163b You'll be able to watch as GoLive CS2 processes the pages. When the export is complete, click OK to dismiss the dialog box.

TIP 164 Finding and Selecting Package Objects

Open an InDesign Package in GoLive, and you can select objects by hovering your mouse pointer over them in the Package window. The colored highlight lets you know which item you can grab, but sometimes you'll have arranged or layered objects in InDesign so that they are difficult to select in the Package window. An easy way to select overlapping objects is to Control-click (Mac) or right-click (Windows) in the InDesign Layout tab of the Package window and select the object you want from the Select submenu (**Figure 164a**).

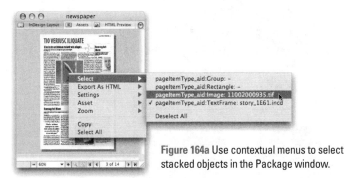

Figure 164a Use contextual menus to select stacked objects in the Package window.

Another way to select hard-to-grab objects in the Package window is to switch to the Assets tab where you can see a simple list view of all your stories, images, and multimedia content. You can search for items by filename in this list view. Control-click (Mac) or right-click (Windows) on a file in the Assets list and choose Reveal in InDesign Layout to focus the selected object in the Package window so you can confirm that it's the correct item. When you have the right item, you can drag and drop directly from the Package window into your GoLive layout (**Figure 164b**).

Figure 164b The Assets list makes it easy to find an object when you already know its filename.

TIP 164: Finding and Selecting Package Objects

Viewing Thumbnails in the Assets List

There are several ways to view images in a Package window, including the InDesign Layout view and the List view in the Assets tab. One of our favorite ways to view images in the Package window is also a new feature in GoLive CS2: the Thumbnail view in the Assets tab of the Package window (**Figure 165**).

Size Retention

The other advantage of browsing thumbnail images from the Assets tab of the Package window is that when you place them in a Web page they retain a usable size that corresponds to their size in the original print publication.

Figure 165 View images in the Package as thumbnails.

Open the Package window, switch to the Assets tab, and click the Thumbnail view icon in the bottom left corner to see image thumbnails. You'll want to scroll past all the stories because they're just XML files and don't have an interesting thumbnail icon. When you get to the Images section, you'll see a nice large thumbnail for each image. It's much easier to find the image you want based on these visual thumbnails instead of switching pages or looking at a long list of filenames.

TIP 166 Using InDesign Layers to Customize Web Layout

Most designers are comfortable with using layers in Photoshop, but using layers in a page-layout application such as InDesign can be a relatively new concept for many. We really encourage designers to use the document-wide layers feature in InDesign because there are so many practical benefits. For example, in the world of print design it can make it easy to create documents with multiple languages, avoid common transparency problems, and simplify handing off projects to coworkers and freelancers.

If that weren't enough, using layers in InDesign can also make it easier to convert print designs to Web pages using GoLive CS2. If you expect to repurpose an InDesign layout for the Web, you should consider using layers that will streamline the process later. For example, you might create one layer for text and another layer for images.

After you package the InDesign layout (see Tip 160) and open the Package window in GoLive, open the Layers palette to see the original InDesign layers. Now click the eyeball icons in the Layers palette to toggle the visibility of the layers in the Package to make it easier to select just the content you want for your Web page (**Figure 166**).

Hiding Master Page Elements

Another great way to use InDesign layers for Web conversion is to place all master page elements on one layer. Now, with one-click you can exclude master page elements such as headers, footers, and page numbers that you'll never use in a Web page.

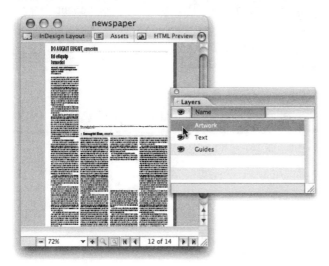

Figure 166 The empty white areas on this page were photographs that were temporarily disabled using the Layers palette in GoLive.

TIP 167

Placing Text, Tables, Images, and Movies from InDesign

Placing assets from an InDesign Package into your GoLive layouts is as easy as drag and drop. This tip gives some details and explanations of the process.

Text and Tables

When you drag text stories from the Package window into GoLive's Layout Editor, they are placed as XML components (**Figure 167**). These XML components behave just like normal components (see Tip 131), so updating your Web pages based on updates in your InDesign print layouts is a piece of cake (see Tip 174). If the InDesign story was threaded across multiple frames or multiple pages, and you drag the story from the Assets tab of the Package window, the entire story is placed in GoLive when you drag and drop. This is a huge timesaver compared with the typical copy and paste method of content repurposing. If you drag a text frame from the InDesign Layout, just that chunk of the story will be placed, but the red plus icon at the start or end of the component reminds you that there may be overset text and you need to make sure to drag all the necessary text frames. InDesign tables work the same as text stories and are placed as an HTML table in a component.

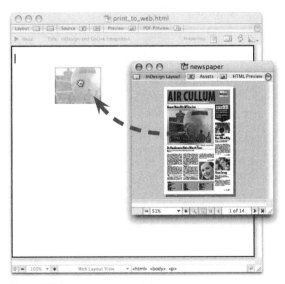

Figure 167 If you can drag and drop, you can convert InDesign layouts into Web pages with GoLive.

Images

Drag images into your Web page from the Package window, and the image will be converted to a Web-friendly format according to the compression option selected at the bottom of the Inspector palette. If you want to customize the settings for an image instead of using one of the optimization presets, select it in the Package window and choose Open Save For Web Dialog from the Web Format pull-down menu at the bottom of the Inspector palette. Now when you drag and drop that image into the Layout Editor, you can select the appropriate image format, adjust the compression options, control the image size, and click Save (see Tip 142).

When you drag an image from the InDesign Layout tab of the Package window into your Web page, you might be surprised that the image looks so tiny. The dimensions of the target file match the dimensions of the image in the Package preview, so zoom in to increase the size of the Package window to get a target image with a more useful size without adjusting each one individually.

Part of the magic of the Package integration between InDesign and GoLive is that CMYK images are automatically converted to RGB, and high-resolution images are instantly downsampled to 72 dpi. It's also convenient that GoLive CS2 automatically creates an Accessories folder for each package you work with. GoLive uses this Accessories folder as the default save location for all images, movies, and external CSS. These features make repurposing print content for the Web easier than ever before.

Movies and Sounds

InDesign CS2 lets you place multimedia files such as QuickTime movies in your layout. To use a movie or sound from the Package window, drag and drop it into the Layout Editor just like an image. Smart Objects don't work for movies because the files tend to be larger and have very different compression factors. If you need to resize or recompress the video, you should always go back to the source footage instead of resizing the movie in the Layout Editor.

Managing Package Preferences

New in GoLive CS2: You can select multiple stories or multiple images and adjust their conversion settings all at the same time. If you want to start from scratch, choose Delete InDesign Package Preferences from the flyout menu of the Package window to reset the conversion options of every item in the Package.

TIP 168

Customizing Text Conversion Options

When you drag a text story or an image from a Package window, GoLive makes some assumptions about how you want to use the content. Most of the time GoLive will guess correctly, but sometimes you'll want to override the defaults and customize the options for an object in the Package.

The default behavior for text is to place the story as an XML component based on the Adobe InCopy file format. This is what most users will want because your GoLive Web pages can be updated automatically based on changes to your InDesign layout (see Tip 174).

However, if you want to break the connection between the print and Web layouts, or if you want to edit or stylize the text in GoLive, you can place the story directly as plain text instead of as an XML component. Select the story in the InDesign Layout or Assets tabs of the Package window and use the Insert As menu in the Inspector palette to choose if you want to place the text as editable text, a component, or an image (**Figure 168**).

Bonus Tip

Select any frame of a threaded text story in the InDesign Layout view of a Package window, and conversion settings chosen in the Inspector apply to the entire story.

Figure 168 Adjust text-conversion options in the Inspector palette to control how InDesign stories are converted to HTML and CSS for the Web.

To place stories as plain text with no styling attributes, uncheck the Use CSS Styles option in the Inspector. If you prefer to retain the text formatting, make sure Use CSS Styles is enabled and choose Internal or External to control where the CSS styles are defined. Only choose None if you've already created the CSS styles manually.

TIP 169 Converting InDesign Text Styles to CSS

When you drag text stories from the Package window into a Go-Live Web page, the character, paragraph, and nested styles can be converted to a close approximation using CSS. This is a significant timesaver that helps ensure visual consistency between print and Web publications without requiring any extra effort. Be aware that certain InDesign typography features—such as baseline shift, ligatures, tracking, kerning, hyphenation, and optical margin alignment—cannot be retained in a Web page because equivalent features don't exist in CSS.

First, select the story in the Package window and look at the Inspector palette (**Figure 169**). To translate InDesign text styles to CSS styles, make sure the Use CSS Styles option is enabled. Then in the CSS Style Definition pull-down, choose from None, Internal CSS, and External CSS. (You probably don't want to use None because that means none of the styles will be defined for you.) You can use Internal CSS, but that writes the CSS definitions into every page, which is usually redundant and makes the pages harder to update. We recommend choosing External CSS and using the default .css file from the InDesign Package. Now when you place InDesign stories in your GoLive Web pages, the external .css file in the accessories folder (see Tip 167) can be the default style sheet for all the Package content, and GoLive will automatically link to the .css file.

Figure 169 Retain the text style options so that text from InDesign Packages uses an external style sheet.

Customizing the Package CSS

The ability to automatically use one external CSS file for all the content from an InDesign Package is a significant timesaver, but the fonts definitions in the CSS are likely to refer to fonts from print design that may not be common Web design fonts. To address this issue, choose Package CSS... > Edit... from the package menu, and adjust the font definitions as necessary.

TIP 170
Distributing Long Stories Across Multiple Web Pages

In InDesign, a *story* is defined as text that flows through a series of threaded text frames. You can have a very short story that begins and ends in one text frame, or a very long one that spans multiple frames and pages. If you want to place a long story onto Web pages in GoLive but distribute the text across multiple pages, you can use the Text Crop feature available for stories in InDesign Packages. This allows you to keep the text styling as defined in InDesign, but change the layout and flow of the text.

First, let's take a closer look at what happens when you drag text from the package window into a GoLive page. Imagine a three-column layout from InDesign, which was subsequently packaged and opened in GoLive. You don't want the story to have multiple columns on your Web page, because that would force the user to scroll up and down, which would be very annoying. When you drag one column from the Layout tab of the package window into your GoLive page, you get only the text from that column. If you instead drag the story from the Assets tab of the Package window, you'll get the entire story.

How do you get more text than what's in one column, but less than the full story? Answer: Text cropping. Let's say we wanted to take a chapter from this book, which is one long text thread, package it in InDesign, and open in GoLive with the goal of cropping the long story into pieces, resulting in one tip per page in GoLive. Here's how we do it.

Drag the story from the Assets tab of the Package window onto a page and then use the Crop tool in the Inspector palette to select the portion of the text that we want on the page (**Figure 170a**). In our hypothetical example, we'd choose the text of one tip.

Figure 170a Drag and drop a story from the Package window onto the GoLive page and then use the Text Crop tool in the Inspector to select only the portions you want to retain.

Once the text is selected, click the checkmark in the toolbar to confirm the crop. You can also click the X to cancel the crop, or the curved arrow to remove the crop (**Figure 170b**).

Figure 170b Once you've selected the Crop tool in the Inspector palette, the toolbar will show these three options: Remove Crop, Cancel, or Accept Crop.

You'll see an icon in the upper left corner of the text box indicating that the text is a component (see Tip 131) that retains a link back to the original InDesign document. You'll also see a red plus sign that indicates that there is more data to the story than what is visible in the cropped area (**Figure 170c**).

Figure 170c When cropped, a text component shows a red plus sign in its upper left and lower right corners.

To use a different portion of the story on another page, simply drag and drop the same story onto another page and crop it differently. In our example we used the Crop tool to take chunks of text from one InDesign chapter that had multiple tips and turned it into multiple pages in GoLive with one tip per page.

TIP
171 **Locating Used Assets**

TIP 171 Locating Used Assets

If you have used an image from an InDesign package on one or more pages and need to know what pages they are on, you can use this neat trick. Open the Package window and then find the asset in the Layout or Assets view. Right-click (Control-click on Mac) and choose Asset > Open Related Smart Object Pages. Note that there is a number following the menu item. That number indicates the amount of pages on which the Smart Object is being used. Once selected, this command will open all of those pages (**Figure 171**).

Figure 171 A plethora of options in the contextual menu make it easy to locate a package asset.

From this same contextual menu are options that make it easy for you to find the original asset in other locations, namely in the Site, in the Bridge application, or in the Finder (Windows Explorer on Windows).

Finally, you can also choose to open the asset in your default Web browser or edit it in the original authoring application. And last but not least is a quick way to see the asset's Properties. Selecting Show Properties opens the Get Info box in the Finder on Mac and the Properties box on Windows.

TIP 172 Using InDesign XML Tags

If your InDesign document contains XML tags, those tags will be brought into the GoLive Package as well. When you open a Package that contains a tagged InDesign file, you will notice a fourth tab across the top of the Package window (**Figure 172a**).

Figure 172a Packages of InDesign with XML structure reveal a fourth tab in the package window in GoLive.

If you find the highlighting of tagged page items distracting, you can turn it off (or back on again) in the View palette (**Figure 172b**).

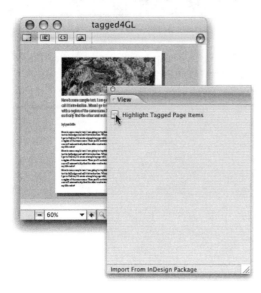

Figure 172b XML highlighting can be turned on or off in the View palette.

(continued on next page)

TIP 172: Using InDesign XML Tags

If you have created a template page that has regions whose names exactly match the names of the XML tags, you can drag and drop from the XML tab of the Package window into the template, and the items will automatically be placed into the correct region. You can even drag multiple items at once, and they'll drop into their designated space.

Note

This method should be used only when the XML is simple and flat. Use the Structure pane in InDesign to make sure there are no nested tags.

When you have the InDesign document set up properly, create the Package, open it in GoLive, and select the tags from the XML tab of the Package window. Drag the tags into the GoLive template page to place the items (**Figure 172c**).

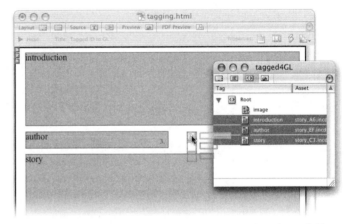

Figure 172c Drag and drop XML elements from the package into a GoLive template page with matching region names.

TIP 173 Placing Package Text as Images

Placing InDesign stories as text in GoLive is what you'll want to do most of the time, but there are always exceptions. For example, if a typographic or drop shadow effect on a headline cannot be reproduced with HTML and CSS, you may prefer to place that text as a graphic. You sacrifice some editability and download speed, but you can match the look and feel of the original print piece perfectly.

To place text or a table from an InDesign Package as a PDF Smart Object, select it in the Package window and choose Snapshot Image from the Insert As pull-down menu in the Inspector palette (**Figure 173**).

Figure 173 If you can't reproduce the same text effect with HTML and CSS, consider placing the text as an image.

You can even control the optimization settings for the graphic that is created with the Web format menu at the bottom of the Inspector palette to choose the compression settings. The list of options corresponds to the optimization presets available in the Save for Web dialog, but if you'd rather optimize the images on a per-image basis, choose Open Save For Web Dialog instead of a preset. When the optimization is complete, save the target image into your Web site's root folder.

Smart Objects created from text update just like any other Smart Objects, which means if you repackage the InDesign layout, your text-based graphics can be updated automatically (see Tip 174).

TIP 174

Repackaging Print Layouts for GoLive

We think it's obvious that the Package feature connecting InDesign CS2 and GoLive CS2 integrates print and Web design in unprecedented ways, but what happens when your clients change their minds? Do you have to start all over again? Of course not!

Just make the changes to the print piece in InDesign CS and repackage the layout with the same filename and location as before with the File > Package for GoLive command (**Figure 174a**).

Figure 174a Repackage the InDesign Layout to update the content in your Web pages.

Now switch to the GoLive Site window, select the updated InDesign Package in the Site window, select Site > Update > Files Dependent On Selection, and watch GoLive update all the necessary Web pages with changes to the text and images that were made in InDesign (**Figure 174b**).

Figure 174b Update your Web site by repackaging the layout in InDesign and updating files dependent on the Package in GoLive.

TIP 175 Automatically Converting Just the Text into a Web Page

Sometimes users ask for a quick and easy way to export just the text of an InDesign layout into a Web-friendly text format. Using an InDesign Package, this is really easy trick to do in GoLive.

Open the Package in GoLive, switch to the Assets view, and select all the files in the Stories category (**Figure 175a**). Now drag and drop all the stories into a Web page in GoLive and you've converted all the text from the entire InDesign document with one click!

Figure 175a Drag and drop all the stories from the Package window into a Web page to convert the text into a Web-friendly format.

By default, GoLive places the text stories as XML components. If you want to edit the text after it's been placed in GoLive, you'll want to convert the components to editable text. Choose Special > Component > Detach All Components (see Tip 176) to break the link between the InDesign Package and the Web page layout so that you can edit or copy the text as much as you want.

If you find yourself doing this frequently, you can force GoLive to place the stories as plain text from the very beginning. Select all the stories in the Package window and set the Insert As option in the Inspector palette to Editable Text (**Figure 175b**). You can also control whether the text is formatted using internal CSS, external CSS, or nothing at all.

Figure 175b Control text-conversion options in the Inspector palette before you drag and drop the stories.

TIP 176
Detaching Placed Text Components

When you place text from an InDesign Package, the copy is used in GoLive as an XML component. This makes long-term content management and updates much easier, but it also makes it difficult to edit or stylize the text in GoLive.

To break the connection between the component and the InDesign Package, select the component in the Layout Editor and choose Special > Component > Detach Selected Component (**Figure 176**). Now you can edit and stylize the text in GoLive, but if you repackage the InDesign layout, this detached text doesn't update automatically.

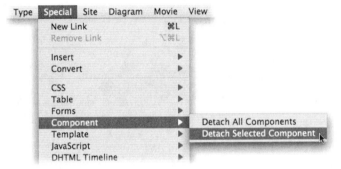

Figure 176 Detach a component and you can edit and stylize the text as much as you want.

If you don't need or want the automatic updating of Package contents, select Special > Component > Detach All Components to break the connection of every component on the open page.

TIP 177
Creating HTML Conversions with Adobe Acrobat

The improved Package workflow between InDesign CS2 and GoLive CS2 gives you the ultimate control over how you want to repurpose your text and images in a print-to-Web workflow. That said, it could take some time to get the content positioned just how you want it for the Web.

Although we think the Package feature will ultimately give you the best results, we realize there are times when you just need a down-and-dirty conversion and don't have the time to make things perfect. In those cases, you can use InDesign and Acrobat together for a cool little Web page creation trick.

Start by exporting a PDF of your document from InDesign. Make sure to set the PDF compatibility in the PDF Export dialog to at least 1.4 so you don't inadvertently flatten and slice any of the images in the document.

Next, open the PDF file in Adobe Acrobat (not the free Reader), choose File > Save As, and choose HTML 3.2 (uses font tags) or HTML 4.0.1 (uses CSS styles) from the Format menu (**Figure 177a**).

Figure 177a Use Acrobat to save a PDF from InDesign as HTML.

(continued on next page)

TIP 177: Creating HTML Conversions with Adobe Acrobat

Before you click Save, click the Settings button to adjust some of the advanced preferences for HTML output. Make sure the Generate Images option is enabled, and we also suggest use the subfolder option, especially if your design has a lot of images. Set the output format to JPEG for the best results and downsample the images to 72 dpi to keep the file sizes small (**Figure 177b**).

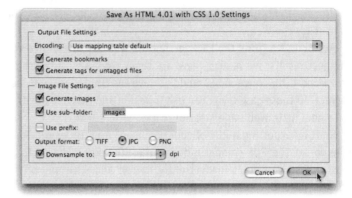

Figure 177b Adjust these output settings before saving the HTML from Acrobat.

CHAPTER NINE

Adding Interactivity

We adore clean-looking, well-organized Web sites that offer pertinent and timely information. We abhor gratuitous glitz used for no other reason than the designer felt like playing with cool software. That doesn't mean we are against interactivity on a Web site, though. Quite the contrary—a bit of well thought-out interactivity can make the user's experience go from mundane to delightful.

In this chapter we take a look at various ways you can add interactivity to your Web site. We cover everything from rollovers and JavaScript Actions all the way to forms, QuickTime, Flash (SWF), and imagemaps. Just remember that interactivity used on a Web site should have a reason behind it. Simply sprinkling your page with flashing, flying, blinking goodies won't endear you to your audience. In fact, it may alienate them entirely. Use your judgment when adding interactivity. Ask yourself, "Does adding this animation/pop-up window/other-flashy-goodie make my visitor's experience more useful?" If the answer is no, or even maybe, then forget it. If the answer is yes, then GoLive's full collection of interactive tools is just what you need.

DHTML Drop-down Menus

If you want to create a navigation bar that's more advanced than just rollover images, check out MenuMachine (see Tip 237) for building DHTML Drop-down menus. MenuMachine is a very popular third-party extension for GoLive that's worth every penny.

TIP 178 Creating Rollovers

A very popular effect found on even the simplest Web sites is called a *rollover*. The name describes the effect itself, because as you *roll* your mouse pointer *over* an image, the image's appearance is altered. But the effect can also be used when you click the image or move the mouse pointer away from it.

Rollovers add subtle feedback to a page so visitors know what is clickable and what's important. Here's how to do it: Add an image to the page, open the Rollovers palette from the Window menu, select the Over state, and click the New icon 🔖 near the bottom of the palette. Now use the Fetch URL tool to assign the rollover image in the URL field at the bottom of the palette. If you want to add other rollover states, such as a Click state, follow the same process.

When you assign an image to a rollover, make sure the Preload option is enabled, and GoLive will write JavaScript that automatically loads all the images when the page loads in a Web browser (**Figure 178**). If Preload is unchecked, the Over state image won't download until the visitor moves the mouse pointer over the image, where he'll probably see an undesirable delay while the second image downloads.

Figure 178 Edit your rollover states and status message in the Rollovers & Actions palette.

You can also add a status message that appears in the bottom left corner of the browser window when a visitor hovers the mouse pointer over the rollover image. With the Over state selected, click the Create New Message icon 💬 and type the status message in the Message field in the bottom of the Inspector.

Adding Interactivity

TIP 179 Saving Time with Automatic Rollover Detection

Creating rollovers isn't very hard, but if you have to create lots of them for a site or a complex navigation bar it can become very tedious. GoLive makes this tedious process easier than any other Web-authoring application in the world, and it happens to be one of our favorite features.

GoLive is one smart puppy. It can learn new tricks, such as recognizing how you name the image files that make up the multiple rollover states. When you train GoLive, it can sniff out all the required images and write all the JavaScript code, including the Preload option, automatically. To teach GoLive how you name your rollover images, choose GoLive > Preferences (Mac) or Edit > Preferences (Windows) and select Rollover in the Images category on the left.

The rollover settings are case sensitive and support several unique naming patterns, and the bottom of the Preferences dialog includes a good explanation of how this feature works (**Figure 179a**). The default settings match the output defaults for Adobe ImageReady, and you can add your own file naming schemes.

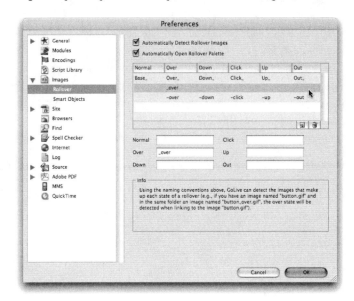

Figure 179a The rollover detection settings let you teach GoLive how you name your rollover images.

(continued on next page)

TIP 179: Saving Time with Automatic Rollover Detection

After you teach the rollover detection settings how you name your rollover images, the rest is a piece of cake. Just drag and drop the Normal state image into the Layout Editor and watch in amazement as GoLive automagically finds all the images for multi-state rollovers, writes all the JavaScript code, and includes preloading code. You can see all the new rollover states listed in the Rollovers palette (**Figure 179b**).

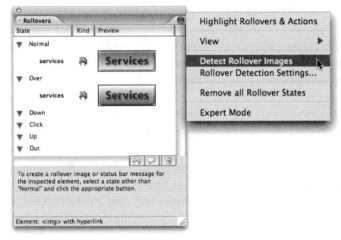

Figure 179b After GoLive detects your rollover images, you can see the results and customize the rollovers in the Rollovers palette.

If you have already placed a Normal state image on your page, there's still an easy way to automatically detect the rest of the rollover images. Select the image in the layout and select Detect Rollover Images from the Rollovers palette. Voila!

Using GoLive's JavaScript Actions is quite simple. A JavaScript has to be attached to an event to run—an event such as a movement of the mouse, a keystroke on the keyboard, a browser window being opened, and so on. One of the most common triggers for a JavaScript Action is the click of a link.

Select in the Layout Editor the text or an image that will be the trigger and then open the Actions palette from the Window menu. On the left side is a list of events to choose from. Select an event such as Mouse Click, click the New button on the right (**Figure 180a**), and then select an Action from the Action pull-down menu at the bottom of the palette (**Figure 180b**).

The numbers you see next to the Action's name indicate the minimum browser versions the selected Action is compatible with. If you want to limit the available Actions to only be compatible with certain browser versions, then choose Set Action Filter in the flyout menu.

Figure 180a Select an event in the Actions palette and then click to add a new Action.

Figure 180b Choose an Action from the Action pull-down list.

Creating Your Own Actions

If you are familiar with Java-Script, you may want to make GoLive Actions of your own. To find instructions on how to do so, see the SDK Programmers Guide.pdf, part of the GoLive Software Development Kit (SDK) that ships with GoLive.

Make It Your Actions Palette

The divider lines that separate the different areas of the palette allow you to resize the different sections. Customizing the layout of the Actions palette lets you access the entire list of events or the controls for really advanced Actions.

TIP 180: Using JavaScript Actions

Creating Remote Rollovers

When visiting a Web site, you may roll your mouse pointer over a text link or image and find that an image appears elsewhere on the page. This is referred to as a *remote rollover,* and in GoLive the effect is created with the Set Image URL Action.

To use Set Image URL, you'll need at least two images that are the same size (see sidebar). Put the one that will be swapped out on the page, select it, choose Name from the Name/ID pull-down in the Basic tab of the Inspector, and give it a name (**Figure 181a**).

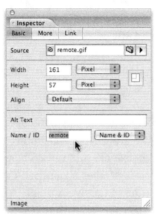

Figure 181a Give a name in the Inspector to the image that will change.

Next, select the image you want to use as the trigger. Now assign a Set Image URL Action from the Image category of Actions to the image on the Mouse Enter event using the Actions palette.

Note
You may also use a text link or any element that accepts the name attribute as the trigger for Set Image URL.

From the Image pull-down, select the name you assigned to the first image you placed on the page and then use the Fetch URL tool to point to the image that will be used for the remote rollover (**Figure 181b**). Save the page and click Preview to test the Action.

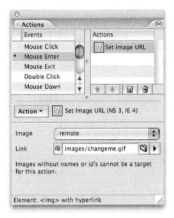

Figure 181b Choose the name of the image that will be swapped out in the Actions palette and then choose the alternate image.

If desired, you can create another Set Image URL Action and assign it to the Mouse Exit event. This controls what happens when you move the mouse pointer away from the trigger. Choose the remote image by its name and reassign the image to the original state with the Fetch URL tool.

Image Placeholders

When you create remote rollovers, it's important to use two images that are the same size so that you don't run into odd rendering flaws in some browsers. But what happens if you want to have a remote rollover in a part of the page that's empty? Just create a blank GIF placeholder image with the same dimensions as the remote rollover image. You can also try the ShowHide Action (see Tip 182).

TIP 181: Creating Remote Rollovers

TIP
182 Showing and Hiding Layers

A striking but easily accomplished effect created by GoLive Actions is the ability to show or hide layers. For example, you may have a text link on a page that when clicked reveals a hidden layer with additional information in it. In this tip, we show you step-by-step how to set this up. Complete the following steps to use the ShowHide Action:

1. Open a blank page and type **Hello**. Select it and enter the pound sign (#) into the URL field of the Inspector to create a null link.

2. Drag a layer onto the page and in the Layer tab of the Inspector palette name it greeting (**Figure 182a**). Type **Hello to you, too!** inside the layer. In the Inspector palette, turn off the Visible check box. The layer will now be hidden.

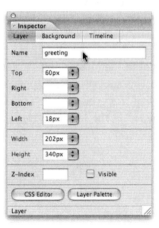

Figure 182a Name the layer and make it invisible in the Inspector palette.

3. Select the linked word Hello. In the Actions palette, choose Mouse Click for the Event, click New to create a new Action, and then select Multimedia > ShowHide from the Action pulldown menu.

4. Select greeting from the Layer pull-down menu and select Show from the Mode pull-down menu (**Figure 182b**).

Figure 182b Choose a ShowHide Action and designate the layer you want to show or hide.

Alternate Endings

If you want the layer to show when you hover your mouse pointer over the link instead of when you click, just attach the ShowHide Action to the Mouse Enter event. Then you can also set up a separate ShowHide Action for the Mouse Exit event that hides the layer.

Now click Preview at the top of the page and click the word Hello. The hidden layer should appear, showing you the response. It's that easy. You may also choose Toggle as the mode, which would allow the layer to be shown and then hidden with each subsequent click of the link.

TIP 182: Showing and Hiding Layers

Closing Windows

This Action is the simplest of all. To close a page, add a link saying something like, "Close this Window." Then attach the Close Window Action to the Mouse Click event. When the user clicks the link, the window goes buh-bye.

TIP 183 Opening New Windows

Little windows that pop up without warning are a nuisance, but a window that opens when a user needs more information can be a very effective design solution. In this tip, we show how easy it is to create just such a new window. Follow these straightforward steps:

1. Select text and create a null link by typing a pound sign (#) into the URL field of the Inspector palette. (You can also use an image for the link—just select the image and use the Link tab of the Inspector to create the link.)

2. In the Actions palette, select the event to use as a trigger. In this example we'll use Mouse Click.

3. Create a new Action by clicking the New button 🖫 on the right.

4. Select Link > Open Window from the Action pull-down list.

5. In the Actions palette, choose the options for your window. In this example, we made a window 300x300 pixels in size and disabled the browser's Menu and Tools (**Figure 183**).

6. Create a new window in any size and with or without the browser interface features such as scrollbars and menus. Use the Fetch URL tool to link to the page that will load into the new little window.

You'll need to preview this Action in a browser, because GoLive's preview will not open a new window for you. Click the Preview in Browser button on the toolbar and click the link to open the new window.

Figure 183 Set options for your pop-up window in the Actions palette.

TIP 184 Randomizing Images

If a picture is worth a thousand words, what are three pictures worth? Six pictures? Instead of forcing yourself to pick that one perfect image for a Web page, you can pick from several images and let GoLive randomize the display every time a visitor loads the page. It's easy to set up with JavaScript Actions when you follow these steps:

1. Add the base image to the page just like a normal image. If all the images are the same dimensions, leave the dimensions as Pixels in the Inspector. If the images are not the same size, then set the image dimensions to Image in the Inspector.

2. Select the image in the page and give the image a unique name in the Basic tab of the Inspector. Limit the name to letters and numbers to keep things simple and remember that the Name field can't start with a number (**Figure 184a**).

Figure 184a Name the image in the Inspector so you can control it with JavaScript Actions.

3. Drag a Head Action object ![A] from the Smart section of the Objects palette into the Head section (see Tip 36) of your Web page and open the Actions palette.

(continued on next page)

Six Random Images

If three images aren't enough, you can try the free 6 Random Images Action from http://share.studio.adobe.com/axAssetDetailSubmit.asp?aID=3867. Make sure you remove the default RandomImage Action so they don't conflict.

4. With the Head Action still selected, choose On Load in the Events menu and pick Images > RandomImage in the Action pull-down menu (**Figure 184b**).

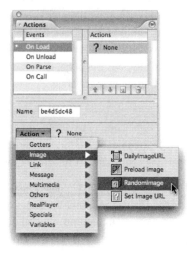

Figure 184b Set the Random Image Action to occur when the page loads so the visitor instantly sees the random image.

5. Decide which three images you want to randomize and assign them in the bottom of the Actions palette (**Figure 184c**).

Figure 184c Assign the random images in the Actions palette.

6. To see the Random Image effect, preview the page in a Web browser (see Tip 94). Reload the page several times to see the image change.

TIP 185 Targeting Two Frames

When you create a link in a page of a frameset, you always assign a target to the link so the Web browser knows which frame to open the link into (See Tip 75). Usually this works fine, but what happens when you have a more complicated frames design? For example, maybe you need one link to change two frames to update a navigation frame and a content frame. Use the Target2Frames Action to change two frames simultaneously with one link. Just follow these steps:

1. Create a frameset with at least three frames and make sure all the frames have unique names.

2. Select the text or image you want to use and assign the link by clicking the Link icon in the toolbar 🔗.

3. Open the Actions palette from the Window menu, select the Mouse Click event on the left, click the New Action icon 🔲 on the right. Then choose Link > Target2Frames from the Action pull-down menu. Notice GoLive automatically adds a pound sign (#) as the link destination in the Inspector. Leave this as is and don't add a custom link because the Action will do all the linking for you.

4. Enter the two frames and the pages you want to load into those frames at the bottom of the Actions palette (**Figure 185**).

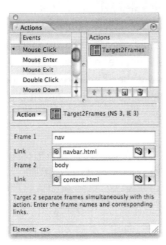

Figure 185 Set the Action parameters in the Actions palette and test in a Web browser.

5. Preview the frameset in a Web browser to check the results. Voila!

Kill That Frame

While it's common to want two frames to load at the same time when a link is clicked, it's also common to want a link to break out of a frameset. To force a frame to reload outside the frameset but in the same window, use the KillFrame Action found in the Link section of the Actions pull-down. Simply add the action to a link and you're done!

TIP 186
Finding and Installing New Actions

GoLive Actions—pre-built JavaScripts that are easily configured in the GoLive interface—make building interactivity into your Web site simple and trouble free. GoLive ships with almost 100 Actions pre-installed. The included Actions perform tasks from the very simple (open a new window, set the status) to the relatively complex (write a cookie, create a password). You'll find the Actions in the Adobe GoLive CS2:Modules:Jscripts:Actions folder; they are separated into subfolders related to the types of tasks they perform (**Figure 186**).

Figure 186 Actions are nestled in subfolders of the Actions folder.

When you download new third-party Actions for GoLive, we recommend you install them in a subfolder called something like Third Party, because it will make it really easy for you to migrate your Actions the next time you upgrade GoLive to a new version. In that event, all you need to do is remove the Third Party subfolder from the Actions folder, install the upgrade, and then return the Third Party folder to the Actions folder.

Note
For a detailed look at how to install, use, troubleshoot, update, and organize GoLive Actions, we highly recommend the excellent reference ebook by Mads Rasmussens called Adobe GoLive Actions for Newbies, *found at http://www.rasmussens.dk/newbies/index_newbies.html.*

TIP 187 Flattening the JavaScript Library

The source code for every JavaScript Action that you have used throughout your site is stored in an external JavaScript library called CSScriptLib.js, and GoLive automatically creates the file when you use an Action or a rollover in a Web page. This library file, placed into a folder called GeneratedItems at the top level of your Site, includes all the necessary JavaScript for the Actions for the entire site to function properly (**Figure 187**).

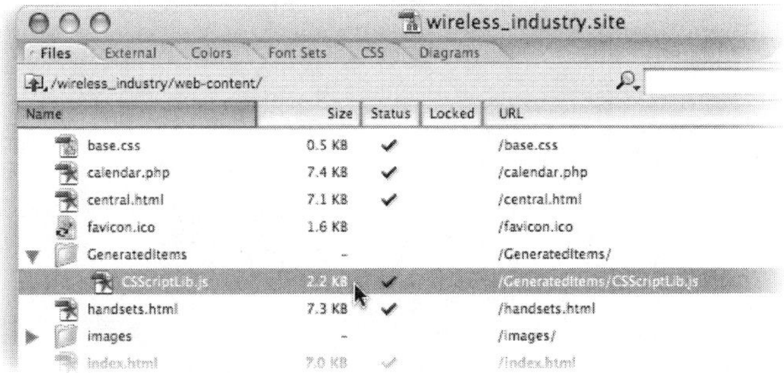

Figure 187 The CSScriptLib.js file can drastically reduce the download time of the overall site.

Other Web-authoring applications store the JavaScript code in each page, which is repetitive, unnecessary, and can cause your source code to become really bloated. Using an external JavaScript library means that the code for Actions or rollovers used on multiple pages does not have to be reloaded with each and every page that utilizes the Action. Instead, the library loads the code once, the browser caches it, and you get faster-loading pages. Not only that, but GoLive manages all URLs in the JavaScript library, so you can move pages around or even rename them, and all the referenced URLs are updated as necessary by GoLive.

Previous versions of GoLive included the JavaScript code for every installed Action, not just the Actions used. This meant you had to flatten the library for maximum efficiency every time you uploaded the site. GoLive CS2 keeps the JavaScript library lean and mean and only uses the code necessary for the Actions you've used on pages in the site.

(continued on next page)

**Action! Action!
Read All About It!**

To learn more about some impressive third-party Actions (and extensions, too), see Chapter 13. To see how GoLive's handling of JavaScript Actions stacks up against the competition, download the excellent GoLive JavaScript Actions white paper: http://www.adobe.com/products/golive/pdfs/gl_whtpr_js.pdf.

If you delete any actions from pages in the site, though, the CSScriptLib.js does need to be flattened. By default, GoLive handles the flattening process automatically when the file is uploaded. You can also flatten it manually if you want to see what the file size will be. Choose Site > Flatten JavaScript Library or use the contextual menu to access the Flatten JavaScript Library command.

Trivia
The filename CSScriptLib.js has absolutely nothing to do with CSS. The CS stands for CyberStudio, which was the original name of the application before Adobe acquired it from the company named GoLive Systems.

TIP 188 Highlighting Actions

To get a quick idea of where Actions are being used on your page, employ GoLive's ability to highlight Actions. Highlighting is an easy way to get an overview of how many Actions you're using and where they're located on the page. Select one of the following two methods to invoke highlighting:

- Open the View palette to the Highlight section, click the Special button, and then choose JavaScript Actions (**Figure 188a**). Click Clear to turn off the highlighting.

Figure 188a You can highlight Actions on a page by using the Highlight feature.

- Open the Actions palette and then choose Highlight Rollovers & Actions from the flyout menu (**Figure 188b**). This command is a toggle, so you'll need to select it again to turn the highlighting off.

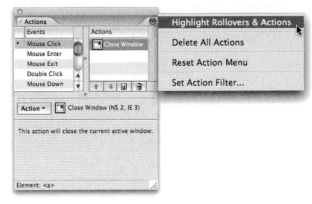

Figure 188b Alternatively, turn on highlighting from the flyout menu of the Actions palette.

TIP 188: Highlighting Actions

Deleting Actions

You could locate and delete each Action by hand, but that would take a long time on a complex page. Instead, just choose Delete All Actions in the flyout menu of the Actions palette.

TIP

189 Copying and Pasting Actions

GoLive Actions are powerful, pre-built JavaScript functions that make it easy to create interesting, useful, and interactive effects in your Web pages. With GoLive you can copy and paste Actions from one link to another or from one event to another. For example, if you accidentally create an Action for the wrong event, just cut and paste the Action to the correct event. Also, if you create a sequence of complicated Actions, you can copy and paste all those Actions from one link to another!

To copy or cut an Action, select it in the Actions list (on the right side of the Actions palette) and then choose Edit > Copy or Edit > Cut. To paste the Action and all of its settings onto a new link, select the link and then in the Actions palette select an event from the list on the left. Now put your cursor into the Actions list and choose Edit > Paste (**Figure 189**).

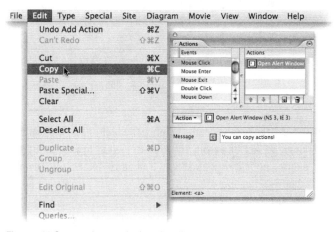

Figure 189 Copy and paste Actions just like text.

TIP 190 Resetting the Actions Menu

As mentioned in the sidebar for tip 189, GoLive remembers the last six Actions you've used and lists them at the top of the Action pull-down menu. This helpful feature was added in GoLive CS as a convenient way to access the Actions you use most frequently instead of drilling down into the long submenus of Actions (**Figure 190a**).

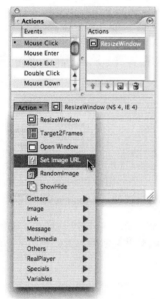

This was a nice idea for GoLive CS, but a few flaws annoyed some users. For example, sometimes the list of recent Actions would get really long and even remember duplicate Actions. Another problem was that you couldn't clear out the list without deleting all the application preferences.

The good news is the GoLive product team has improved this feature in GoLive CS2. To reset the recent Actions list, choose Reset Action Menu from the Actions palette flyout menu for that factory-fresh scent (**Figure 190b**).

Figure 190a GoLive remembers the last six Actions you've used in the Action pull-down menu.

Missing Menu Options?

In GoLive CS, the Rollovers and Actions palettes were combined in one palette called Rollovers and Actions. The palette menu options for both were also combined. If you are looking for a palette menu option in the Actions palette that you can't find, it could be that it's now located in the Rollovers palette menu instead.

Figure 190b Reset the Action list from the flyout menu.

TIP 190: Resetting the Actions Menu

TIP
191 Creating Forms

Forms are a great way to gather information and feedback (and maybe even orders) from your Web site's visitors. To create a form, start by dragging a form container 🟦 from the Forms section of the Objects palette into the Layout Editor.

You must place the rest of your Form objects inside the form container for them to work properly. Adding a table inside the form container is generally a helpful way to organize and align all the form fields and their labels. There are more than a dozen different form elements you can use within GoLive. Here are descriptions of the items you'll use most frequently:

- **Text Field** 🔲: Use these for short text entry such as name, email, and street address.

- **Passwords** 🔲: This works the same as a text field except that when the user enters text it is rendered as bullets or asterisks. This is an effective way to guard sensitive information such as passwords and credit-card numbers from prying eyes.

- **Text Area** 🔲: This is like a special text field that can have multiple lines for longer entries. It's perfect for a comment or question field.

- **Check Box** 🔲: Use check boxes when more then one answer might be appropriate. For example, if your form asked for our favorite flavor of ice cream, we'd want to check vanilla, strawberry, AND chocolate.

- **Radio Button** 🔘: Use a radio button when asking an either/or question.

- **Popup** 🔽: These are great when you want to ask your visitor to pick from a predetermined list of options. For example, what state are you from?

- **Label** 🔲: After you create all your form elements, you should label each one with a Label object.

- **Submit Button** 🔲: Every form needs a Submit button so the visitor can send a response.

- **Reset Button** : A Reset button isn't necessary, but it's helpful if the visitor makes mistakes and wants to start over.

- **Hidden** H: The visitor won't actually see hidden form fields (thus the name), but the values of hidden fields are stored in the code of the page and submitted with the rest of the form data. You may or may not need to use these, depending on how your hosting provider supports form submissions.

When you're done creating the form, select the form container again in the Layout Editor and give it a name in the Name/ID field in the Inspector (**Figure 191**). You also need to set the form Action in the Inspector according to the instructions you receive from your hosting provider or system administrator. Set the Method to Post and you're pretty much done.

Figure 191 Set the form's name, Action, and method in the Inspector palette.

Contact Your Hosting Provider

We wish there were an easy solution, a proverbial silver bullet, that we could tell you about to make your forms submit to a database or send to an email account. Unfortunately, there are so many different ways to do it (PHP, ASP, JSP, Lasso, Perl, and AppleScript, to name a few) that it depends in each case on the configuration at your hosting provider. Please contact your hosting company or server administrator, not us, for details.

TIP 191: Creating Forms

192 Creating a Form Inventory

Field Validator Action

For simple forms you can use the Filed Validator Action to ensure that the form is submitted according to your specifications. To use it, select the small form icon on the form container and then in the Actions palette, scroll down the events list to Form Submit. Select it and add an action. Next choose FieldValidator from the Getters list and set the options for the field that you want to validate. You can add as many instances of the Field Validator as you need in order to ensure all the fields are correctly submitted.

Depending on how your hosting provider sets up its form-to-email solution, you might need a little configuration file that lists all the fields in the form. Instead of retyping all these by hand, select the form and click the Inventory button in the Form Inspector to open the Form Inventory dialog (**Figure 192**). Click the top Export button to export the form element names to a text file and click OK when you're done.

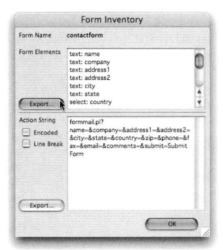

Figure 192 Export all the field names with the Form Inventory dialog.

There are also a few key form-related Actions and extensions you should know about:

- **Form Element Extractor:** For an even better form inventory, check out this free extension from Ken Martin at www.kpmartin.com/Downloads/.

- **Smart Forms:** Save yourself tons of time creating repetitive form elements with this free extension (see Tip 193).

- **VerifyForm:** Use this powerful commercial Action to verify and reformat form data before your visitors click the Submit button (see Tip 249).

Automating the Creation of Complex Forms

Creating a complex form with lots of form elements or long popup menus can be really slow and tedious. To make this process faster, GoLive includes several pre-built form elements in the Library palette. Open the Library palette from the Window menu and navigate to the Forms section of the application-wide snippets (**Figure 193a**). Here you'll find snippets of several common form popup lists, such as countries of the world, credit-card types, and months of the year. Just drag and drop these snippets into the Layout Editor.

Figure 193a The Library palette includes several pre-built form elements.

If you need even more pre-built form objects, check out the handy Smart Forms extension, which adds dozens more of the most common, pre-built form elements in a new section of the Objects palette (**Figure 193b**). The feedback regarding Smart Forms has always been really positive, and we've even heard stories of Web designers completing a new form design before their managers were even done making the request! They could save you a lot of time, too.

(continued on next page)

Figure 193b Smart Forms can save you time and eliminate typing mistakes.

First, create a form on your Web page. Now when you need a common form element, such as states in the United States, days of the week, or connection speeds, just grab it from the new Smart Forms section of the Objects palette. There are 35 pre-built form elements, including the following:

- Form Starter
- Ecommerce Form Starter
- Countries
- U.S. Postal
- States and Provinces
- Canadian Provinces and Territories
- U.S. Time zones
- 9-digit U.S. Zip Code
- 10-digit U.S. Phone Number

- Credit Card Types
- Credit Card Expiration
- Delivery Methods
- Gender
- Marital Status
- Age Groups
- Education Level
- Household Income

TIP 194 Placing QuickTime and SWF Objects on a Page

You can really go a long way with HTML, CSS, and images, but adding rich media content such a QuickTime movies and SWF animations can improve a site dramatically when done appropriately. The good news is that adding this multimedia content to a page with GoLive is as easy as drag and drop. Select the .mov or .swf in the Files tab of the Site window and drag it into the Layout Editor. GoLive will automatically add the correct height and width attributes, plug-in information, and the <object> and <embed> tags to make everything work smoothly in the browsers.

Figure 194a Adjust QuickTime-specific attributes in the QuickTime tab of the Inspector.

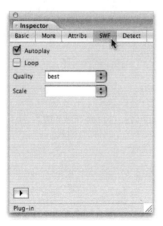

Figure 194b Control special SWF attributes in the Inspector.

What's interesting about how GoLive handles multimedia content is the way the Inspector changes depending on the type of file you've placed. For example, when you place a QuickTime movie in a page, there's a special QuickTime tab in the Inspector that gives you one-click access to options such as showing the controller, autoplaying the movie, and looping the video (**Figure 194a**).

When you place a Flash animation, the Inspector includes a SWF tab that lets you adjust if the animation autoplays, if it loops, the quality of the playback, and how it scales when resized (**Figure 194b**).

See Tip 241 to learn how to use the Detect tab in the SWF Inspector and deploy intelligent plug-in detection code.

Creating Clickable QuickTime Poster Frame Movies

Many Web designers choose QuickTime to deliver their multimedia content. Because of QuickTime's incredible quality, they want an impressive user experience to match. Visit Adam's tutorial at www.golivein24.com/tips/qtposter/ to learn a technique that allows the user to control when a QuickTime movie is played.

Placing Real Objects on a Page

RealAudio and RealVideo are popular media formats that you may wish to include on your pages. GoLive provides a Real object that can be used for both audio and video. To use the Real object, drag it from the Basic set of the Objects palette and place it onto your page. The Inspector palette will offer several options, the most important being the link to the source file.

Next, you'll want to choose whether or not to have the clip begin playing automatically when the page is loaded and what type of controls you want to offer. To edit those settings, click the Real tab. When using video, leave the Controls popup on Image Window. If you choose one of the other options, the sound will play, but there will be no video showing. When using audio it's fine to choose Control Panel, which gives the user a set of controls for pausing, stopping and starting the clip, simplifying matters even more and only giving a play button or one of the other options. Of course, a savvy visitor will know that they can access controls by right-clicking (Control-clicking on Mac) and selecting from the contextual menu in the browser (**Figure 195**).

Figure 195 Choose Image Window if you want a video to play.

TIP 196 Placing Windows Media on a Page

To use Windows Media files in your pages, you'll first need to place a Windows Media object onto the page. With the object selected, you will see four tabs across the top: Basic, More, Attribs, and Windows Media. Link the Windows MediaObject to the source file in the Basic tab of the Inspector palette. Clicking the Windows Media tab reveals an additional set of four subtabs where you can set attributes for

Figure 196 The Windows Media tab of the Inspector palette reveals four subtabs where you can set additional attributes.

the Windows Media object, such as Autoplay, which begins playing the clip as soon as the page loads into the browser, and Enable Controls, which gives the viewer a set of controls to pause, stop, and start the clip (**Figure 196**).

It's important to note that the Windows Media Object only writes the <object> tags into the source code and not <embed> tags. This is fine for Windows browsers, but for the clip to play on Macintosh browsers you'll need to include <embed> tags. To do so follow these steps:

1. Select the Windows Media object on the page.

2. Click the Split Source button to reveal the source code. The code for the selected object will begin with <object> and end with </object>.

3. Type the following into the source code within the object tags: <embed type="application/x-mplayer2" src="filenname.ext" width="xxx" height="xxx"></embed>. Replace *file-name.ext* with the filename of the source clip and enter the actual pixel dimensions of the clip instead of *xxx*. (If you are unsure of the path and/or filename, look for the code that says <param name="url" value="your/filename/here.wmv"> and copy the path written into the value.)

Finally, be aware that if the visitor to the page does not have the Windows Media Player, the content will not play for them.

TIP 197 Placing MP3 Audio on a Page

To embed MP3 audio in your page, you can use the Real object, the QuickTime object, or the Windows Media object. In some cases, if you are not certain which of the plug-ins the visitor would have, you may consider offering several options. If you do so, it's important to turn the Autoplay option to False on each of them so that they don't both begin playing when the page is loaded into the browser. Do so by deselecting the Autostart options in the Inspector for both plug-ins (**Figure 197**).

Figure 197 When using multiple clips on a page, turn off Autostart by deselecting the checkmark. The image on the left shows the options in for the QuickTime plug-in, and the one on the right shows options for the Real plug-in.

Another option is to simply create a text link to the audio file. When clicked, the clip will open in a separate window and play by means of whatever plug-in the user has installed that supports MP3. The advantage of this method is that you don't need to guess which plug-in(s) the user may have installed. The disadvantage is that each clip opens a separate window with no other content than the clip, and the visitor needs to press the browser back button to go back to your page again.

TIP 198 Creating QuickTime Slideshows

GoLive includes an impressive QuickTime Web video editor, and one of its coolest features is the ability to easily create QuickTime slideshows. Follow the step-by-step instructions below and have fun!

1. Select File > New > Web > Multimedia > QuickTime Movie and enter the dimensions of the QuickTime movie you want to create. Click OK (**Figure 198a**).

Figure 198a Create a new movie and pick the dimensions.

2. Choose Movie > Show Timeline Editor to reveal the Timeline window.

3. Drag a Picture Track ![icon] from the QuickTime section of the Objects palette to the left side of the Timeline window. Change the dimensions of the Picture Track in the Inspector so that they match the dimensions of the movie (**Figure 198b**).

Figure 198b Match the dimensions of the picture track with the dimensions of the movie.

(continued on next page)

TIP 198: Creating QuickTime Slideshows

4. With the Picture Track still selected, look at the Slideshow tab of the Inspector palette. Use these options to control how long each image is visible and which transition effect, if any, you want to use between each picture (**Figure 198c**).

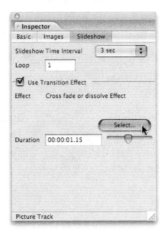

Figure 198c Adjust the slideshow delay, loop, and transition in the Inspector.

5. Now switch to the Images tab of the Inspector and prepare to import your still images. Before you press the Import button, you have a few settings to check. GoLive will scale down images that are larger than your movie dimensions, so make sure the Images Constrain Proportion option is checked. If any of your images are not the same proportions or orientation as your movie, you'll get a matting effect which can be controlled by setting the Background Color option (**Figure 198d**).

Figure 198d Adjust the image settings before you import the files.

6. Click the Import button and select the images you want in the slideshow. Hold down the Shift key to select multiple images. Because GoLive uses QuickTime technology, you can include images in many different formats (layered Photoshop, GIF, JPEG, PNG, Pict, BMP, Targa, TIFF, and so on), resolutions, and dimensions. You can even combine images from multiple sources. Click Choose when you're done.

7. The next dialog prompts you to compress the images for the movie (**Figure 198e**). Because the slideshow consists of still images, we suggest using the Photo JPEG compressor at your preferred quality setting. Click OK, and GoLive will import, compress, and sequence your images with a transition.

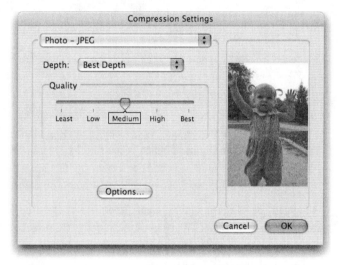

Figure 198e Choose Photo JPEG to compress the pictures in the slideshow.

(continued on next page)

TIP 198: Creating QuickTime Slideshows

8. When the slideshow is created, your Timeline window will be filled with all your still images, and a transition will be placed between each image (**Figure 198f**). To further customize your movie, double-click any of the A/B transition icons in the Timeline window to select a different transition.

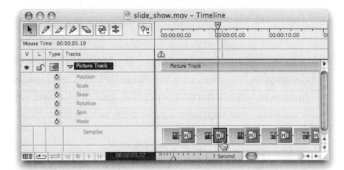

Figure 198f GoLive automatically sequences the still images and transitions for you.

9. When you're ready to save the movie, don't use the export commands because that would render each individual frame and cause the movie to have a much larger file size than necessary. Instead, choose Files > Save As and save the movie so it uses the native QuickTime transitions and minimizes the file size.

Now you can play the movie in the QuickTime Player or place it on a Web page (see Tip 194) for visitors to enjoy (**Figure 198g**).

Figure 198g Anybody can view your slideshow with the free QuickTime Player available at www.apple.com/quicktime.

TIP 199 Creating Imagemaps

Imagemaps are just one more way to create interesting navigation bars in a page. Instead of slicing a design in Photoshop or creating a DHTML drop-down menu, imagemaps can be a simpler solution. Follow these easy steps:

1. Place an image in the Layout Editor and enable the Use Map checkbox in the More tab of the Inspector. GoLive automatically adds a unique name for the map in the Name field, but you can customize this if you want (**Figure 199a**). Also, notice the addition of a little yellow square with the letter M  in the Layout Editor. This is a visual indicator that there's an imagemap on the page.

Figure 199a Make a normal image into an imagemap by clicking the Use Map option in the Inspector.

2. Now look at the toolbar and see how it changed to offer the tools you need to draw *hotspots* (clickable areas) with hyperlinks (**Figure 199b**). To create a rectangular or circular hotspot, select the tools in the toolbar and click and drag on the imagemap graphic in the Layout Editor. To create a polygonal hotspot, select the tool and click repeatedly with the mouse to create the corner points of the custom shape.

Figure 199b Use the tools in the Toolbar to draw out the imagemap regions.

(continued on next page)

Zooming

You can zoom in on an image-map without zooming the entire page. To get better control over very intricate image maps, hold down your Shift key and resize the image proportionally from the bottom-right corner so that it's larger. Your image will get larger, and the hotspots will stretch accordingly. Now adjust the hotspots as required. Click the Set to Original Size icon ☐ in the Basic tab of the Clickable Image Map Inspector, and the hotspots will scale proportionally to fit.

3. When you're done creating the hotspots, select each one and assign a hyperlink in the URL field of the Inspector (**Figure 199c**).

Figure 199c Assign hyperlinks to the hotspots just as in a normal link.

Now that we have the basics out of the way, we want to show you a few power user tips you're going to love:

- To create several hotspots of the same size, as for a navigation bar, create one hotspot and copy and paste the rest. This will create multiple hotspots with the exact same dimensions.

- If you have a hard time positioning an imagemap hotspot exactly where you want it, select the hotspot and use the Transform palette to fine tune its size and position.

- Use Smart Guides (see Tip 60) to help you align the edges of hotspots on an imagemap.

- It can also be challenging to line up your hotspots evenly. Hold down Shift to select multiple hotspots and use the Align palette to tidy things up.

CHAPTER TEN

Advanced Site Management

One of our favorite true stories happened the day Adam was finishing a huge 7,500-page site with GoLive. Two hours before the site was supposed to go live, the client called and asked for some "minor last-minute changes." Adam knew that no last-minute change was minor, but he listened to the requests anyway.

What would surely have been a real nightmare with other Web-design software turned out to be a two-minute change with GoLive. It took longer to upload the updated files than to make the actual changes. The project was on time to the day and 15 percent under budget, and Adam wouldn't have done the site with anything other than GoLive.

There are so many cool things you can create with GoLive, but at the end of the day one of the most important factors to meeting (or even beating) a project deadline is powerful site management. We like the fact that GoLive can handle really large sites faster than ever before. We love the fact that we have multiple undos even with site-management tasks. And we appreciate that GoLive tracks hyperlinks in HTML, XHTML, CSS, JavaScript, PDF, QuickTime, and SWF.

Features like these allow you to work quickly and creatively, and you never have to worry about broken links or missing images. Even all the third-party actions and extensions (see Tips in Chapter 13) work seamlessly with the link-tracking features of the Site window.

TIP 200 Diagramming New Sites

You're probably used to drawing out site maps (on paper or with the computer) and then regenerating the file structure in HTML. Put those late nights of confusion and chaos to an end with the powerful diagramming features in GoLive. Actually, GoLive offers three different site-mapping modes, so let's start by explaining the different options.

Navigation View

Choose View > Site Tabs > Navigation to open the Navigation view of a site. The Navigation view generates a visual site map for an existing site based on a combination of the folder structure and the hyperlinks between the pages (**Figure 200a**). To customize the orientation and presentation of the map, use the variety of options in the View palette. Using the Navigation, Display, and Filter options, you can really customize the site map to look any way you want. To add pages to the site in this view, simply drag pages from the Objects or Library palette.

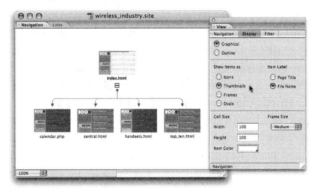

Figure 200a Use the Navigation view to get a hierarchical site map view of an existing site.

Links View

The Links view is grouped together with the Navigation view and is accessed by choosing View > Site Tabs > Links. The Links view is an interesting way of examining existing sites to better understand all the link relationships between various files (**Figure 200b**). It's sort of like a more intense version of the In & Out Links palette (see Tip 201). To customize the presentation and options for the Links view, make changes to the settings in the View palette. If the Links view starts to get unwieldy, turn on the Panorama pane so you can easily navigate around the site. Turn on the Reference pane to see which files a selected page references.

Creating Hyperlinked Site Maps

To create a hyperlinked site map, choose Diagram > Create Table of Contents when the Navigation view is open. Any pages that are visible in the Navigation view (click the plus icons) will be included in the site map.

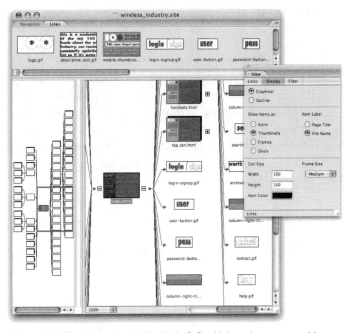

Figure 200b The Links view is like the In & Out Links palette on steroids.

(continued on next page)

TIP 200: Diagramming New Sites

Diagrams

The first two views are for existing sites, but Diagrams are for mapping out new sites or new sections of existing sites.

1. To create a new diagram, choose Diagram > New Diagram and give it a name when prompted (**Figure 200c**). The new diagram will be added to the Extras tab of the Site window, and the easiest way to open it is to select its name from the Diagram > Diagrams submenu.

Figure 200c Create a new diagram, name it, and open it with the Diagram menu.

Bonus Tip

The file extension for diagrams is .aglsd, which is short for Adobe GoLive Site Diagram.

2. So that GoLive knows how the new diagram fits in with the rest of the site, you need to add an anchor page to the diagram. To add an anchor page, drag the home page or any other page in the Files tab of the Site window into the diagram window (**Figure 200d**). Notice the anchor page has the special anchor icon next to it in the diagram window.

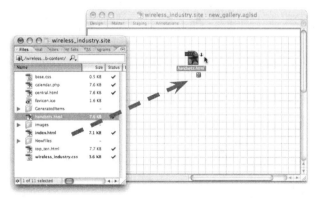

Figure 200d Drag and drop a page from the Site window to create an anchor page.

3. Now plan out the rest of the site map by dragging objects from the Diagram section of the Objects palette into the diagram window. You can add basic objects such as pages, sections, and groups as well as advanced objects including references to wireless content, server-side scripts, and multimedia content (**Figure 200e**).

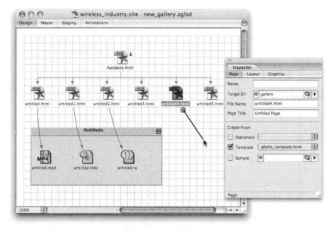

Figure 200e Use objects from the Diagram section of the Objects palette to build your site map.

4. Use the Point and Shoot (Fetch URL) tool next to any files in the diagram window to create link relationships between multiple files.

Figure 200f Assign a template to the pages in the diagram before submitting them into the site.

5. After the organization of the site map is complete, you can assign templates (see Tip 133) to the pages to accelerate the rest of the site design process. Just select a page in the diagram, open the Page tab of the Inspector, and choose a template in the Template pull-down menu (**Figure 200f**).

(continued on next page)

TIP 200: Diagramming New Sites

6. Before you're done with the site map, you can customize the presentation of the diagram using all the options in the View palette (**Figure 200g**). The variety of controls is utterly amazing. You also might want to customize the diagram by putting your company logo or the name of the project on the diagram using the Master tab of the diagram window.

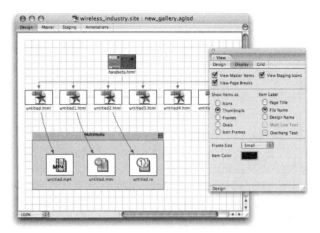

Figure 200g Adjust the Design and Display settings for the diagram in the View palette.

7. When you're ready to start adding content to the pages in your diagram, click Diagram > Staging> Submit All and watch GoLive move all the pages from the diagram into the Files tab of the Site window. It's incredible how much time this can save you, but even more amazing is the fact that all the links and references within all your pages and templates are updated perfectly by GoLive. By default, pages in a diagram are submitted to the top level of the Site window, but you can control this behavior. Before you submit a diagram, select files and sections in the diagram window and name a folder in the Folder or Target Dir(ectory) fields in the Inspector (**Figure 200h**).

Figure 200h Assign the target directories for the diagram pages in the Inspector palette.

Exporting Site Maps to PDF

Choose File > Export > Diagram, select PDF in the format pull-down menu, and click OK. This turns your diagram into an Adobe PDF that anybody can view with the free Adobe Reader. It's a great way to get feedback and approval on a project before it starts.

8. If you change your mind after you submit a diagram and want to try a different design idea or navigation bar, you can recall all the pages of a diagram. Just select Diagram > Staging > Recall All and try a different approach.

Managing Files with the In & Out Links Palette

The In & Out Links palette in GoLive CS2 offers a unique way to manage links and view file relationships in your site. Open the In & Out Links palette in the Window > Site menu and select a file in the Files tab of the Site window. The selected file is automatically positioned in the middle of the palette (**Figure 201a**). On the left are all the files that reference the selected file, so if you select a file such as the home page, an external .css file, or a template, you'll probably have tons of referencing files on the left. On the right side of the palette you see all the files referenced by the selected file. If you select a JPEG, you should have no files on the right, but if you select the home page or a navigation component, you should have lots of files listed on the right.

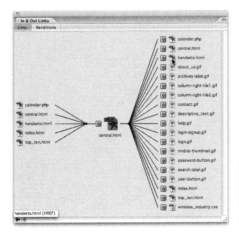

Figure 201a In & Out Links palette lets you quickly view file and link relationships for any selected file.

To determine which file is which, position your mouse pointer over a file in the palette; its file path, relative to the root level of the Web site, is displayed in the bottom left corner of the palette. This is really helpful if you have multiple files with the same name, such as index.html, in the same site.

The good news is that In & Out Links isn't just a pretty way to look at file links—it's also an easy way to redirect links and fix errors. If you want to change links from one file to another file, use the Point and Shoot (Fetch URL) tool next to the filename in the palette to point to a new file in the Files tab of the Site window

Advanced Site Management

(Figure 201b). If there's a broken link or missing file error in the palette, you can redirect the reference to the correct file.

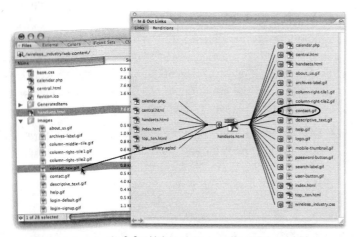

Figure 201b Use the In & Out Links palette to redirect links and fix errors.

The In & Out Links palette is one of the most powerful site-management features in GoLive and it has a few hidden options many users are not aware of. When you look at the In & Out Links palette with a large site, it might be overwhelming based on how you need to use it. To control what is shown in the In & Out Links palette, select Palette Options from the Palette menu in the top right corner of the palette (**Figure 201c**).

Figure 201c Control what you see and how it's sorted with the In & Out Links Palette Options window.

With these palette options you might choose to hide the links to the selected file and show only HTML files linked from the selected file. Select the filtering options you need from the Options dialog and click OK.

TIP 201: Managing Files with the In & Out Links Palette

Fixing Problems in the Errors Tab

TIP 202

If you use the site-management features in GoLive, it's unlikely that you'll see any errors in your site, but in the rare case you do, it's easy to fix them. If you see any bug icons in the Files tab of the Site window or errors in the Errors tab of the Site window, refresh the Site window ⟳ first before you panic. It's possible that you inadvertently moved or renamed some files in your operating system that GoLive doesn't know about yet. If that doesn't solve the problem, open the Errors tab of the Site window and read on for how to fix various common problems.

- **Missing Files:** Select the missing file error in the Site window and use the Point and Shoot tool in the Error Inspector to update the links to the correct file (**Figure 202a**). Confirm the warning dialog and you're done.

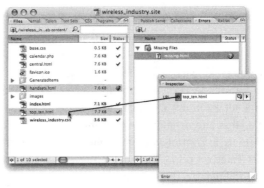

Figure 202a Point and Shoot from the Error Inspector to fix missing files.

- **Orphan Files:** Orphan files are files that GoLive can find on your hard drive but that are not located in your web-content folder. This means that unless you fix these errors, the orphan files will not be uploaded to the server and will cause errors for your visitors. To fix an orphan file error, drag it from the Errors tab to the Files tab in the Site window (**Figure 202b**). GoLive will copy the orphan file into the root folder and update all links throughout the site to the new location.

Figure 202b Drag and drop orphan file errors to copy
the files to the site and update the necessary links.

- **Filename Constraints:** If there's a certain way you want to
name all of the files and folders in a site, choose Site > Settings. Under Filename Constraints, click Site Specific Settings
and select one of the presets (**Figure 202c**).

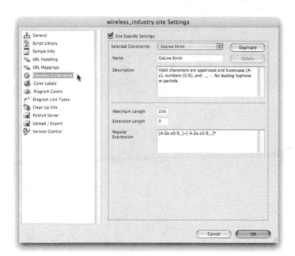

Figure 202c Customize the Filename Constraints for a site
in the Site Settings dialog.

(continued on next page)

TIP 202: Fixing Problems in the Errors Tab

Now the Site window will warn you about file and folder names that violate this preference, but it won't automatically change filenames or prohibit you from creating new filenames that don't follow the rules. The feature warns you, but you have to fix the error. You can easily fix the error by selecting the file in the Errors tab and changing the filename in the File Inspector (**Figure 202d**).

Figure 202d Select a Filename Warning in the Errors tab and change the filename in the Inspector.

TIP 203 Changing References Across a Site

Sometimes you need to change references throughout a site from one file to a different file. You can try to make these changes with complicated Find and Replace sequences, but Change References makes it easy with just a few clicks.

Select a file in the Files tab of the Site window that needs to be redirected and select Site > Change Links. The selected file is automatically added to the top field, so now all you have to do is tell GoLive what file you want to replace the links with. Use the Point and Shoot tool to locate the new file in the Site window and click OK when you're ready (**Figure 203a**).

Warning About Image Sizes

If you change references for an image, you should try to make sure the two images have the same pixel dimensions. The Change References command only updates the image reference, not the image dimensions. If the two images are different sizes, you should perform a quick site-wide Find and Replace (see Tip 205) to update the image dimensions.

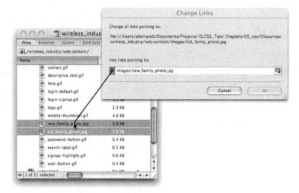

Figure 203a Assign the new and old references and click OK.

Confirm the changes in the Change Links dialog (**Figure 203b**) and click OK. Kick back and watch as GoLive does all the heavy lifting and updates all the necessary pages.

Figure 203b Confirm the site-wide link changes.

TIP 203: Changing References Across a Site

TIP 204 — Using Find and Replace in a Document

Situation: You've landed a job renovating the neglected Web site of a medium-sized business. None of the pages is currently based on a template, nor is data stored in a database. You have every intention of implementing both of those features in the future, but the task at hand is to immediately correct and update the information on the static pages.

Save yourself a lot of time by using Find and Replace to quickly handle these kinds of edits. The Find commands are found in the Edit menu. A number of sub-menu items are nested under Find: Find Text, Find Next, Find Previous, Find Selection, Enter Find String, Replace, Replace & Find Next; some of these options will be grayed out until you've performed at least one find operation. Knowing when and how to use these commands is the key to successfully performing edits with ease.

Open the page where you want to perform a Find operation, choose Edit > Find > Find Text, and choose Top Document from the pulldown menu at the bottom. You can type, paste, or drag text or syntax into the input box at the top (**Figure 204**).

Figure 204 To run a Find operation on the active page, choose Top Document from the menu at the bottom of the Find Text window.

Toggle open the Options section to select options for your search:

- **Match Case:** Enable Match Case if you want the case of letters to be considered—for example, you want to find *web* but not *Web*.

- **Entire Word:** Select Entire Word if you want a word to be found only if it exists on its own—for example, to find *hand* but not *handsome*.

- **Regular Expression:** Enable Regular Expression if you want to use wildcards in your search operation, but be careful! If you don't know what you're doing, you could wreak havoc on your pages.

- **From Top:** If you click From Top, the search will start at the top of the page. Otherwise it will begin at the location of the cursor.

- **Wrap Around:** Wrap around will perform the search from the cursor to the end of the page and then go to the top and end up back at the cursor position again.

- **In Selection:** To run the find operation on the current selection only, enable In Selection.

Note

To search for text, run the Find operation in the Layout, Source, or Outline Editor; to search for syntax, use the Source or Outline Editor.

To replace the found text with different text, type the replacement into the Replace input box. With your options selected and replacement in place, you're ready to run the search. To begin, click the Find button. If a match is found, it will be highlighted on the page. Click Find Next to move on to the next instance or click Replace to replace the found item with what you have in the Replace input box. Click Replace & Find to both replace the found item and move on to the next instance. If you want to replace all found instances, click Replace All.

Look What I Found!

GoLive has a clever feature that enables you to run additional searches without reopening or bringing the Find Text window back into focus. If you've previously run a search, you'll notice that additional Find commands such as Find Next become available in the Find submenu. Simply by using the associated keyboard shortcuts, you can run find operations on your page without even using the Find Text window!

TIP 204: Using Find and Replace in a Document

TIP 205 Using Find and Replace in Multiple Documents

The Find Text window has a drop-down list labeled Work On that enables you to run searches on more than one document at a time. Choose an option from this list if you need to perform a global Find and Replace operation across multiple pages in a site, on a selection of pages, on the Files or Extras tabs, or on a Collection or Query (**Figure 205a**). The options in this section are the same as those used in the Top Document area (see Tip 204). The difference here is that you must specify whether to search for text in Layout Mode or Source Mode by clicking the appropriate radio button.

Figure 205a You can search your whole site, a selection of files, or particular tabs of the Site window.

If you elect to search for text, you'll see the standard Replace options in the input box below. If, however, you need to search for Code Elements, select Find Code Elements from either the Find window menu or choose Edit > Find > Find Code Elements. Upon doing so, the Find window changes to display a series of pull-down lists that allow you to customize your search. Toggling open the Change portion shows options for how the found element should be treated. Use the plus and minus buttons to add or delete criteria to your search. If you are adept at using regular expressions, you can click the Advanced button and type in your own grep patterns (**Figure 205b**).

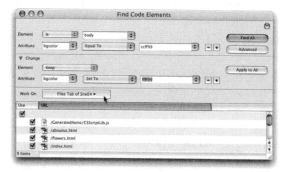

Figure 205b The Find Code Elements window is very robust allowing you to run incredibly granular searches based on multiple criteria.

Click Find All to find all matches. In the Results window, a number in the Hits column indicates how many times the item was found in each searched document (**Figure 205c**). You can also select whether to show Matches Only, Non-matches Only, or to Show All by selecting one of those options from the popup list. Double-click a file in the results list to open the file and see the first match highlighted.

Figure 205c The results list not only shows which documents contain the found item, but how many times the item was found within each page.

TIP 205: Using Find and Replace in Multiple Documents

Using Regular Expressions

If you would like to use wildcard searching, also known as *regular expressions* or *regex*, GoLive gives you a head start by offering a number of frequently used search patterns that you can select from the Find Text flyout menu under Saved Searches > Regular Expressions.

TIP 206 Saving and Loading Searches

If you need to get *really* granular when you run a search, you can take advantage of GoLive's ability to run searches on the results of previous searches. Say you want to find a set of files that contain the word *heartache* and also contain the word *backache*. You can first search for *heartache* and then use the results from that search to run another search for *backache*.

To save a search, you first run a Find operation and then choose Save Search from the Find window menu. GoLive will bring up the Save dialog box and points you to the TextSearch folder inside your GoLive that is several directories down in the GoLive settings folder. Name your search and save it into the TextSearch folder. To use a saved search, choose Load Search from the Find window menu. GoLive opens the TextSearch folder and allows you to choose from the saved searches.

To use the results of one search as the basis of another search, click the Use Results button in the results list. The results will automatically be loaded into the Search In input box in the Find Text window. You can remove items from the list before using the results if you'd like.

To save the results as a collection, click the Save Collection button (see Tip 210). A dialog labeled Create a New Collection will open displaying a descriptive name for the Collection. You can change the name if you'd like (**Figure 206**). As with the Use Results option, you can delete files from the results list before saving it as a collection if necessary.

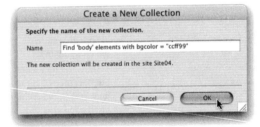

Figure 206 You can save the results of a Find operation as a collection. See Tip 210 for more info.

Note
Remember that a collection can only be saved into one site. If you searched in multiple sites, you can still create the collection but can only save it into one site.

TIP 207 Finding Site Assets

Let's say you know you have a certain file somewhere in your site, but you couldn't find it for a million bucks. Instead of wading through all the folders and subfolders in your site, choose Edit > Find > Find Site Assets. Type your search criteria in the Find Site Assets dialog and choose what part of the site you want to search in **Figure 207**. Searching for assets in the Files tab is the most common use, but you can also search in the Collections, Colors, Errors, External, Extras, and Font Sets tabs of the Site window.

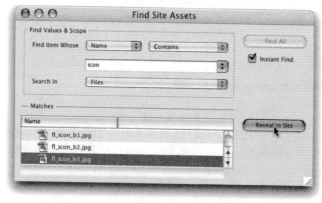

Figure 207 Enter your search criteria and click Find All to quickly locate site assets.

After you get the search results, you can select any file in the list of matches at the bottom and click the Reveal in Site button. Now that the file is selected in the Site window, you can open the In & Out Links palette (see Tip 201) to see what files, if any, are referencing the found file.

Bonus Tip

See Tip 28 to learn about using Quicksearch to locate files directly from the Site window.

Enabling Instant Find

To see the results of your search as an instantaneous filter, make sure the Instant Find option is enabled, and you don't even have to click the Find All button.

TIP 208 Finding File Differences

Whether you're troubleshooting an obscure coding problem, experimenting with different solutions to a CSS problem, or just looking for text changes, the ability to compare the source code of two files side by side can be very helpful. GoLive has a file-differencing command that is activated by selecting Edit > Find > Find Differences. Use the Point and Shoot tools in the Find Differences dialog to select the two files to compare and click OK (**Figure 208a**).

Figure 208a Select Edit > Find > Find Differences and choose two files to compare.

The next dialog shows a side-by-side code view of the two files and highlights any differences for you (**Figure 208b**). To make sure the two files scroll together, leave the Synchronize Scrolling option enabled. All the differences between the two files are listed at the bottom of the dialog where you can click on an entry to jump to the correct line of the pages.

Figure 208b The Find Differences dialog lets you navigate and compare and code differences between two files.

TIP
209

Running Site Reports with Queries

GoLive CS2 has a powerful search feature called *queries*, which give you the ability to search through your site for files based on a variety of criteria. A query can be run on a whole site, on selected files in a site, or on the results of another query.

You define queries in the Query Editor. To get to the Query Editor, first select Edit > Queries (**Figure 209a**). Click the New Query button to define a brand new query or select an existing query in the list and click the Edit Query button. Either way, the Query Editor will open (**Figure 209b**).

Figure 209a Choosing Run Query from the Edit menu opens the Query dialog.

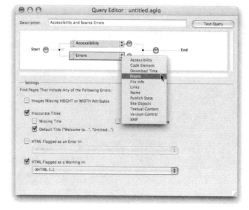

Figure 209b Choosing New Query or Edit Query opens the Query Editor.

(continued on next page)

Search for XMP Metadata with Queries

New in GoLive CS2 is the ability to create queries that search for XMP metadata (see Tip 27). This makes it very easy to search for images with a specific caption, copyright, or keyword.

Finding Default Page Titles

Included with the built-in queries is a criterion for errors, which includes an option to find any page that still has the default page title. Run this query to quickly gather up those pages and change their titles to something appropriate for your page. Remember, most search engines rely on page titles to properly index Web pages. The more precise the page title, the better.

Click the double-facing arrow ⬍ where it says Find What? to reveal a pull-down menu of search criteria. When a criterion is selected, its options are shown in the lower portion of the Query Editor. Make the appropriate selections for your search from those options.

To add additional criteria, click the small round button containing an arrow ⊙. From there you can select another criterion with Boolean options such as *and*, *or*, and *not*. Use the round button to the right of the Find What menu to delete a criterion.

When your query is ready to go, click the Test Query button to see how the Query works. After the query is complete, you can save the results as a collection or use the results as the basis of another query, syntax check, or find operation. When you close the Query Editor, you'll be asked if you'd like to save your query. If you do, then go ahead and name and save it into your Site folder.

TIP 210   Exploring Collections

Often there are some files in your site that will receive more frequent edits than others. Wouldn't it be nice to be able to access only those pages without having to drill down into various folders to find them? Use GoLive's new Collections feature, and the problem is solved.

To create a collection, follow these easy steps:

1. Click the Collections tab at the top of the Site window.

2. Click the Create New Collection button in the Toolbar .

3. Name the Collection.

4. Drag files from the Files tab of the Site window into the new collection folder in the Collections tab.

That's it. Now when you need to get to that collection of files, just open the collection and use the pages as usual (**Figure 210**).

Figure 210 Collections are useful for grouping together sets of files that you often need to edit, especially those buried deep in the folder structure.

Making a Backup First

As with any major site-wide operation, be sure to back up your site first in the rare event you make a mistake or something goes wrong. Take our word for it—you'll thank us later.

211 Cleaning Up a Site

GoLive offers a method for removing unused files and cleaning up orphan file errors (see Tip 202). Open the Site window and choose Site > Update > Clean Up Site to clean up these stray nuisances and get rid of unnecessary files. A dialog box appears, offering options for removing and adding files to the site (**Figure 211a**).

Figure 211a Choose the options you want in the Clean Up Site dialog box.

Once you have made your selections, click OK. GoLive will cycle through the files and then display another dialog showing which files will be removed or added (**Figure 211b**).

Figure 211b A list of the files that will be added or deleted is shown before any operation is completed.

You can check or uncheck files in this list to customize the process. When you are finished, click OK to complete the process.

In rare cases, GoLive may tell you that no files in the site are referenced and that all the files in the site should be deleted. This alarming situation occurs when GoLive doesn't know which file should be considered your home page. To fix this, select the home page in the root level of the Site window and click Home Page in the Page section of the Inspector palette.

Advanced Site Management

CHAPTER ELEVEN

Publishing Your Site

You've learned a lot, put in a lot of hard work, and you're eager to share your Web site with the world. Before you upload your site to a Web server, of course, you need to purchase a domain name and establish a hosting account if you haven't done so already. There are plenty of domain registrars, but www.godaddy.com and www.dotster.com are two of our favorites, and their prices are great. Whomever you choose as your registrar, make sure the company is approved at www.icann.org/registrars/accredited-list.html.

The next step is to find a hosting provider who can give you the service and support you need at a price you can afford. GoLive uses standard Internet protocols such as FTP and WebDAV, so you don't have to worry about finding a special company to host your GoLive sites. If you're looking for a particularly GoLive-savvy hosting company, we recommend you check out www.golivehost.com or www.mediatemple.net.

When you've got those two tasks squared away, it's time to upload! The first few tips in this chapter cover basic settings and uploads, but we quickly advance to some really cool power tips.

Save Password Now on by Default

Notice that the Save Password checkbox is on by default. If you're not worried about security on your computer, you can leave this on and save yourself time and hassle every time you connect to a server. If you are worried about security, uncheck this box and don't include the password here. You'll be more secure if somebody gains unauthorized access to your computer, but you'll have to enter the password every time you connect.

TIP 212 Creating and Editing Server Settings

GoLive manages all your server settings in a centralized location instead of saving settings in each site and forcing you to repeatedly enter the same options over and over again. Select File > Server > Favorites..., and you see the Edit Server dialog (**Figure 212**). Enter your settings here once, and they're instantly available to every site you work on, as well as to the FTP browser that's built in (see Tip 223).

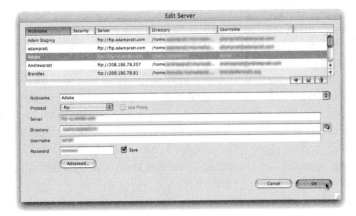

Figure 212 Manage all your publish server settings in one place.

Click the New button ⬛ to create a new entry and give it a nickname in the first field. You'll probably select FTP for your protocol, but notice you can also pick from http (WebDAV) and File for a local file server. Now enter the information for server address (IP or name), directory, username, and password as provided by your hosting provider or server administrator. If you don't know the directory path, click the browse icon ⬛ in the Directory field and let GoLive try to find it for you.

To create a new entry that's similar to an existing entry, select it in the list and click the Duplicate button ⬛ to duplicate it. This is a great way to save time if you just need to make a small variation for a different site on the same server.

TIP 213 Testing Server Connections

In Tip 212 you learned how to enter your FTP server settings so that you can upload your site to the Web, but how do you know if you entered everything correctly? You could enter the settings, assign them to your site, and try to connect and have no idea if it's going to work until the very end. That's way too tedious for us, which is why we thought up this great little trick for testing your FTP settings.

After you enter all your FTP server settings including server, username, and password, click the browse button [image]. This will force GoLive to talk to the server and test the connection as it tries to resolve the directory path. If you see a file listing for the folder you expected, you know you entered the settings correctly (**Figure 213a**).

Figure 213a If you get a directory listing that's a good sign.

However, if you get a warning dialog you know you've entered something incorrectly (**Figure 213b**). A mistake in the username or password is the most common error, but verify all fields and try again.

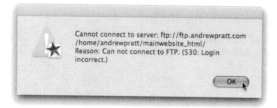

Figure 213b An warning lets you know something is wrong with the settings or your connection without leaving the Edit Server dialog.

TIP 214 Using Secure FTP

FTP (File Transfer Protocol) was originally defined in the early 1970s and it's the method virtually every Web designer uses to upload files, download files, and move files around on the Web server. However, what many Web designers don't realize is that standard FTP doesn't encrypt or obscure the transferred data or even the login password. This means that standard FTP transfers are susceptible to data interception or simple password guessing. Needless to say, this is especially important for anybody dealing with ecommerce, credit-card transactions, or very sensitive information.

The solution to this potential security risk is to use a secure connection between the FTP client (GoLive) and the Web server. Click the Advanced button when you edit the server settings and choose SSL (Secure Sockets Layer), SSH (Secure Shell), or SFTP (Secure File Transfer Protocol). Contact your hosting provider or server administrator for details on which method you should choose and what security credentials you should enter into the Security section of the Advanced FTP Options dialog (**Figure 214**).

Figure 214 Contact your hosting provider for details of what to enter for security settings.

TIP 215 Entering FTP Settings for Web Sites

After you've entered all your publish server settings as described in Tip 212, open your Site window and choose Site > Settings. Select Publish Server on the left and choose the server nickname from list of server entries you've already entered (**Figure 215**). If the server you need to connect to isn't already stored as a favorite, you can still enter its setting in the bottom of this window. After you enter the site-specific settings, you can always click the Favorites button ✱ and add the new server settings to the application-wide list of server favorites.

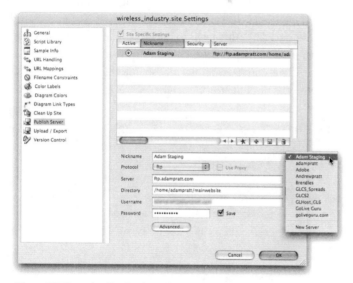

Figure 215 Open the Site Settings dialog and assign a publish server to your Web site.

The publish server settings you assign to a site are stored in the application preferences and in an encrypted format in the site-name/web-settings/siteServersettings.xml file. This means that if you deliver this site to a client or move the site to a different computer, all the login settings travel with the site, and you don't have to re-enter any server settings. Just make sure to copy the entire project folder including the Site file, root folder, Data folder, and Settings folder.

Connecting to the Publish Server

After you enter server settings and assign them to the site, you can connect to the publish server in a few different ways. The easiest method is to click the Connect to Publish Server icon in the toolbar (**Figure 216a**). You can also choose Site > Publish Server > Connect.

Figure 216a Connect to the Web server with the Connect to Publish Server toolbar icon.

When you're connected, you can see your local files in the Files tab on the left and the server files in the Publish Server tab on the right (**Figure 216**). This means you can connect to the server and do all your uploading and downloading right inside the GoLive Site window. There's no need to buy any shareware or launch any other utilities—it's all built in.

Figure 216b See your local and server files side by side in the Site window.

To disconnect from the server, click the Disconnect icon in the toolbar or Control-click (Mac) or right-click (Windows) in the Publish Server tab of the Site window and choose Disconnect (**Figure 216c**).

Figure 216c Disconnect from the server the same way you connected.

TIP 217
Connecting to Multiple Servers

Let's face it: connecting to an FTP server really isn't that big of a deal. Lots of people do it every day. However, one thing that makes GoLive's server connectivity really outstanding is the ability to connect to and synchronize with multiple servers at the same time. That's right, you can switch from one server to another with a single click. Make sure you have multiple servers assigned in the Publish Server pane of the Site Settings as seen in **Figure 217a**.

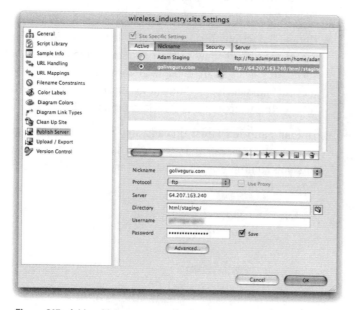

Figure 217a Add multiple servers to the Site Settings so you can switch between them later.

When you're connected to a server you can easily switch to a different server by choosing a different server nickname from the list in the Site > Publish Server > Active Server submenu (**Figure 217b**).

Figure 217b Switch between servers on the fly in the Site > Publish Server menu.

Managing Staging and Production Servers

Many Web designers upload their sites first to a staging server for review and then upload the same files to a production server after they've been approved. GoLive's ability to connect to multiple servers makes this tedious workflow much easier.

TIP
218 Uploading Files

You can drag and drop files between the Files and Publish Server tabs of the Site window to upload and download files, but this process is prone to error. Instead, let GoLive keep track of the files you need to upload. There are three upload commands you need to learn (**Figure 218a**):

- **Upload All:** You'll use this command the first time you upload a site because it uploads all the local files in your site to the Web server.

- **Upload Selection:** This uploads all selected files in the Files tab of the Site window to their correct location on the Web server. It's even smart enough to correctly upload multiple files that are selected in different folders, even multiple nested folders, to the appropriate locations on the Web server.

- **Upload Modified Files:** Uploads only the files on your hard drive that are newer than the ones on the server. A dialog lets you confirm exactly which files are uploaded before the process begins.

Figure 218a Three upload commands in the Site menu give you time-saving options for uploading.

Use the Upload button on the toolbar to easily begin the process of transferring files to the Web server. The button can be used two ways. Click and hold the button to access and select from the same list of commands defined above. A single click on the button defaults to the behavior enabled in the Change Button To submenu. If set on "Upload Modified..." Command, a single click will begin uploading the modified files (**Figure 218b**).

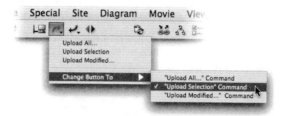

Figure 218b Customize the behavior of the Upload button in the toolbar.

Come On Down!

The toolbar button directly to the right of Upload is Download. Just as you can transfer files to a Web server, you can also download files from the server. The Download button's behavior mirrors that of the Upload button. Click and hold to access a list of commands, or click once to begin the download process as set in the Change Button To submenu.

TIP
219 Handling Invisible Files

It's common for a Web designer to use text files called .htaccess to control visitor access to special directories on the Web server. If you're not familiar with these files, you can check the documentation that comes with Apache, a popular Web server, or contact your hosting provider for assistance.

Configuring a Web server with these .htaccess files is relatively simple and very common, but it poses a real nuisance for Mac users. The problem is that Mac OS X treats any file that begins with a period as an invisible file. Previous versions of GoLive and the Mac OS X Finder won't display these hidden files without special tricks and workarounds. The good news is that GoLive CS2 understands that these invisible files are important to the work of a Web designer and displays them just as you'd expect in the Files tab of the Site window (**Figure 219**).

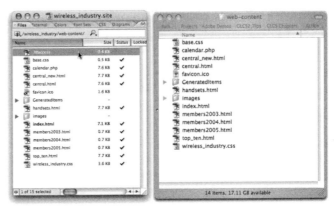

Figure 219 The Finder doesn't display the .htaccess file, but GoLive gives you what you want.

TIP 220 Synchronizing Modification Times

Several things can cause the files in your Site window to get out of sync with your Web server, including

- Somebody else moving or updating files on the server.

- A corrupt or re-created GoLive Site file.

- Changes to Web-server configurations including daylight savings time changes.

If the Site window insists on uploading files that you know are up to date, open your Site window and choose Site > Publish Server > Sync Modification Times > All (**Figure 220**). It might look like new files are uploading, but it's just synchronizing the modification times of the files on the remote server with those on your local computer.

Figure 220 Sync modification times on the server when things get out of whack.

If you have a specific set of files that need to be synchronized, select the appropriate files and folders in the Files tab of the Site window and choose Site > Publish Server > Sync Modification Times > Selection. This process can be very helpful if you move large files such as videos on the server and don't want to have to unnecessarily upload the files again just to get the Site window synchronized.

TIP 221 Synchronizing Files and Deleting Server Extras

When you have multiple offices or different people working on the same site, it can be tricky to keep all the files synchronized and not accidentally copy over newer files. The new Synchronize command helps keep everything up to date and also satisfies a long-standing feature request from customers, making it easier to delete unnecessary files on the server.

To use the Synchronize command, open the Site window, connect to the publish server, and choose Site > Publish Server > Synchronize All. You can also click the Synchronize icon ◀▶ in the toolbar to open the Synchronize dialog. GoLive takes a moment to compare the local and remote files and shows a dialog with two side-by-side files lists (**Figure 221**).

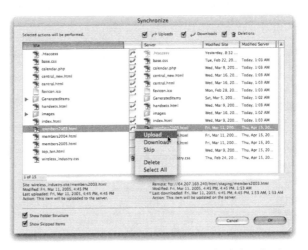

Figure 221 The Synchronize dialog lets you upload, download, and delete files so everything is synched up again.

Scan files in the list and click the pull-down menu between each pair of files to specify the action that you want to occur. When you're ready to synchronize, click OK and let GoLive synchronize all the files.

- **Skip:** This is the default action, and unless you have a lot of files out of sync this will apply for most files.

- **Upload:** If the local file is newer, choose Upload.

- **Download:** If the remote file is newer, choose Download.

- **Delete:** If the remote file is unnecessary, you can delete it, but be careful not to accidentally delete server files such as scripts and databases.

TIP 221: Synchronizing Files and Deleting Server Extras

222 Stripping Extra Code

Automatically Flattening the JavaScript Library

Check this option to optimize the site-wide JavaScript library (GeneratedItems/ CSScriptLib.js) every time you upload files from your site. When the library is flattened, it only uses the functions necessary for your site and will optimize overall download time of your site (see Tip 187).

GoLive offers very powerful authoring tools that can save you a lot of development time, but sometimes the tradeoff is a little bit of extra source code. For example, if you use templates, some extra comment tags are inserted in the source code, and if you want your source code formatted nicely, some extra space characters are added.

If you're really picky about your source code or need it to validate perfectly against certain standards, GoLive can strip out these extra tidbits and upload the most pristine code you've ever seen. To enable code stripping, choose Site > Settings and select the Upload/Export pane on the left. Enable the Site Specific Settings checkbox at the top of the dialog and look at the Cleanups section (**Figure 222**). You can tell GoLive to strip the following code every time you upload or export your site.

Figure 222 Enable code stripping in the Site Settings dialog to control the final output.

- **Adobe GoLive Elements:** Special tags for features such as JavaScript Actions and Components.

- **Comments:** Any source code comments including those used to manage templates.

- **Spaces:** Any extra spaces for formatting your source code.

Stripping extra code doesn't affect how the pages work in a Web browser, but removing spaces does reduce the readability of the code. If you strip GoLive elements, it will be all but impossible to easily re-edit advanced GoLive features such as components and JavaScript Actions.

Using the Built-in FTP Client

Most of the time you'll just use the FTP tools that are integrated with GoLive's Site window and the Publish Server tab. However, every once in a while you'll need to quickly upload something to an FTP server that might not be associated with a site you're editing. For example, while writing this book we've uploaded many screen shots and PDF files to our project server. Instead of launching a separate FTP client, we use the one built into GoLive, which you can open with the File > Server > Connect to FTP... command (**Figure 223**).

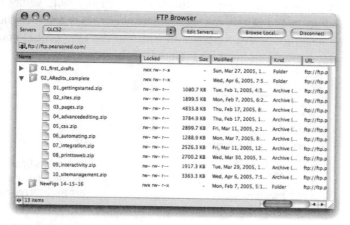

Figure 223 Use the FTP client in GoLive for all your file transfer needs.

From here you can choose the server you need to connect to and click the Connect button. After you connect, you can create new folders and delete files with the buttons in the toolbar, and you can upload files by dragging them into the window. When you're done, click Disconnect.

Downloading a Page

Surfing the Web for design inspiration is a great way to get your creative juices flowing. When you find a cool design or technique, you can learn from the example by choosing File > Server > Download Page… in GoLive and pasting the URL into the dialog that opens. GoLive will download the page and render it in the Layout Editor where you can deconstruct the design. Just remember: Learn, don't steal.

Troubleshooting with Server Logs

If you've ever tried to connect to a server, you've probably at some point encountered some kind of error. Did you type the wrong password? Maybe the server timed out? Whatever the cause, you know there are a lot of reasons why server connections can be a problem. Fortunately, GoLive includes diagnostic tools to help you troubleshoot these annoyances.

If you have server connection problems, choose File > Log. The Log window opens to show you any recent errors (**Figure 224a**). Use the information tracked here to diagnose connection problems with your hosting provider. To make the logging more verbose, choose the Log pane in the application preferences and turn on the Warnings and Status Messages options. You can even control how many log sessions are stored (**Figure 224b**).

Figure 224a Open the Log window to troubleshoot recent connection errors.

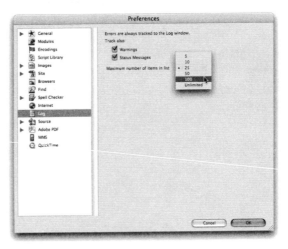

Figure 224b Use the Log preferences to control how much detail is recorded in the log.

Publishing Your Site

TIP 225 Browsing With the Local File Browser or Adobe Bridge

Located under File > Server is another command called Browse File System.... Selecting this option opens a standard OS dialog box that lets you browse to a folder on your network. Upon choosing a folder, GoLive opens and displays the folder's contents in the Local File Browser. You can change the view options of the Local File Browser window by Control-clicking (Mac) or right-clicking (Windows) and choosing an option from the View submenu. Selecting Thumbnails makes the window look similar to the new Adobe Bridge that comes with GoLive CS2 and the other CS2 applications from Adobe. You can even drag and drop files from the Local File Browser to the Files tab in the Site Window.

Although this is a convenient feature, it can be a slow and tedious process to browse through hundreds or thousands of digital photographs in the search for the perfect shot using this method. Adobe Bridge to the rescue!

The new Adobe Bridge makes it easy to browse your images and add your favorites to your Web sites in GoLive. To open Bridge, choose File > Browse in GoLive or click the Bridge button 🖼 in the toolbar.

Bridge is a standalone application that will remind you of the old Photoshop File Browser, but now it works for all the Creative Suite applications. It's like a virtual dashboard for your entire creative workflow. You can navigate your hard drive in the top left corner of the Bridge window, view image thumbnails on the right, and see a large preview on the left. You can even change the size and layout of the image thumbnails using the various controls on the bottom right corner of the Bridge window (**Figure 225**).

(continued on next page)

Compact Mode

Adobe Bridge is an awesome new addition to the Creative Suite, but in the default configuration the Bridge behaves like a window instead of a floating palette. This means if you switch from Bridge to another application such as GoLive you won't be able to see the Bridge window anymore. To see both applications at the same time, click the Compact Mode icon ⬜ in the top right corner of Bridge and make sure "Compact Window Always On Top" is enabled in the flyout menu. Now your Bridge window will behave like a floating palette and will be available to any open application.

Figure 225 Browse images for your site using the new Adobe Bridge.

When you find the image you want to use in your Web site just drag the file directly into the Files tab of the GoLive Site window. This will copy the file into your Site where you can use the image as is or as a Smart Object source. If you'd rather place the image directly in a Web page as a Smart Object (see Tip 141), you can drag the source image from the Bridge directly into the Layout Editor in GoLive. This works especially well for large JPEGs from a digital camera (see Tip 143).

CHAPTER TWELVE

Versioning Files with Adobe Version Cue

Adobe GoLive CS2 offers a variety of versioning tools, including directory-based versioning, support for Concurrent Versions System (CVS), versioning via FTP, and support for Perforce. But GoLive's integration with the rest of the Creative Suite is what makes Version Cue, the suite's built-in versioning system, so compelling.

In this chapter, we show how to make a new Version Cue project, how to take an existing site and turn it into a Version Cue project, how to administer the project, and when and how to access the features that Version Cue offers. You'll learn how to create a version of a document, revert to a previous version, compare versions, and more.

For additional information beyond what is covered in this chapter, take a look at the new Adobe Help Center application (see Tip 10). It's chock-full of detailed information on how to use Version Cue in conjunction with the other Creative Suite 2 applications.

226 Introducing Version Cue

Run Version Cue on a Separate Server

The default Creative Suite installation installs Version Cue CS2 on your machine and turns it on automatically. If you would instead prefer to run Version Cue on a separate machine so that all users on your network can access it, you can do so by doing a custom install of the Creative Suite. Simply deselect Version Cue in the list so it won't be installed on the local machine. Then, run the installer on the second machine (the server) and deselect everything *except* for Version Cue CS2. This will install Version Cue CS2 on the second machine. You can find the network address that the users will need to access Version Cue in the login screen of the Advanced Administration area (see Tip 227 sidebar).

What exactly *is* Version Cue? Simply put, Version Cue is a file-management and version-control system specific to the Adobe Creative Suite. It made its debut in the first edition of the Creative Suite, but in CS2 has become more discoverable, more robust, and easier to use. If you have a standalone copy of GoLive CS2, you will not have Version Cue because it ships only as a component of the Adobe Creative Suite 2. However, each of the individual Adobe products, GoLive CS2, Photoshop CS2, Illustrator CS2, InDesign CS2, and Acrobat 7 Professional, can hook into a running installation of Version Cue.

Version Cue is a server, a holding area in which you create projects that you want to manage with the Version Cue features, such as sharing files with a co-worker. Version Cue projects can contain documents of all kinds, and those documents are accessed either via the new Adobe Bridge application or, in the case of GoLive, from the Site window.

After completing a default installation of the Adobe Creative Suite 2, Mac users will see a new icon in their Finder menu bar whereas Windows users will find the icon in their Taskbar. This means Version Cue is up and running on the local machine. In both cases, you'll be able to access several important functions of Version Cue from this icon, such as the Version Cue preferences and the Advanced Administration area (**Figure 226**).

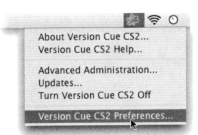

Figure 226 The Version Cue preferences and Advanced Administration area are easily accessed via the Version Cue menu found in the Finder menu bar or in the Windows task bar.

You can also turn Version Cue on or off directly from this menu. When Version Cue is off, its icon displays a little red stop sign on it . Choose Turn Version Cue CS2 On to enable it and Off to disable. As it is starting up, the leaves in the icon first turn gray and then turn green one-by-one until the whole icon is colored in. When the icon is completely green, Version Cue is ready to go.

Versioning Files with Adobe Version Cue

TIP 227 Creating a Version Cue Project

There are several ways to create a Version Cue project, so we cover two of them in this tip. First, we show how to create a project in the Adobe Bridge, and then we create a project from inside GoLive CS2. Other methods that are not covered in this tip are creating a project from Photoshop, Illustrator, InDesign, or in the Advanced Administration area of Version Cue.

Create a Project in Adobe Bridge

A very simple way to create a Version Cue project is to open the Adobe Bridge application and choose Tools > Version Cue > New Project... The New Project dialog box will open with fields in which you can type the project name and info. If you plan to work with others on the project, enable the checkmark next to Share this project with others (**Figure 227a**). When you are finished, click OK.

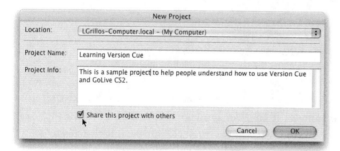

Figure 227a When creating a new project from Adobe Bridge, use a descriptive name. It's a good practice to put a bit of info about the project in the Project Info box as well.

(continued on next page)

Once the project has been created, you can click on Version Cue in the Favorites tab of the Bridge to see it. Hovering your mouse over the project's icon will bring up a Tool Tip showing the metadata for the project, including the project info you entered when you created the project (**Figure 227b**).

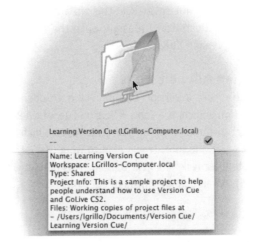

Learning Version Cue (LGrillos–Computer.local)
--

Name: Learning Version Cue
Workspace: LGrillos–Computer.local
Type: Shared
Project Info: This is a sample project to help people understand how to use Version Cue and GoLive CS2.
Files: Working copies of project files at – /Users/lgrillo/Documents/Version Cue/Learning Version Cue/

Figure 227b You can access Version Cue projects and any data about them via the Adobe Bridge application.

Now that you have a project, you can take an existing GoLive site, convert it to a Version Cue site, and save it into that or any other existing Version Cue project. However, it is not necessary to have a Version Cue project prior to converting a GoLive site into a Version Cue site. In the next half of this tip, you'll learn how to create a new Version Cue project directly from within GoLive.

Creating a Project in GoLive CS2

You can create a new Version Cue-enabled site or take an existing site and convert it into a Version Cue site directly from within GoLive. To convert an existing site, follow these steps:

1. Open the site and then choose Site > Settings... from the menu.

2. Select Version Control at the bottom of the list on the left.

3. Enable Use Version Control at the top of the Settings dialog box (**Figure 227c**).

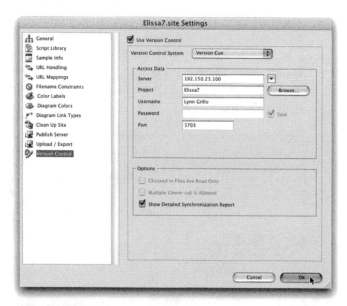

Figure 227c To convert an existing site into a Version Cue site, turn on Version Control in the Site Settings.

4. Choose Version Cue from the Version Control System popup list.

GoLive will automatically fill out the information for Server, Project Username, and Port. If the server IP address is not correct, click the down arrow to the right of the input field to choose the name of the computer on which Version Cue is installed from the list or type in the IP address. You can find the IP address in the login screen of the Advanced Administration page (see sidebar "Logging into the Advanced Administration Area"). Check to make sure your username is correct and if it is not correct it before continuing.

5. Rename the project if you'd like or click Browse to select a different project to save the site into.

(continued on next page)

Logging into the Advanced Administration Area

Using the Version Cue CS2 icon in the Finder or in the Windows Taskbar, choose Advanced Administration. Your Web browser will open and display the login page. The default login and password *system* is noted directly on the page above the login and password fields.

If you do not need secure access to the Version Cue administration features, you can leave the defaults as they are. If you prefer more security, change the defaults in the Users area after you have logged in. *Be sure to note your new username and password before logging out.* See Tip 235 for more info.

TIP 227: Creating a Version Cue Project

Adding Users to a Project

To allow other users to access your projects, make sure that your Version Cue workspace is visible to others. This setting is found in the popup next to Workspace Access in the Version Cue preferences.

To add users to a project (or deny a user access to one), log into the Advanced Administration area and go to the Users area. You'll be able to add or delete users and set their access privileges, including which projects they may have access to and whether they have administrator privileges.

6. Click the options to Show Detailed Synchronization Report and then click OK.

If you are placing the site into an existing project, the synchronization screen will come up next. If you are creating a new project, you'll first get a dialog box saying that the project does not exist and asking if you'd like to create it. Choose Yes, and then the synchronization screen will appear (**Figure 227d**).

Figure 227d To convert an existing site into a Version Cue site, turn on Version Control in the Site Settings. You can see all of the files that will be uploaded to the Version Cue server and make any changes you deem necessary.

7. To finish the process, click OK. The files will be uploaded to the project, and a report will be displayed.

Note

When converting older GoLive sites into Version Cue sites, you may get an alert saying that the site must be converted to the new site structure. Do so by dismissing the dialog box, and then with the site opened, choose Site > Convert Site to New Structure… before proceeding with the steps outlined here.

To create a new Version Cue site, follow the steps outlined in Tip 14, and when you get to the Version Cue screen come back to step 1 in this topic.

TIP 228 Mounting a Version Cue Site

To begin working on a Version Cue site you must first mount the site from your local machine. This means that a working copy of the site will be created on your computer, whether the site you are accessing resides in a project on your own machine or in a project on a Version Cue server elsewhere on your network. Mounting a Version Cue site is very simple. From the File menu, choose Connect to Version Cue (**Figure 228a**).

Figure 228a To mount a Version Cue-managed site, select Connect to Version Cue from the File menu.

A window will open showing a list of projects that you have access to. Select the project containing the site you want to work on and click OK, or double-click the project name in the list (**Figure 228b**).

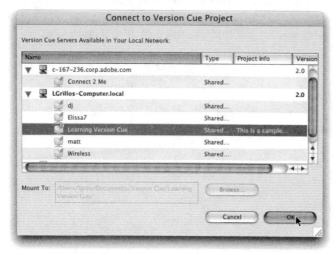

Figure 228b Double-click the name of the project that holds the Version Cue site you want to open to mount it to your computer.

You may get a dialog box asking you to synchronize the site. You can click OK to synchronize or Cancel to mount the site without synchronizing it. For more on synchronizing, see Tip 233.

TIP 229 Saving a Version of a Page

Opening a file in a Version Cue site is just like opening any other file. Simply double-click the file in the Files or Extras tab to open the page, or from the Version Cue workspace in Adobe Bridge. If no one else is using the document you have opened, the title bar of the document will say *Available* in parenthesis. Alternatively, the file could say *In Use by Someone*, indicating that the person named is working on the file. Additionally, the Version Cue status icon at the bottom of the document window will show that the file is in use and by whom, even if that person is you (**Figure 229a**).

Figure 229a You can easily see the status of a Version Cue file in the lower left portion of the document window. The Tool Tip gives a status report.

When you first begin working on a document you will get an alert asking you if you'd like to mark the file as in use. In a multi-user environment, you'll want to say yes. If you attempt to make changes to a page being worked on by someone else, you will get an alert warning you that you risk a conflict (**Figure 229b**).

Figure 229b More than one person editing a file at once can cause a conflict. GoLive gives you fair warning.

You can make as many changes as you want to a document and save it as many times as you'd like without affecting the version of the file in Version Cue. That's because you are editing a *working copy*, one that is local to your computer. In order for the changes you made to be reflected on the copy managed by Version Cue, you'll need to *Save a Version*. Do so by clicking the Save a Version button in the Version Cue toolbar (**Figure 229c**). You can also use Site > Version Control System > Save a Version, or Control-click (Mac) or right-click (Windows) the file in the Files list and select Save a Version.

Figure 229c Use the Save a Version button to create a new version of a file.

When the Save a Version dialog box appears, you can add a comment if desired. These comments aren't necessary, but they might help your co-workers understand your contributions to a project as you collaborate on a Version Cue project. Then, click OK to save the new version back into the Version Cue workspace (**Figure 229d**). To see the versions of a document, select it in the files list and click the Versions button on the Toolbar.

Figure 229d Every time you save a version, you have the opportunity to add comments. The comments can be seen in the Version Cue workspace in Adobe Bridge as well as in the Versions list in GoLive.

The Version Control Toolbar

The GoLive toolbar is actually four toolbars side by side. One of them is strictly for use with Version Control, and like the others it can be dragged out of its default docked location at the top of the screen or floated wherever you'd like. From this little toolbar you can mark individual or multiple files as In Use, synchronize local files with Version Cue, monitor user activity, and more.

TIP 229: Saving a Version of a Page

TIP 230 Reverting a Page to a Previous Version

If you find that you need to revert a Version Cue-managed page back to a previous version, you can do so quite easily by following these simple steps:

1. Select the page in the Files list of the Site window.

2. Click the Versions button in the Version Control toolbar or choose Site > Version Control Systems > Versions.

3. When the Versions window opens, select the version you want to promote in the list.

4. Click the Promote to Current Version button.

5. Click Done.

The newly promoted version of the page will open, and the Versions dialog box will close (**Figure 230**). When you promote a previous version to current status, a new version is created, complete with new version number.

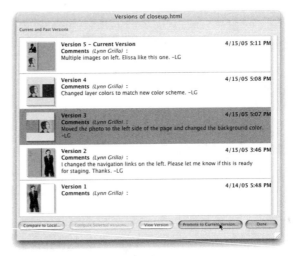

Figure 230 Click the Versions button in the toolbar to see the list of versions for the active document. You can promote a previous version to a current status.

What Are Alternates?

Nestled in the Version Control System submenus is an item named Alternates. What is an alternate and when would you use it? Let's say you are working on a prototype for a site and you design several sample pages. Version Cue allows you to designate these pages as alternates of one another. To create an alternate, select two or more documents in the site window and choose Site > Version Control System > Alternates > Make Alternate.

One of the alternates will always be considered the primary, or the first choice, but you can change the primary alternate designation by selecting one of the other alternates and choosing Site > Version Control System > Alternates > Make Primary Alternate.

Alternates 🔲 and primary alternate 🔲 each have a unique symbol associated with them in the Alternates column of the site window.

TIP 231 Comparing Two Different Versions

You may want to compare two versions of a document to determine exactly what has changed between them. To do so, follow these easy steps:

1. Select the page in the Files list of the Site window.

2. Click the Versions button in the Version Control toolbar or choose Site > Version Control Systems > Versions.

3. When the Versions window opens, select the two versions you want to compare and click the button marked Compare Selected Versions... (**Figure 231a**).

Figure 231a Select two versions from the list and then click the Compare Selected Versions button.

A window will open showing the source code of the two documents side-by-side. To hone in more easily on only the changed bits, enable the checkmark next to Hide Identical Lines. By keeping Synchronized Scrolling on, both pages will scroll together when you are looking through the code (**Figure 231b**).

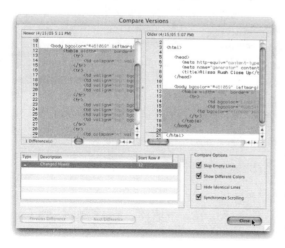

Figure 231b The code for each of the two pages is displayed in the Compare Versions dialog box side-by-side.

So Many Differences

If there are a number of differences between the two versions of the file, you can use the Previous Difference and Next Difference buttons in the Compare Versions dialog box to examine each difference individually.

TIP 231: Comparing Two Different Versions

TIP 232 Using Version Cue Link Management

GoLive has world-class site management, and you won't lose any of that functionality when using a Version Cue site. However, it's important to understand what is marked as *In Use*, and what happens if you cancel the *In Use* mark. When a file is marked as in use, you'll see an icon in the Version Cue status column in the Site window (**Figure 232a**) as well as in the lower left portion of an opened document window.

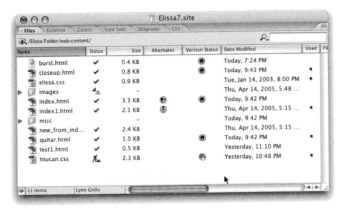

Figure 232a Files that are In Use have an In Use icon in the Version Cue status column of the site window. If you don't see that column, close the right pane of the Site window and stretch it a bit larger until the column appears.

When you make changes to the site that affect links within the site, such as renaming a file or moving it to a different directly, you normally get an alert asking if you want to update the references. With a Version Cue site, you may also be asked if you would like to mark those files as in use, depending on what change you are making. In some cases, GoLive will automatically mark the necessary files as in use for you. Here are some examples.

Files are automatically marked as in use when:

- Renaming a checked out file affects the page.

- Moving a checked out file affects the page.

- Deleting a checked out file affects the page.

- Changing references to a checked out file affects the page.

Important!

It's very important to understand that if you mark a file in use, make changes to it, and then choose *Cancel Mark In Use*  in the Version Control toolbar, or from the menu, all the changes you made will be lost. It is essentially reverting the file back to its state prior to opening it. *This is true even if you have made changes to the file and saved those changes and closed the file without saving a new version.*

If you select multiple files in use in the Site window and cancel the In Use mark for all of them, you could easily end up with a site full of errors. Before canceling the In Use mark choose Site > Version Control System > Save a Version for All (**Figure 232b**).

Figure 232b Choosing Save a Version for All is a shortcut for saving new versions of all the pages you worked on.

This safely saves your work back into the Version Cue project and allows you to enter a comment for multiple files all at once.

TIP 232: Using Version Cue Link Management

Synchronizing Files with Version Cue

After updating files in the working version of your site (the copy on your local computer), or after adding to or deleting files from the project, you'll need to synchronize the local version with those in the Version Cue-managed workspace. To begin the synchronization process, click the Synchronize button on the Version Control toolbar or choose Site > Version Control System > Synchronize All... from the menu (**Figure 233a**).

Figure 233a One easy click on the toolbar begins the synchronization process.

The Synchronize window opens and shows which files are marked for upload, for download, and for deletion. Items on the left are those on your local machine, and items on the right are those in the Version Cue project. To see the status for any file, click the file in the list and look at the info beneath both the right and left panes. GoLive gives a description of the status of the file locally (left) and on the Version Cue server (right) (**Figure 233b**).

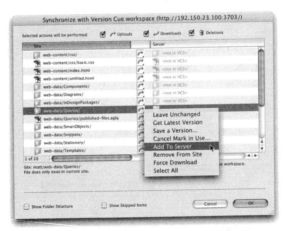

Figure 233b You can let GoLive synchronize the files, or change the default options by choosing from the popup menu in the Synchronize window.

You can change the upload designation for any item by clicking the icon between the two panes. A list of options for handling the file such as Add To Server or Get Latest Version pops up. Simply select the handling option of your choice for any particular file.

Versioning Files with Adobe Version Cue

TIP 234 Working Offline and Publishing

Publishing a Version Cue site to a Web server works the same as with any non-Version Cue site in that you simply connect to the publish server in GoLive and then choose upload modified, upload all, or upload selection just as you normally would. (For more on publishing, refer to Chapter 11.)

However, it's important to first synchronize the files on your computer, the working copies, with those in the Version Cue project prior to publishing the site (see Tip 233 for info on synchronizing). This ensures that the both the Version Cue project and the Web server have the most up-to-date versions of the site and all its associated files.

One point to note is that it is possible to upload files to the Web server even when you are working offline. Working offline means that you have mounted a Version Cue site, which copies the site to your local computer, and then disconnected from the Version Cue server. The local site is your working copy, and as mentioned earlier you can edit and save to your heart's content. When you are ready, log back into Version Cue to synchronize your local copy with the one on the Version Cue workspace.

You may prefer to do all your work offline, connect to Version Cue to synchronize, and then go offline again to publish to the Web server. To work offline, first mount the Version Cue site (see Tip 228) and then choose Site > Version Control Systems > Work Offline (**Figure 234a**). Alternatively, if you've already got working copies of your site on your local computer, simply choose File > Open to open the site and begin working on it.

(continued on next page)

Publish from Advanced Administration

You can publish to a Web server directly from the Advanced Administration area. To do so, login to the Advanced Administration and then click the Projects tab. Enable the checkbox next to the project you want to publish and click Export. In the next screen, choose the project name and the protocol of your choice. Enter the publish server information and click Export again.

Figure 234a When offline, you use a *working copy* of the site that has been downloaded to your local computer from the Version Cue workspace. You can edit, add, delete and even publish files in the offline state; however you should synchronize with the Version Cue project before publishing.

When you are offline, the Version Control status in the title bar at the top of the Site window will display *(Offline)*, and the menu options will be reduced to only one. That option is to uncheck the Work Offline command, which you do by choosing Site > Version Control Systems > Work Offline again (**Figure 234b**).

Figure 234b When offline, the site's title bar tells you so, and the Version Control System submenus are reduced to one.

235 Backing Up Version Cue

Something we highly recommend is to take a moment to set up backup configurations for your Version Cue projects. You can schedule backups to occur daily, weekly, or monthly for each individual project, or you can manually back up all Version Cue data at once. To perform either backup routine, you need to access the Advanced Administration area.

Use the Version Cue icon in the Finder menu bar or in Windows Taskbar, choose Advanced Administration, and log in. To back up a project, follow these steps:

1. Choose the Projects tab, enable the checkbox next to the project you want to backup, and then click the Backup button (**Figure 235a**).

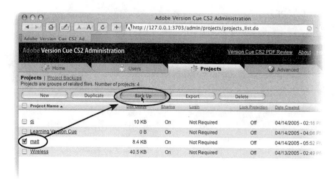

Figure 235a Put a checkmark next to the project you want to backup.

2. Click the checkbox next to the options you want to include in the backup: Project File Versions, Project Metadata, and Users/User Assignments. The Files option is always selected by default (**Figure 235b**).

(continued on next page)

The Whole Shebang

To back up all projects in your Version Cue workspace, click the Advanced tab in the Advanced Administration area and then click Back Up Version Cue Data. In the next screen you have the opportunity to give the backup a name. After doing so, click Save to begin the backup process.

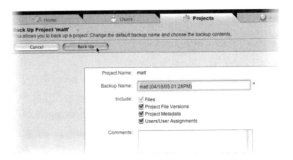

Figure 235b Select which options you want to include in the backup.

To schedule an automatic backup:

1. Go back to the main Projects screen by clicking the Projects tab.

2. Click the name of the project in the list.

3. In the Backup Configurations area at right, click New (**Figure 235c**).

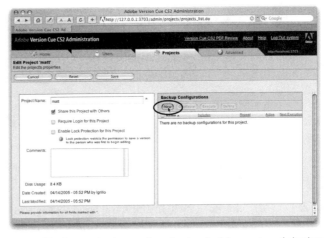

Figure 235c Create a backup configuration to schedule an automatic backup.

4. Choose Daily, Weekly, or Monthly from the Repeat popup.

5. Set your other preferred options in the Schedule area and then click the Save button in the upper left.

To delete a backup configuration, enable the checkbox next to its name and click the delete button. After you've backed up a project you'll see a project list. From this list you can restore a previous backup by clicking on it and then clicking the Restore button.

CHAPTER THIRTEEN

Third-Party Actions and Extensions

Hundreds of third-party actions and extensions are available for GoLive. *Actions* are pre-built JavaScript functions that add powerful interactivity to your Web site with the ease of point and click, meaning you don't have to know how to program or understand source code to add great features to your Web sites. Verifying forms data entry and creating interactive slide shows are two examples of what third-party actions can add to your Web sites.

Extensions are different from actions in that they add features, such as new menus and palettes, to the GoLive authoring environment. GoLive comes with a few extensions to get you started, and many more are available at Adobe's Action Exchange at http://share.studio.adobe.com.

Most serious Photoshop users enhance their digital toolbox with third-party plug-ins that add specialized features. GoLive actions and extensions work in a similar way to increase your productivity, enable your creativity, and expand the possibilities. The first tip in this chapter shows you how to install new extensions. Then we introduce you to several of our favorite actions and extensions, many from trusted Adobe partners.

TIP 236 Installing Extensions

A few extensions might include their own installers, but most require you copy them to the correct location in the GoLive application folder. Follow the instructions below to install extensions:

1. Install GoLive CS2 if you haven't done so already.

2. Copy the folder for the new extension, such as Smart Forms 2.0, into the Adobe GoLive CS2:Modules:Extend Scripts folder (**Figure 236**). If you look inside an extension folder, you'll notice there's always a file called Main.html and there might also be a few other script or image files. Don't copy these individual files—always install the entire extension folder.

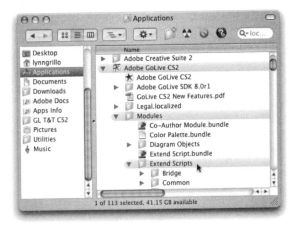

Figure 236 Copy the new extension folder into the Extend Scripts folder and relaunch GoLive.

3. Quit and relaunch GoLive to enable the new extension.

You can check to ensure that the newly installed extension is turned on by opening Preferences > Modules and scrolling down the list until you see the name of the extension. If there is no checkmark next to the name of the extension, enable it and restart GoLive.

To temporarily disable an extension, open the application preferences, select Modules on the left, and in the list of extensions on the right uncheck the ones you want to disable. Your new configuration will be active after you quit and relaunch GoLive.

TIP 237 Building DHTML Drop-down Menus

Name: MenuMachine

Developer: Big Bang Software

Source: www.menumachine.com

Cost: See site for details

MenuMachine 2 is a major update to this popular extension that creates DHTML drop-down menus. The source code created by MenuMachine has been improved and is the fastest, most reliable, and most compatible of any DHTML menu system we've ever seen.

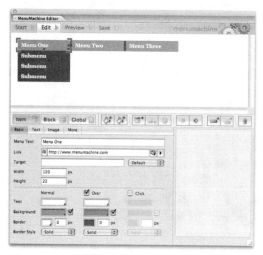

Figure 237 MenuMachine 2 uses the familiar GoLive interface and integrates flawlessly with the powerful site management to keep everything up to date.

We've always loved MenuMachine, but new features such as animated effects, variable opacity, and an extensive arrow and icon image gallery make it even better. The fact that MenuMachine 2 has improved accessibility support, CSS integration, and easy new themes for instant menus make us wonder how we ever lived without MenuMachine.

There are tons of cool features we don't have space to cover here, so make sure you check out the great documentation that comes with MenuMachine.

TIP
238 # Adding a Secure Shopping Cart

Name: CatalogIntegrator Cart

Developer: CatalogIntegrator

Source: www.catalogintegrator.com

Cost: Free–$1,995 US

Building an online storefront has never been easier. Install Catalog-Integrator Cart into GoLive and you'll get a full set of BuyObjects in your Objects palette that you can simply drag and drop onto your GoLive pages to set up a store.

After installing the extension, restart GoLive and in the Object palette click the button for the BuyObjects. There are quite a few objects there, so it's helpful to use the Toggle Orientation button in the lower left of the Objects palette and then widen the palette a bit to get a full view of the available BuyObjects (**Figure 238**).

Figure 238 The CatalogIntegrator Cart BuyObjects.

Each BuyObject is a fully contained HTML form object. After you've dropped one onto a page, use the Inspector palette to configure fields such as SKU number, Product Name/Description, price, size, color, and so on. The basic CatalogIntegrator Cart is a free download and comes in two varieties: one version for Windows servers and one for Unix and Mac OS X servers. Whether you build the site on Windows or Mac makes no difference; it's only the type of server that will be used to host the site that matters when deciding which version to choose.

Once you have created the shopping cart pages, you'll need to hook up to a server in order to receive the store's orders. To that end, CatalogIntegrator offers a full line of products to meet your needs, everything from a small-scale PayPal interface to a hosted cart to a full-blown, real-time merchant account.

CatalogIntegrator now has several expanded plug-ins for inventory importing and invoice exporting that are included in the new Pro and Enterprise cart versions, including real-time FedEx, UPS, and USPS shipping rating plug-ins.

TIP 238: Adding a Secure Shopping Cart

TIP
239 Adding PayPal eCommerce

Name: PayPal eCommerce Extension

Developer: Transmit Media

Source: www.transmitmedia.com/golive/paypal/

Cost: Free

The PayPal eCommerce Extension allows you to add basic ecommerce to your Web sites by creating payment buttons and basic shopping-cart functionality. Visitors to your site can use credit cards to pay for items, allowing you to accept credit-card payments for items or services that you sell on your site. To receive payments, you will need to open up a free PayPal business account (unless you already have one). Customers making payments to you need not have a PayPal account, only a valid credit card. Payments made to you will be credited to your PayPal business account. PayPal even supports payments in several currencies, including US$, CA$, Euro, British pound, and Japanese yen.

The extension consists of four new objects that are added to the Objects palette. When you drag any of the objects onto a page, a helpful wizard pops up (**Figure 239**), asks you a few questions, and writes all the necessary PayPal code for you.

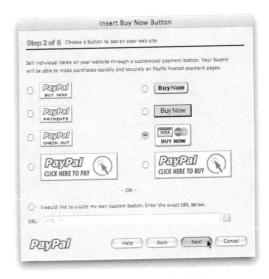

Figure 239 Add one of the four PayPal objects to a page, and the wizard gathers all the required information.

The palette objects are:

- **Buy Now:** Inserts a PayPal button that visitors can click to pay you with any major credit card. Visitors will be taken to the PayPal Web site where they can then enter payment information, which will be credited to your PayPal account.

- **Add to Cart:** This button allows visitors to add multiple products or services on your site to their personal shopping cart.

- **View Cart:** This button allows visitors to view the contents of their shopping carts without having to add a new item.

- **Subscription:** Recurring payments can be used to set up an ongoing charge or payment plan for customers—for example, a monthly or quarterly fee instead of a one-time charge.

TIP 240 Cleaning Up Garbage Code

Name: DocCleaner

Developer: Oliver Michalak

Source: http://golive.werk01.de/DocCleaner

Cost: $15 US

This is an extension that we simply cannot do without. In fact, we might even get physical if someone tried to take DocCleaner away from us. For cleaning documents of unwanted fonts tags or non-breaking spaces, for removing width or height attributes from a table, for getting rid of tag attributes or even tags themselves, your best friend is DocCleaner (**Figure 240**).

Figure 240 DocCleaner handles a variety of cleaning tasks quickly and efficiently.

If you need to clean legacy HTML pages that are riddled with <font> tags in order to use CSS to style text on pages, you will find this extension indispensable. Conversions of multiple documents can be time-consuming and challenging, but DocCleaner makes this and similar tasks a piece of cake. You can run DocCleaner on one page, a selection of pages, or on an entire site.

TIP 241 Detecting SWF Plug-in Compatibility

Name: Advanced SWF Authoring

Developer: GoLive Product Team

Source: http://share.studio.adobe.com/axAssetDetailSubmit. asp?aID=8802

Cost: Free

The GoLive product team put together a nifty extension that sniffs out whether or not a visitor to your page has the proper SWF plug-in needed to see Flash animations. This is a very cool extension because it offers a lot of flexibility as to how the detection happens, and it creates the necessary code in your page.

After installing the extension, you'll notice a new section in the Inspector palette when a SWF is placed onto a page. The section, called Detect, offers three detection methods: You can create a page that will direct the user to the Flash page if the plug-in is detected or to an alternate page if the plug-in is not installed (**Figure 241**); you can specify a GIF or JPG which will replace the SWF if the plug-in is not detected; or you can specify HTML to replace the SWF if the plug-in is not detected.

Figure 241 This extension adds a new Detect section to the SWF Inspector.

In all three cases, you simply choose a detection method from the Type pull-down in Inspector palette and then click the Create Page button, which creates a new detection page, or click the Insert Detect button to insert the code into the current page.

In our tests we got an alert when using the image-replacement method. The alert is to let you know that you need to enter the pixel dimensions of the GIF or JPG into the inspector because the extension doesn't automatically do so itself, but its wording is a little unclear and even a bit scary. Don't let it throw you, though. Just click the OK button and enter the width and height of the image into the Inspector palette. It works like a charm!

Viewing Server Side Includes in Layout Mode

Name: Translate SSI

Developer: GoLive Product Team

Source: Sample Extension in the GoLive SDK folder

Cost: Free

Server Side Includes, more commonly called SSIs, are similar to GoLive components in that you include part of one page inside another. The difference is that GoLive components are client-side technology, and SSIs are server-side technology. When updating a GoLive component, all affected pages must subsequently be uploaded to the Web server. However, when updating an SSI, all you need to upload is the include page itself.

The Translate SSI extension allows you to view the included page, more accurately known as the virtual include file, in GoLive's Layout Editor, which makes it much easier to visually lay out the page. You can find the extension in Adobe GoLive application folder > Adobe GoLive SDK folder > Samples > Translate SSI. Copy the whole folder and install it as directed in Tip 236.

To use the extension, follow these steps:

1. First, create the HTML snippet that you want to use as the include file and save it into your site. You should not include a DOCTYPE or other header info, nor the body tags. Confine it to just the piece of HTML that you want to show up in the other page.

2. Choose Dynamic Script Tags from the list of object sets in the Objects palette.

3. Drag and drop the SSI object **ssi** onto the page where you want to use it (**Figure 242**).

4. Use the Fetch URL tool to point and shoot at the include file.

Figure 242 Drag the SSI object onto your page and link to the include file using the Inspector palette.

TIP 242: Viewing Server Side Includes in Layout Mode

TIP 243 Adding a Search Engine

Name: Atomz Express Search

Developer: Atomz

Source: http://www.atomz.com/golive/

Cost: Free for sites up to 500 pages

Atomz Express Search is an easy way to add search capabilities to your site. The service is free for sites up to 500 pages, but you should contact Atomz directly for pricing for larger site installations. With the Atomz extension for GoLive, you can quickly and easily insert the Atomz Search form into your Web pages. The extension supports multiple Atomz Search accounts and multiple Atomz customer logins so a Webmaster can easily manage multiple sites and accounts all from within GoLive. If you don't already have an Atomz account, sign up at www.atomz.com.

Once you've installed the extension, be sure to quit and restart GoLive. Then select Special > Insert Atomz Search to insert the search form into the current document. You can also drag and drop the Atomz Search object 🖰 from the Atomz section of the Objects palette in the Layout Editor.

You'll be asked for your email address, password, and site name, and the extension instantly writes all the code you need for a fully functional search engine (**Figure 243**). It really is that easy!

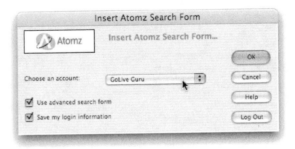

Figure 243 If you can drag and drop, you can add a search engine with Atomz.

TIP 244 Automatically Converting Hyperlinks

Name: URLize

Developer: GoLive Product Team

Source: Sample Extension in the GoLive SDK folder

Cost: Free

Converting a bunch of email addresses or Web site URLs in a page to hyperlinks can be a really tedious task. Links pages and employee directories are perfect examples of Web pages with lots of hyperlinks or email addresses. It's not hard, but it's really boring and error-prone.

The URLize extension automates hyperlinking and is included for free as a sample extension with GoLive. If you don't have the Adobe GoLive SDK:Samples folder in your GoLive application folder, you can always download the latest version of the SDK and the sample extension at http://partners.adobe.com/asn/golive/download.jsp.

To convert a link, select the email address or URL in the Layout Editor and choose Extensions> URLize text > Convert a selected URL or email text to a link (**Figure 244**). GoLive instantly converts the selected text, such as http://www.adobe.com, into a link to itself.

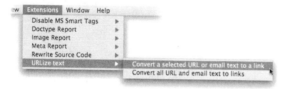

Figure 244 Select one of the URLize commands to automatically convert hyperlinks.

You can also convert the entire page at once. If you have several URLs and email addresses to convert in a page, select Extensions> URLize text > Convert all URL and email text to links. What a timesaver!

TIP 245 — Developing Data-driven Sites with OmniPilot Lasso

Name: Lasso Studio 8 for GoLive

Developer: OmniPilot Software, Inc.

Source: www.lassostudio.com

Cost: $199 US

Lasso Studio enables Web developers to build visually rich, powerful, data-driven Web applications using the familiar GoLive interface (**Figure 245**). Solutions built using Lasso Studio can be deployed on any server running Lasso Professional 8 on any platform. Lasso Studio can connect to a variety of databases, including FileMaker Pro, MySQL, Microsoft SQL Server 2000, Frontbase, Sybase, Openbase, PostgreSQL, Oracle, and hundreds more.

Site Builder Target

Figure 245 Lass Studio adds dozens of new objects to the Objects palette, a Lasso Studio menu, and three new palettes in the Window menu.

Some of the features Lasso Studio adds to GoLive include the following:

- Display database tables and fields right within GoLive.

- Preview data live from your database right within GoLive.

- Syntax coloring for LDML code, including tags, keywords, strings, and expressions.

- Code completion for all LDML tags.

- Quickly build an entire data-driven Web site using the Site Builder wizard.

- Lasso tags are represented as icons to minimize visual disruption of your layout while designing.

- Instantly change the active database via the Database Selector.

- Visual editing environment provides more than 1000 Lasso tags.

- Build and edit robust programming expressions with guided ease.

- Allow workgroup editing on a shared database without requiring direct access to databases.

- Includes single-user version of Lasso Professional 8 server software for development and testing.

TIP 245: Developing Data-driven Sites with OmniPilot Lasso

TIP
246 Adding a Tell a Friend Link

Name: Tell a Friend

Developer: Rasmussens Design

Source: www.rasmussens.dk/action

Cost: $10 US

GoLive users ask us all the time how to put a link on their Web sites that functions as a "tell a friend" feature. The aptly named Tell a Friend action from Rasmussens Design does exactly that, without the complexity of server-side scripting or difficult configurations, and it splits up the email address into bits, which the email harvesters can't pick up.

You can now choose this action in one of two flavors: a text or image version. It launches most email clients and automatically puts the window title in the email subject line and the URL of the page in the email body. All the visitor has to do is click the link text, enter the recipient email address, and send the message. You can also have text before and after the actual link text, so it's completely customizable.

To use the Tell a Friend action, follow these steps:

1. Drop a body action ⬚ from the Smart section of the Objects palette into the body of a Web page.

2. With the action placeholder still selected, choose the Tell a Friend or Tell a Friend Image action in the Actions section of the Rollovers & Actions palette.

3. Customize all the action parameters in the Actions palette (**Figure 246**). Make sure you resize the palette to be very tall so you can see all the options.

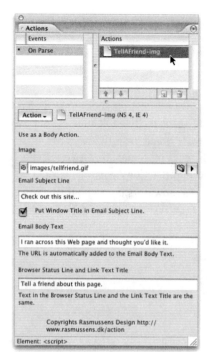

Figure 246 Experiment with the settings for the Tell a Friend action and test the results by previewing in a Web browser.

TIP 246: Adding a Tell a Friend Link

TIP 247
Creating Interactive Slideshows

Name: SlideShowKit

Developer: Mind Palette

Source: www.mindpalette.com/actions

Cost: $15 US

There are several ways to create interesting slideshows, but many of them require browser plug-ins, which can complicate the issue. Nate Baldwin of the Mind Palette group has written dozens of amazing actions. One of our favorites is his SlideShowKit action set. This powerful action is actually eight actions combined together to perform some impressive slide-show effects, without the need for any plug-ins or special viewer software (**Figure 247**).

Figure 247 Just one example of what can be achieved with the SlideShowKit actions.

The SlideShowKit actions are very flexible and can be configured in a variety of ways:

- Adding unlimited slideshows (user triggered or automatic) to your page, each with unlimited images.

- Toggling Play/Pause button option for autoplaying slideshows.

- Adding a link for each image in your slideshow to either open a new page or a popup window.

- Automatically generate a dynamic form selection menu for easy navigation through images.

- Automatically generate a count sequence as the slideshow progresses (1 of 20, 2 of 20, and so on).

- Assign a text caption or description that is automatically displayed with the corresponding image.

The actions come with a very detailed PDF manual explaining all the options, and there's a demo page at www.mindpalette.com/actions/natebaldwin/slideshow_kit/Examples. If you have questions about any of the Mind Palette actions, they have great support forums at www.mindpalette.com/forum.

TIP 248 — Adding a Scrollable Area to a Page

Name: ScrollArea 1.1

Developer: Ahgren's Actions

Source: www.golivecentral.com/pages/ahgren.shtml

Cost: Free

Michael Ahgren's ScrollArea action enables you to easily build attractive scrolling areas on your page. The action combines Go-Live layers, which act as the container that scrolls, and either text or images that trigger the scrolling effects. Behind the scenes, the ScrollArea action writes the necessary JavaScript that makes the scrolling happen. All you need to do is use the GoLive Inspector, the CSS Editor, and the Actions palette to click your way to happy scrolling (**Figure 248**).

Figure 248 Set the options for your scrolling area in the Rollovers and Actions palette.

It's simple to do. Place a layer on the page called "container" and put another layer inside that called "scroll." Next select the text or image that will be the trigger, make it a link, and add the ScrollArea action. Selecting a Mouse Enter event will cause the scroll to begin when the user hovers over the link, which is a nice effect. In the Action palette, match up the layer names in the pull-down menus, designate the direction of the scroll, and you're pretty much done. There's an input field where you can control the speed of the scroll and a place to assign how much of the area should scroll, called the *step size*.

ScrollArea action also includes great PDF documentation with directions on how to add text and images to the layer, how to set the options for step size and scroll speed, and how to scroll the area in as many as eight directions.

TIP 249 Verifying Form Field Entries

Name: VerifyForm

Developer: Walter Blady's Actions

Source: www.actionscafe.com

Cost: $45 US

If you have any forms on your Web site, you've probably wasted a lot of time correcting or reformatting some of the submitted data. Walter Blady of Actions Café has developed a commercial-grade product that verifies and reformats up to 15 selected fields in a single form (**Figure 249**) so that the data you receive is complete, verified, and formatted just how you need it.

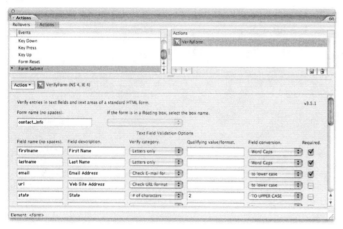

Figure 249 Set the VerifyForm action to work on the FormSubmit event so it can verify the data before it's submitted.

The VerifyForm action goes to work as soon as the visitor clicks the Submit button. All data-entry errors are displayed to the visitor and must be corrected before the form is submitted. VerifyForm can also block blank and duplicate forms from being submitted as well as guard against profanities or other inappropriate entries. Walter's actions include exhaustive documentation to get you started.

(continued on next page)

Some other benefits of using the VerifyForm action include the following:

- Relieves server load by checking forms before they are sent.

- Great features for Web site owners who don't have access to CGI form handlers.

- Comprehensive set of form checking and field-formatting features.

- Checks text fields, radio buttons, and single and multiple select lists.

- Can send form data as a delimited string ready for importing into a database.

- Customizable form-entry error messages.

- Uses cookie technology to repopulate forms if a user revisits the form page.

TIP
250 **DJ Design Actions**

Name: 20 Actions Collection

Developer: DJ Design

Source: http://actions.golivetutor.com

Cost: Free

Dave Jones at DJ Design packages all 20 of his free actions together in one Zip file so users can download them all and use the ones they want. Some of his actions offer general-purpose features, such as printing pages (**Figure 250**) and custom window opening, as well as some very advanced JavaScript variable and code snippet actions.

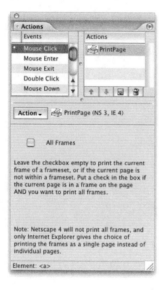

Figure 250 The Print Page action is helpful and easy to use.

All 20 actions are useful, but here are a few of our favorites:

- **AutoFrameset and IntoFrameset:** Use these two actions together to force a page into a frameset. This is useful when a page is linked via a search engine, because the search engines tend to index the individual pages, without the frameset.

- **PrintPage:** Prints the current page, even if it's a frames page.

(continued on next page)

- **Current Date:** Displays the current date on the page. You can even customize the font, size, and color of the type or apply a CSS class style.

- **Open Window 1.2:** This action is based on the original GoLive Open Window action and adds a new checkbox to force the new window to fill the entire screen. It also leaves all the checkboxes unchecked by default, because most people seem to prefer that in their new windows.

GoLive Resources on the Web

Adobe Resources

GoLive Product Page
http://www.adobe.com/golive

GoLive Tips
http://www.adobe.com/products/tips/golive.html

Adobe Studio
http://studio.adobe.com

Adobe Studio Exchange
http://share.studio.adobe.com/

GoLive Top Issues (Adobe Technical Support)
http://www.adobe.com/support/products/golive.html

Tips and Tutorials Sites

GoLive Central
http://www.golivecentral.com/

GoLive in 24
http://www.golivein24.com

GoLive 911
http://www.futurastudios.com/golive911/

GoLive Basics
http://www.golivebasics.com/

GoLive Tutor
http://www.golivetutor.com/

GoLive After Hours
http://www.afterhours.org.uk/

MindPalette Tutorials
http://www.mindpalette.com/tutorials/index.php

Rasmussens Design
http://www.rasmussens.dk/tut/

Lists and Communities

Adobe User to User Forums
http://www.adobeforums.com/

OmniPilot GoLive TalkList
http://www.listsearch.com/GoLiveTalk.lasso?tab1=about

GoLive Mod
http://groups.yahoo.com/group/golivemod/

Actions and Extensions

Adobe Studio Exchange
http://share.studio.adobe.com

Good collection of third-party actions, extensions, and modules
http://www.actionext.com

Index